PATHWAYS FOR REMEMBERING AND RECOGNIZING INDIGENOUS THOUGHT IN EDUCATION

Philosophies of Iethi'nihsténha Ohwentsia'kékha (Land)

Indigenous scholars have been gathering, speaking, and writing about Indigenous knowledge for decades. These knowledges are grounded in ancient traditions and very old pedagogies that have been woven with the tangled strings and chipped beads of colonial relations.

Pathways for Remembering and Recognizing Indigenous Thought in Education is an exploration into some of the shared cross-cultural themes that inform and shape Indigenous thought and Indigenous educational philosophies. These philosophies generate tensions, challenges, and contradictions when considered within the context of current educational systems that reinforce colonial power relations. Sandra D. Styres shows how Indigenous thought can inform decolonizing approaches in education as well as offer possibilities for truly transformative teaching practices. This book offers new pathways for remembering, conceptualizing, and understanding these ancient knowledges and philosophies within a twenty-first century educational context.

SANDRA D. STYRES is an assistant professor in the Department of Curriculum, Teaching, and Learning at the Ontario Institute for Studies in Education, University of Toronto.

Pathways for Remembering and Recognizing Indigenous Thought in Education

Philosophies of Iethi'nihsténha Ohwentsia'kékha (Land)

SANDRA D. STYRES

UNIVERSITY OF TORONTO PRESS
Toronto Buffalo London

© University of Toronto Press 2017
Toronto Buffalo London
www.utppublishing.com

ISBN 978-1-4875-0180-8 (cloth)   ISBN 978-1-4875-2163-9 (paper)

Library and Archives Canada Cataloguing in Publication

Styres, Sandra D., 1961–, author
Pathways for remembering and recognizing indigenous thought in education :
philosophies of Iethi'nihsténha Ohwentsia'kékha (land) / Sandra D. Styres.

Includes bibliographical references and index.
ISBN 978-1-4875-0180-8 (cloth).   ISBN 978-1-4875-2163-9 (paper)

1. Indians of North America – Education – Canada.   2. Indian philosophy –
Canada. I. Title.

E96.2.S79 2017   371.829'97071   C2016-907820-5

This book has been published with the help of a grant from the Federation
for the Humanities and Social Sciences, through the Awards to Scholarly
Publications Program, using funds provided by the Social Sciences and
Humanities Research Council of Canada.

University of Toronto Press acknowledges the financial assistance to its
publishing program of the Canada Council for the Arts and the Ontario
Arts Council, an agency of the Government of Ontario.

Canada Council   Conseil des Arts
for the Arts   du Canada

ONTARIO ARTS COUNCIL
CONSEIL DES ARTS DE L'ONTARIO
an Ontario government agency
un organisme du gouvernement de l'Ontario

Funded by the   Financé par le
Government   gouvernement
of Canada   du Canada

Contents

Foreword

Indigenous education in Canada has been identified within Canadian society as an issue, a concern, or a "problem" from the 1800s to the present day. In her work on Aboriginal education in Canada, Verna Kirkness traces the history of imposed colonial influence on Aboriginal education to the mission schools of the early 1800s. There have been various ways of conceptualizing and framing Indigenous education as a "problem," but most of those conceptualizations are based on the use of a pathologizing lens that positions Indigenous peoples as the problem and fails to take into account the complex histories that have brought us collectively to this point in education. Indigenous education has been the subject of many books, research studies, journal articles, and newspaper and magazine articles, as well as documentaries and other films. An inquiry to Google will produce 7,110,000 hits in under a minute. We do not lack for quotes from government officials stating that Indigenous education is in "crisis." The clear tendency to conceptualize Indigenous education as being in crisis has been present for decades. When former Assembly of First Nations National Chief Shawn A-in-chut Atleo resigned amid the controversy over proposed reforms to Indigenous education in Canada, he did not speak of education as being in crisis but rather spoke about the need to "smash the status quo." Styres's work in this volume smashes the status quo by deconstructing it and offering insights on how what she describes as "a wampum philosophy of education" can move us beyond the status quo to a new understanding of both Indigenous education and mainstream education in Canada.

Styres's voice in this volume is a counterpoint to the multitude who proclaim Indigenous education is in crisis and to those who search for

quick fixes and tools that will bring the "crisis" of Indigenous education safely into the fold of current Canadian mainstream educational
priorities and conceptualizations of what education should be and
what education should produce. Her work speaks to the status quo of
Canadian education and guides the reader through the complicated
philosophical underpinnings of education that have been informed by
the entangled histories of the colonized and the colonizer. She offers a
finely nuanced narrative that provides a rare combination of strong theoretical reasoning and practical considerations of how positive change
could be undertaken. Styres resists essentialism to offer an analysis of
the complex contemporary realities of education that have their roots
in rich philosophies and ways of being that existed before first contact.

Linda Smith has written, "[I]ndigenous work has to 'talk back to'
or 'talk up to' power" (2012, p. 127) and Styres has accomplished this
within her work. Not only does this volume openly engage relations
of power and privilege that are central to understanding how we have
gotten to this place in Canadian education, but the work itself also
challenges those relations of power and privilege on multiple levels.
Styres has consciously chosen to bring a voice to her work that resonates
with respect and reverence for Indigenous traditional knowledges,
communicates a deep understanding of Western academic knowledge
and conventions, and offers intimate and at times personal insights
into complex realities. The voice in this volume is only one aspect of
what sets her work apart from many of the others written about Indigenous education. Styres's ability to "talk back to" power is evident in
how she has structured her narrative, in her recentring of Indigenous
knowledges, and in the tough questions that she asks and explores.
While she speaks directly to differences between circularity and linear
thought and engages readers in intense explorations of philosophies
and Indigenous thought, the structure of her narrative offers readers
an embodied experience of what she explores in her writing. Readers
are immersed in a multidimensional experience wherein they are challenged to engage in the theoretical arguments that are presented and
with the finely nuanced and carefully crafted voice of the work that
provides readers with a first-hand experience of Indigenous thought
and circularity. Styres strikes that fine balance between respecting and
honouring those knowledges, philosophies, and histories that have
brought us to the current status quo and critiquing and challenging
them in ways that can move us beyond the status quo to new understandings of education.

In my work as an educator and a researcher, I am frequently asked how pre-service and current educators can better understand Indigenous education within the Canadian context and ensure that they are sensitive to the needs of Indigenous students. My answer has been a long reading list of key Indigenous authors and research and the suggestion that it will take many years of study and self-reflection. Styres's volume will be an essential addition to my list. Her work resonates with the strong Indigenous women's voices offered by key scholars, such as Jo-Ann Archibald, Marie Battiste, and Linda Smith. Styres's voice harmonizes with theirs as she offers her honour song, which respects Indigenous knowledges, critically examines decolonizing strategies, and moves Indigenous education within Canada beyond the current status quo to new understandings of relationships and reconceptualizes education in ways that honour Indigenous students' connections to Land, languages, culture, the relational self, and circularity.

In her role as both an insider (through her heritage and ties to Indigenous community) and an outsider (through her engagement in Canadian higher education), Styres has produced a work that speaks both to Indigenous peoples and to those who have colonized Indigenous peoples. Her work is an intimate weaving of those tangled historical strands that each of us brings forward into education through our shared histories of colonized or colonizers. It challenges us to make sense of those histories, own our own baggage, and strip away the preconceptions and assumptions that blind us to current realities so that we can engage collectively in the work that needs to be done to smash the status quo of education and move forward together in ways that respect multiple sovereignties.

Dawn Zinga
Associate Professor and Chair
Department of Child and Youth Studies
Brock University

Dedication and Acknowledgments

I would like to dedicate this book to my best friend and partner in life, tiakení:teron (my husband) Darryl. His consistent support throughout this long journey has meant so much more than I could ever express. I also dedicate this work to kheio'okón:'a (my children) Matthew and Michael, to kheiatere' okón:'a (my grandchildren) Braedyn and Syann, and to all our children who are here now and those yet to come.

First, I want to acknowledge and thank all my ancestors and teachers (Land, human, and non-human) who have come to me when I needed them and shared their knowledge and what I needed to hear in those moments – Nya:weh (thank you).

I want to acknowledge and thank my dear friend and colleague Dr Dawn Zinga for taking that leap of faith with me, for being open to the journey, and for her unwavering friendship. I also want to acknowledge all her hard work in reading my chapters and offering insightful feedback and encouragement during this process.

I would like to acknowledge and thank Dr Celia Haig-Brown and community scholar Kaaren Dannenmann for their early work related to land as first teacher that was the initial inspiration for my own journey.

I would like to thank Dr Robert Jahnke and Dr Huia Jahnke for inviting me into their land, territory, and school and welcoming me so wonderfully. I would also like to acknowledge and thank Dr Spencer Lilley and Mari Ropata-Te Hei, indeed all the faculty, lecturers, and staff at Te Pūtahi-a-Toi: School of Māori Art, Knowledge and Education at Massey University in Palmerston North, New Zealand, for their kindness, friendship, and generosity in sharing their time, knowledge, and experiences with me.

I would also like to acknowledge Robin Hapi, a Hao Moana Fellow with Massey University, who among his many accomplishments is currently the Chair of Business and Economic Research Limited, former chief executive of the Treaty of Waitangi Fisheries Commission, and former chief executive Aotearora Fisheries Ltd., for sharing his stories and knowledge with me about the Manawatu River.

I would also like to thank Arpege Taratoa, a Massey University graduate student with Te Pūtahi-a-Toi: School of Māori Art, Knowledge and Education, who so graciously shared her work related to water and its connections to sustainable relationships between Māori and Pākehā regarding the land and its waterways.

To my long-time friend and colleague Amos Key, Jr. I want to say niawen'kó:wa (thank you so much) for your insightfulness and for generously sharing your knowledge, friendship, and wisdom with me.

PATHWAYS FOR REMEMBERING AND RECOGNIZING INDIGENOUS THOUGHT IN EDUCATION

Philosophies of Iethi'nihsténha Ohwentsia'kékha (Land)

—

Vision – (Re)centring

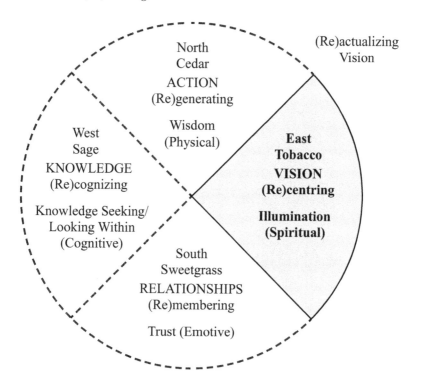

This book is the culmination of my experiences coming to understand Iethi'nihsténha Ohwentsia'kékha, which are Land-centred Indigenous philosophies grounded in ancient knowledges that are continually being (re)cognized and (re)generated within contemporary educational landscapes. Throughout this book, you will see parentheses used as a stylistic way to emphasize the prefix *re-*, which means "once more, afresh, and anew." The parentheses are visually and linguistically aligned with the concept of circularity, which is a key theoretical framework used throughout this book. Note, too, the suffix *-ing* in section titles, indicating fluidity, movement, and progressive action.

I begin by introducing myself in relation to the concepts I will discuss in this book, focusing on my vision and purpose of identifying and articulating Indigenous thought within education by exploring connections to land, iterative circularity, and storying. This section begins by looking at the ways Indigenous philosophies are formed and informed by connections to Land, language use, self-in-relationship, and circular-ity, and how these elements connect to learning processes and teaching practices. Using circularity as a theoretical and conceptual organizing framework, Section 1 enters the circle from the east – the east is where we enter this world from the spirit world. With this spiritual under-standing and sacred connection to Land, I lay down my tobacco, the first of the sacred medicines that the Creator gave to the people. Tobacco is offered before all the other sacred medicines, and its smoke carries our prayers to the Creator. The smoke is the place of visioning – where we imagine what is or could be possible, where we identify and articu-late the importance of doing this work, why now – here – in this time. Visioning opens opportunities for deep and profound insight and intro-spection as we explore and examine the ways we engage with natural, spiritual, and built worlds.

Introduction

The truth about stories is that that's all we are.

(King, 2003, pp. 2, 32)

Locating ourselves in relation to everything we do is one of the key foundational principles of Indigeneity. The only place from which any of us can write or speak with some degree of certainty is from the position of who we are in relation to what we know – in this way I am accountable for my own cultural location, which situates me in relation to my community at home and at large, as well as within this text. Therefore, acknowledging my positionality peels back the layers to expose the centre, thereby uncovering motives, intentions, and subjectivities while identifying the epistemic perspectives informing and guiding my writing of this book. Positioning and locating myself culturally and geographically is a relational, respectful, and reciprocal process.

To situate and introduce myself purposefully, meaningfully, respectfully, and relationally, I acknowledge the multiple shifting identities that compose my reality and sense of becoming in relation to this work, as well as the lands that ground, guide, and inform my writing. Many Indigenous scholars argue that in the realities of our current colonial legacy, *Indigeneity*, the state of being Indigenous, extends beyond the rigid boundaries of colonial constructs of fixed understandings and definitions of identity. These colonial constructed understandings are grounded in the political struggles of assimilationist agendas. For many of us who have mixed Indigenous and European ancestry, issues concerning identity are messy and in many ways ambiguous and convoluted; they often seem elusive or indistinct as we work through the confusion to make sense and meaning from mixed, and at times conflicting, identities.

Cherokee author Thomas King (2003) tells us that "the truth about stories is that that's all we are" (p. 2). As with many Indigenous narratives, time is not perceived as linear but rather as circular and iterative. When events took place is not as important as what happened in those places, what we take away from those experiences, and what we learn. Time, seen in this way, brings these events, in the form of stories, forward in our experience so that yesterday is today is tomorrow. While this book was being written today, it was actually written in another time and place – but not exactly then either. When I look back at myself as a child, swinging as high as I could on my backyard swing, singing at the top of my lungs and feeling transcended, as if I could actually fly, or when we spent summers at our family's country home in Trois Rivières, Quebec, and I would take long walks and listen to the stories my father, uncle, and their best friend – who had lived all his life down the road – would tell about the Indigenous and settler peoples who existed on that land, I always felt a deep sense of connection to Land. When I listen to drumming, hearing and feeling the heartbeat of Iethi'nihsténha Ohwentsia'kékha, or even now as I look out the window and see the land blanketed in winter's mantel of sleep, I feel the quiet energies of Iethi'nihsténha Ohwentsia'kékha (Land) pulsing beneath my feet. In this way this book is part of a circular and iterative journeying process in which I travel through time, place, and shifting realities.

Journeying, in this context, is an expression of movement from one place to another by making a conscious and deliberate decision to move into unfamiliar territory while maintaining an observing and reflective frame of mind. Journeying is a spiritual and relational process where our stories become interwoven with other stories, creating new patterns, telling new stories. In this way journeying may lead us to shifting and transforming the landscapes of our paradigms and philosophies. It is, in the words of Cajete (2000), "a journey of discovery" (p. 42) in which individuals gain knowledge about their purpose as spiritual beings. Journeying brings understanding concerning self-in-relationship and storied connections embedded in ancient knowledges and very old pedagogies.

My First Nations heritage comes from my connection to my ancestors through my father's lineage, Kanien'kehá:ka (Mohawk) and French. My mother's lineage connects me to my English and Welsh ancestors from Europe. My family name was Girard and I grew up in Montreal,

Quebec, speaking both English and French fluently but never knowing or being exposed to my First Nations heritage until my father spoke of it to me and to my husband (in separate conversations). While I still do not comprehend the timing of the revelation of my heritage, the acknowledgment of it gave me an almost immediate sense of understanding, of belonging, of connection – a feeling of coming home – it was the beginning of coming to understand and embrace who I am in relation to my world. It was, in a sense, a coming to know through blood memory. Until that revelation a piece of my being had always felt as if it were missing – disconnected somehow – absent by factors I had no part in creating. My father's sudden death prevented me from talking with him further on this matter. The long-standing rupture of kinship ties between my father and his family and the deaths of those family members makes the search more challenging. My journeying continues ...

The lands that have been particularly impactful in grounding, guiding, and informing this work are Six Nations of the Grand River (Six Nations) in Southern Ontario, the Northern Nishnawbe Aski Nation (NNAN) Territory, and Te Papa-i-Oea (City of Palmerston North) in New Zealand. The philosophies and stories embedded in the lands, mountains, and waterways of each place have enriched my understandings of Land and self-in-relationship and provide the focus for this work.

My family moved from Quebec to Ontario during my later teen years, where I met and later married my husband, who is Kanien'kehá:ka, Turtle Clan from Six Nations. We live on land that carries the tracks of our ancestors and all our relations (animate/inanimate and human/non-human), both near and far, and it is the place I interact with daily as I write and reflect on this work. Six Nations is a unique community comprising six distinct Nations, Kanien'kehá:ka (Mohawk), Onyota'a:ka (Oneida), Onundagaono (Onondaga), Guyohkohnyoh (Cayuga), Onondowahgah (Seneca), and Ska-Ruh-Reh (Tuscarora), united under the traditional Hodenosaunee Confederacy,[1] with each Nation having its own unique cultural traditions and language. The land base is approximately 18,820 hectares, reduced from its original 384,450 hectares under the 1784 Haldimand Proclamation. According to the data collected by the Six Nations Lands and Membership Department, the population in the community is 12,606, but the total band membership is 26,503. Six Nations is generally considered one of the largest and most urbanized First Nations communities in Canada.

It is important to provide some historical context and background on the Six Nations community. However, keeping such a complicated piece of history brief is an injustice to the recounting of it and, therefore, I apologize to my Elders past and present, and trust that the complexities will be apparent.

The Hodenosaunee Confederacy (Confederacy), made up of the original five Nations – the Ska-Ruh-Reh (Tuscarora) joined in 1722 – occupied vast territory in what is now known as Upper New York State. During the American war of Independence (1775–83), the Confederacy, not trusting either side and with good reason, declared itself neutral in the conflict. However, they continued to face immense pressure from both British and American colonists to align themselves with one side. The pressures to take sides finally split the Confederacy, with several of the Nations siding with the British. Following the war, the Confederacy was made very unwelcome in the newly created American nation, and as has been historically well documented, it became increasingly difficult and even life threatening for them to remain in the United States of America. The Confederacy treated with the British government for lands in Canada. Under the Haldimand Deed Proclamation of 1784, the British government, as an expression of its gratitude for their service, and as a demonstration of its commitment to an ongoing relationship, deeded to the Confederacy 9.5 kilometres of land on both sides of the Grand River, from its source near Wareham, Ontario, to where it empties into Lake Erie. Four of the original five nations accepted the proclamation and relocated to the new lands in Canada. But these were the traditional lands of the Mississaugas, an Ojibwa nation. The Mississaugas were pressured to surrender them to the British government for the use of the Confederacy and to relocate east to what is now the City of Mississauga. This created a great deal of tension between the Confederacy and the Mississaugas that, in some ways, continues today. It soon became clear that the Mississaugas would not be able to survive in their new location, and in 1847 they accepted an offer to return to a tract of their homelands given to them by the Confederacy from the lands deeded under the Haldimand Proclamation. The tract of land abuts Six Nations of the Grand River Territory in Southern Ontario and is known today as the Mississauga of New Credit First Nation.

The Six Nations territory has been adversely affected by, and continues to wrestle with, the tensions between the Confederacy and an elected system of government[2] imposed in 1925 by Duncan Campbell Scott, then deputy superintendent of the Department of Indian Affairs, who sought to eradicate the community's ancestral political and social systems, which had been in place since the time of the Peacemaker. These ancestral systems empowered and informed the traditional systems of government, as well as the spiritual practices and daily activities of the Hodenosaunee peoples. Scott was the "principal architect of Indian policy" (Titley, 1986, p. 22) and during his career with Indian Affairs, spanning some 52 years, he created and implemented the policies and political agendas that were instrumental in ushering in one of the most devastating eras in Canadian history for Aboriginal peoples – the residential schools. The purpose of the residential schools was to sever Aboriginal children from their kinship ties and connections to land, languages, knowledges, and philosophies – the ultimate goal being to "get rid of the Indian problem" (p. 50) across Canada through assimilationist policies and practices. Captain Richard Pratt, in a paper he presented at an 1892 convention on the education of Native Americans in the nineteenth century,[3] stated that "all the Indian there is in the race should be dead. Kill the Indian in him, and save the man." Pratt put into words Scott's aim to "kill the Indian in the child" and expressed Scott's overall goal for the residential schools.

Another land that guides and informs this work is located in the NNAN Territory. NNAN is a political organization representing 49 First Nation communities throughout the North in Ontario, with a land base of approximately 543,900 square kilometres (half of Ontario). In 2016 the population of NNAN (on and off First Nations communities) was 45,000 (Nishnawbe Aski Nation, 2016). The traditional languages of the Nishnawbe Aski people are Ojibwa, Cree, and Ojicree. Although I have some knowledge and understanding of the complexities of the NNAN communities that forged a relationship with the federal government under the James Bay Treaty 9 and the Ontario portions of Treaty 5, I do not feel it is my place to comment on it further.

The Aboriginal-focused Bachelor of Education Primary/Junior program, offered jointly by Brock University and the Northern Nishnawbe Education Council (NNEC), has two fundamental aims: first, to certify Aboriginal teachers working or seeking to work in First Nations community schools in the NNEC Territory; and second, to demonstrate ways of integrating Indigenous knowledge and Land-centred curriculum into existing mainstream course content. Teacher candidates in the Aboriginal-focused Bachelor of Education degree program come from several of the 24 NNAN communities in the Sioux Lookout district. They leave their communities and fly to a fishing lodge for three weeks of intensive course sessions with course instructors and faculty from Brock University – I was one such instructor.

I worked closely with a colleague and friend, who is an associate professor at Brock University, to develop, design, and implement the courses. The vision and primary theme woven through my journey to NNAN Territory was exploring the ways the land informed the design and delivery of the courses, and in particular how we were able to draw on land as an approach to pedagogy and practice. Then, my understanding had not yet evolved to conceptualizing land with a capital *L* or as a philosophical construct.

The final land that continues to have an important connection to this work is Aotearoa (New Zealand). The most widely used translation for *Aotearoa* is "land of the long white cloud." I have been to Aotearoa twice. The first time was as a research intern working with the Te Kotahitanga research and development project team at the University of Waikato in Kirikiriroa (City of Hamilton). Te Kotahitanga is a government-funded project designed to raise Māori student learning and achievement levels within mainstream schools. At that time, I also interviewed three of the Kaumātua (Māori Elders) who were instrumental in establishing the Kohanga Reo (language nests) in Tauranga. The second time I was invited to work with Te Pūtahi-a-Toi, the School of Māori Art, Knowledge and Education at Massey University in Te Papa-i-Oea (City of Palmerston North). During my time there I critically reviewed and evaluated the ways Māori immersion pedagogies and the philosophies of Te Aho Matua O Ngā Kura Kaupapa Māori (Te Aho Matua) were or were not being supported within the online delivery system of the Te Aho Tātairangi program, which is delivered completely in te reo Māori (Māori language). Te Aho Matua refers to the main underpinning of Māori philosophies and statements of action about teaching and learning. As of February 2008, Te Aho Matua became an officially recognized Māori philosophy of education under New Zealand's 1989 Education Act. Te Aho Matua is written into the legislation in te reo Māori with an English translation. Te reo Māori is one of two officially recognized languages in Aotearoa (English is the second). Aotearoa also has one very powerful treaty – the Treaty of Waitangi.

Each of these lands has places of significance where my connection to land grounds my thinking and inspires the processes that guide and inform this book. In my home community are two places of significance for me. The first one is my own home, where I frequently walk the land in reflection, touching trees and plants and communing with the animals that visit me. The second is the waterway. The Grand River is the main waterway that flows through this community, and it has a long history of connecting individuals and communities and of journeying. Pauline Johnson, a Mohawk poet and literary artist, wrote many poems about the river. At one time, before industry and pollution, the waterway also provided food that sustained the people. Some say the water still sustains and nourishes us.

The fishing lodge located in the Sioux Lookout district had many places to connect to Land, but one place was special. There was a lake where I would go for long walks, either alone or with my colleague, after class to unwind, debrief, and reflect. From those reflections, I would plan for the following day. Many times the lake offered me a teaching that I would soon need. On one of our walks, I found myself far ahead of my colleague and standing alone on the path. It was one of those windy, stormy days, and I suddenly became very aware of the wind and the trees. I looked up at the tree tops, which were bending to the force of the wind. *Flexibility* was the word that kept coming to my mind. As I watched those trees, I suddenly felt so connected and grounded – I felt that I was a part of the trees and the wind. That feeling stayed with me back to the cabin and into the following day, when flexibility became an important aspect of working through some difficult administrative issues.

In Aotearoa within Te-Papa-i-Oea (Palmerston North), I felt especially connected to and would go for long walks in the Victoria North Esplanade Gardens. I walked the nature trails among the native trees and plants, feeling the sun filtering between the branches, hearing children laughing in the park and birds singing high in the trees. Piwakawakas, or fantails, kept me company, flitting around me as I walked. The gardens are a natural inner-city sanctuary adjacent to the Manawatu River, with a long walkway that follows the river for some distance. The river has deep spiritual significance for those iwi (tribes) and hapu (sub-tribes) connected to it, among many things providing a rich food source and, historically, a way of travelling through the high mountain ridges, connecting peoples across the island when the journey overland was treacherous and unpredictable. Traditional narratives tell us that the river was named by Haunui, an ancestor who on reaching the river, seeing its depth and vastness, named it *Manawatu* meaning "my heart stood still in apprehension."

It is from each of these encounters that I draw wisdom and inspiration and a sense of being that is connected and grounded. In the philosophies embedded in each place, land, learning, identity, and education intersect.

"We know what we know from where we stand" (Kovach, 2009a, p. 7).

The Gift of the Seven Grandfather Teachings

To cherish knowledge is to know WISDOM.
To know LOVE is to know peace.
To honour all of the Creation is to have RESPECT.
BRAVERY is to face the foe with integrity.
HONESTY in facing a situation is to be brave.
HUMILITY is to know yourself as a sacred part of the Creation.
TRUTH is to know all these things.

(Seven Grandfather Teachings in Benton-Banai, 1988, p. 64)

Ojibwa teachings tell us that each gift of the seven grandfather teachings has an opposite, and we must be careful to give clear instructions about using each gift in good and balanced ways. In keeping with these teachings, it is important for me to articulate what this work is *and* what it is not. This book is not an attempt to construct my own sense of becoming or a search for my own identity; however, elements of personal journeying, shifting realities, and storying will be threaded like beaded wampum throughout. I am not going to bleed on these pages for you; this is not a story of abuse and dark places. This is a journey of discovery and within that process a (re)cognizing of self-in-relationship, and in some ways it will disrupt the stereotypical representations of Indigenous intellectualism.

This book is not intended to be *the* answer to all the issues relating to Indigenous education; my purpose is to add to our shifting and growing understandings of land and self-in-relationship within historical and contemporary contexts. Neither is this book an effort to further problematize Indigenous education; it is not intended to continue the stereotypical images of Indigenous people as perpetual victims, socially dysfunctional and hopelessly deficient. This book offers a particular decolonizing framework that acknowledges the complex web of colonial relations while not losing sight of the ways those relationships have informed and continue to inform how we *do* education. I resist the idea that decolonization is *the* means to an end; rather in these chapters I endeavour to complicate decolonization as a construct and to articulate the ways that decolonizing approaches can disrupt colonial relations and, in so doing, inform education, schooling, and possibilities for transformative teaching practices. While recognizing the vast diversity among Indigenous peoples across Turtle Island and, indeed, globally, I will, at times, draw on Spivak's (1993, pp. 4–5) notion of strategic essentialism to make purposeful and strategic sociopolitical and sociocultural generalizations, suspending those extensive cultural and linguistic diversities to bring together shared understandings of collective themes concerning philosophies, self-in-relationship, and identity. At the root of these themes is a shared fundamental essence or intrinsic nature. In other words strategic sociopolitical and sociocultural generalizations and the shared themes that emerge from strategic essentialism are a way for us as Indigenous people to have these conversations first among ourselves – representing ourselves to ourselves while talking back to colonial constructions. I am also not interested in putting forward a pan-Indian or didactic approach to Indigenous education, nor is this book a cookie-cutter model, a list of best practices, or a tool kit with a checklist to be replicated and followed. This book is an attempt to articulate the inarticulable – it is an exploration into some of the shared themes that inform Indigenous thought and the ways they can be used to frame an Indigenous-informed philosophy of education that can be adapted across diverse contexts and places.

This book is a wampum philosophy of education based on contemporary (re)memberings[4] of very old knowledges, woven with the tangled strings and chipped beads of colonial relations.

Wampum

In our hand an old, old, old thread …
Hear this prayer of the wampum
This is the tie that will bind us.
>   ("Wampum Prayer" by Tori Amos, musician and songwriter)

Wampum use predates contact and was an ancient recording device invented by Aiionwatha (Hiawatha) (George-Kanentiio, 2000). When strung together or woven into belts, wampum was used to record events and communicate information, served as a badge of office, and legitimized a nation's legal standing.[5] The Peacemaker[6] used wampum created by Aiionwatha to record the raising of the Tree of

Peace and the creation of the Confederacy, which is why wampum is considered sacred. The beads were originally fashioned from purple-and-white Quahog shells (a type of hard-shelled clam found along the Atlantic coast). The purple beads remind the Hodenosaunee people that they have a sacred responsibility to seriously consider the ways they walk in this world and to think about the impacts of their decisions on the generations yet to come. The white beads represent the good and rational mind that is continually focused on achieving balance and harmony with all of creation. Because of its sacred and spiritual significance wampum was not, as has been assumed by some, used as currency. However, because of the shortage of minted coins in the colonies, the *settlers* did, for a time, mass produce wampum beads and use them to trade for furs with the Hodenosaunee and Algonquin peoples.

To steal, sell, or transfer wampum is considered to be profane and a desecration of the sacred words of the ancestors. Wampum, woven into belts or on strings, is also used in ceremonies to (re)member ancient knowledges that are passed down from generation to generation. Many of the original ancient wampum belts were confiscated and either held captive in museums or sold to private collectors. Those few original wampum belts that the people managed to keep hidden are safeguarded by the Hodenosaunee Fire-Keepers and brought out and read only at certain ceremonies. According to Shimony (1994), replicas of missing wampum are acceptable as long as they are constructed from genuine shells. There is "no resistance [from the Confederacy] to using newly constructed sets" (p. 87). Ken Maracle (n.d.), an artisan and traditional wampum maker on Six Nations, states that "the purpose of making replica belts is to make sure that the words of our ancestors, put into the original belts many years ago, will never be forgotten."

In addition to its use in recording important events and ceremonial practices, wampum has also been used as an articulation of the breadth, depth, and scope of relationships. Originally these relationships were between various sovereign First Nations, and then after contact between sovereign First Nations and the various colonizing nations – French, English, Dutch, and the United Colonies. These relationships took the following forms:

- Sovereign Nation to Nation alliances, such as the Hiawatha Wampum Belt (also referred to as the Confederacy Belt) that sets out the

roles and responsibilities of the relationships between the original five nations of the Confederacy: Kanien'kehá:ka (Mohawk), Onyota'a:ka (Oneida), Onundagaono (Onondaga), Guyohkohnyoh (Cayuga), and Onondowahgah (Seneca);
* Tribute offered to another Nation, as in the case of the Mahican Algonquians' defeat at the hands of the Kanien'kehá:ka;
* Treaty agreements, such as the George Washington Belt (also referred to as the Great Chain or Silver Covenant Chain) made between the Confederacy and the 12 United Colonies, and the Guswhenta (also known as the Two Row Wampum Treaty) between the Hodenosaunee people and the English. These treaty agreements articulated the rights and responsibilities of an egalitarian and sovereign relationship between First Nations people and governments of the United Colonies and Canada. The treaties were not and are not an agreement to surrender power or consent to subjugation.

I am making a clear distinction here between Nation-to-Nation alliances and treaty agreements established between First Nations people and settler groups. Having made that distinction, this wampum threads and beads together two distinct but now interconnected stories. First, the wampum articulates Nation-to-Nation relationships, how concepts and ideas are created and beaded together to story shared themes in Aboriginal knowledges and philosophies. Second, the wampum also stories Indigenous people globally and the challenges of colonial relationships and philosophies. The wampum represented in this text is a deconstruction of the cultural currency of the dominant colonizing influences and, while acknowledging those colonial relationships, (re)centres Indigenous thought and processes.

In maintaining this work as a wampum philosophy of education based on contemporary (re)memberings of very old knowledges, I am referring to wampum belts as an expression of sovereign Nation-to-Nation relationships. Identifying, articulating, and threading a wampum philosophy of education acknowledges and respects the diversity among Indigenous Nations (national and international) and ensures that those original knowledges will not be forgotten but can be (re)membered, (re)cognized, and (re)generated in new contemporary understandings. Further, it serves to centre Indigenous thought, disrupt colonial relations, and eliminate the potential for pan-Indian philosophical approaches to pedagogies.

A Word about Terminology

Understanding paradigms depends on a shared knowledge of terminology and is a crucial element of journeying and understandings of self-in-relationship. With this in mind I have defined some key terms to ground their context and use.

Aboriginal: The term *Aboriginal* derives from the first ancestors of the Romans and from *ab origine*; literally translated, it means "from the beginning." The term referred to the original or first people of a country. In this book the term *Aboriginal* is used to differentiate First Nations, Métis, and Inuit peoples within Canada from Native Americans across all of Turtle Island (North America) and Indigenous populations within a global context. The term *Aboriginal* is a politically charged identification, and its use within this book is not intended to be disrespectful, nor is it intended to minimize or disregard distinctions among First Nations, Métis, or Inuit peoples. It is used here in its broadest sense while acknowledging, honouring, and respecting the diversity of First Nations, Métis, and Inuit populations in Canada. As well, the use of the term *urban Aboriginal* is not intended as a divisive construct but is an effort to distinguish Aboriginal peoples who reside within their First Nations communities or territories and those who live in urban centres.

Hodenosaunee: Hodenosaunee is a traditional self-identifying term meaning "people of the long house" or "people who build long houses." The Hodenosaunee people have also been known as the Iroquois (meaning "snakes" or "killer people," depending on the translation). Nonetheless, it is a derogatory name given to them by their enemies and subsequently adopted by the early European explorers, colonists, and fur traders. The use of the term *Hodenosaunee* is thought by some community leaders to be a politically charged and contested designation. Its use in this book is not intended to be an indication of political positioning but an honouring of the voices of my ancestors.

Sacred medicines: It is a generally acknowledged belief among Indigenous people that the Creator has placed many things on the earth for our use, such as the plant medicines that have a wide variety of medicinal and ceremonial uses. Tobacco, sage, sweetgrass, and cedar are referred to as the four sacred medicines and are integral to ceremonial and spiritual practices; ritual cleansing and purification; and spiritual, emotional, mental, and physical healing. They are vital components of daily life. Ancient teachings regarding the use of the four sacred medicines vary among First Nations and across geographic regions. The use of these sacred medicines is crucial to balancing the emotional, mental, spiritual, and physical health and well-being of Native American people.

Dominant Western/Eurocentric: It is important to challenge the notion of Western thought as a hegemonic European construct. Many European peoples have experienced colonization by other dominating European nations and are now living out the historical and contemporary colonial experience. Therefore, for this book the term *dominant Western* refers to a particular world view that rises out of Eurocentricism – that is, the privileging of dominant Euro-centred cultural values and beliefs in education, scholarship, knowledge production, the legitimization of intellectual capital, and the networks and systems of power. Terms such as *Western*, *European*, or *Eurocentric* in this book are not intended to be racial or hegemonic constructs but rather are ways to articulate a particular world view – *dominant* Western ideology.

Journeying through the Book

This book is an identification and articulation of Iethi'nihsténha Ohwentsia'kékha[7] (Land) as an Indigenous philosophy of education that can be defined and implemented within diverse contexts and landscapes. The book is framed as a circular and storied conversation about the ways Indigenous philosophies are formed and informed by connections to land and understandings of self-in-relationship. Circularity is one of the unifying concepts shared among many Indigenous nations across Turtle Island and across the great waters. It is an expression of the experiences of being an Indigenous person in relation to our lands and territories. I have found that just because two people are conversing does not mean they will understand each other. Therefore, one thing I want to achieve with this particular conversation is to open up opportunities for creating bridges between two distinct world views that can coexist and work together in egalitarian and mutually respectful relationships. At times and where appropriate, I make more liberal use of quotations from other authors, particularly Indigenous authors, to honour their voices and capture the beauty and wisdom of their words.

This book is organized into five sections using the concepts of circularity around four elements – titled Vision, Relationships, Knowledge, and Action – which will be unpacked in more detail in Chapter 1. An ancient Anishinaabe circle teaching that tells us that everyone's experiences of circularity are unique and that if you seek your vision and journey around the circle in deeply thoughtful and respectful ways, you will find something that was previously hidden to you. It is, therefore, important to understand that the fluid and iterative nature of circularity results in similar ideas being expressed in multiple ways and with increasingly more diverse and in-depth understandings throughout each of the four elements.

In this section, Vision – (Re)centring, I began the journey by introducing myself in relation to the concepts I discuss in this book. I then described what this work is and what it is not, provided a brief overview of the iterative circular and storied framework used in this book, and will now relate how the issues will be threaded and discussed throughout the chapters. *Iethi'nihsténha Ohwentsia'kékha*, Chapter 1, outlines the vision for exploring the ways Indigenous philosophies are formed and informed by connections to Land (with a capital *L*), language use, self-in-relationship, and circularity, and the connections of these elements to learning processes and teaching practices. This section concludes with an exploration of decolonization that critically examines understandings of decolonizing processes that serve to continue (re)centring colonial relations. Further, it suggests that Land-centred approaches acknowledge but trouble and (de)centre colonial relations while privileging and (re)centring Indigenous thought.

Section 2, Relationships – (Re)membering, expands on the previous section by exploring some of the ways we think about and move from space to place and Iethi'nihsténha Ohwentsia'kékha (Land). Chapter 2 examines Land as primary and central in legitimizing connections to very old pedagogies as well as to learning processes and relations. Iethi'nihsténha Ohwentsia'kékha is understood as a spiritually fluid, dynamic, and relational consciousness. Chapter 3, Self-in-Relationship, looks at the embedded philosophical underpinnings of Land that inform the principles of self-in-relationship together with an understanding of the responsibilities we have to those relationships. I examine (re)membered understandings of self-in-relationship and the ways (re)membering continues to be critical because colonial relationships continue to influence the ways individuals and community define themselves within contemporary contexts. "You're Not the Indian I Had in Mind," Chapter 4, concludes the section by unpacking (re)membered understandings of self-in-relationship, the ways identity was constructed traditionally, and the sociopolitical complexities of doing so in shifting contemporary landscapes.

Section 3, Knowledge – (Re)cognizing, ignites sacred fires by exploring the complex circular and interrelated concepts informing Indigenous philosophies, ancient knowledges, and very old pedagogies in Chapter 5. In Chapter 6, Relations of Privilege – Relations of Power, I explore aspects of architecture and the ways spaces are inhabited and made placeful. I conclude by examining the ways these inhabited architectural spaces, along with networks and relations of power, continue to influence education, together with connections to Indigenous philosophies grounded in understandings of Iethi'nihsténha Ohwentsia'kékha (Land). Land and Circularity, Chapter 7, is an exploration of rationality, particularly in relationship to Land and understandings of self-in-relationship and circularity. This section opens opportunities for exploring collaborative, collective, and individual knowledge building in which we may (re)cognize, literally come to know again, very old knowledges in contemporary contexts.

Section 4, Action – (Re)generation, focuses on actualizing or making the vision a reality. In Chapter 8, Indigenous and Dominant Western Philosophies, I begin by examining the ways Indigenous philosophies may be reconceptualized, reformed, and revived in contemporary and dynamic ways that consider how Indigenous and dominant Western knowledges can coexist to form new, distinctly sovereign relationships. Indigenous Languages and Thought, Chapter 9, builds on the previous chapter by exploring the emotionally complex and highly charged issues relating to Indigenous languages as verb-oriented expressions and the ways this orientation influences and is influenced by Indigenous thought. This section concludes by examining action as a fluid, dynamic, and sustainable process where the initial vision is actualized and the revisioning process continues.

In Section 5, Iethi'nihsténha Ohwentsia'kékha – (Re)actualizing, we further explore the concepts and philosophies of Land and the processes of reactualizing. Chapter 10, Tensions, Challenges, and Contradictions, explores the philosophies of Land in relation to the challenges, tensions, and contradictions of conducting this work within the academy, and offers some practical examples from my experiences, as well as some conclusions and implications for transformative practices. In Coyote as Trickster, Chapter 11, I explore the ways the principles of Land are distinct from two of the current and trendy approaches that attempt to address the limitations of dominant and prevailing ways of doing education. This chapter also looks at the ways the philosophies of Land disrupt, challenge, and resist the embedded colonial relations of power and privilege in current approaches. Finally, Chapter 12, Conclusion and Implications: Iethi'nihsténha Ohwentsia'kékha – Beyond Responsiveness and Place-Based Education, articulates the culmination of my understandings of the relationships between current scholarship regarding the philosophies of Land in education and the implications for praxis. In essence, this section allows the iterative journey to continue through the circle to form the foundation for (re)imagining, (re)theorizing, and (re)visioning Land-centred approaches to education.

1 Iethi'nihsténha Ohwentsia'kékha: Land, Circularity, and Storying

Far from being irrelevant in the modern world, traditional Indigenous social, political and cosmological ontologies are profoundly important to the development of transformative alternative frameworks for global order and new Indigenous ways of knowing and being.

(Stewart-Harawira, 2005, p. 24)

This chapter focuses on articulating the vision and purpose of the work and explores the relevant issues and why these issues are critically important right now – in this time. Included in this chapter is an introduction to an emergent and responsive theoretical conceptual framework that is grounded in Indigenous understandings of circularity and storying. Storying is essentially the ways we narratively describe *ourselves* as Indigenous peoples. This chapter sets out the vision for exploring the ways Indigenous philosophies are formed and informed by connections to Land, along with the ways Indigenous thought may profoundly inform learning and teaching.

Why Now – In This Time?

Many historical and contemporary systemic factors contribute to the current crisis in Aboriginal education and the importance of looking at why we need an Indigenous philosophy of education now – in this time. In 2008, New Democrat MP Charlie Angus challenged the Conservative government in the House of Commons by describing Aboriginal education as a "third world" form of education and the schools themselves as "holding pens for cattle." Further, he said, "too many

Aboriginal children are being denied the fundamental right to be educated in a school that gives them hope" (Bailey, 2008, p. 16). The Aboriginal population in Canada is growing at a rate approximately 1.5 times faster than the mainstream, and Statistics Canada (2011) confirms that this rate of growth will continue. One-third of the Aboriginal population is 14 years of age or under (Statistics Canada, 2013). Most distressing and heartbreaking is that Aboriginal youth suicides (ages 15–24) for both males and females occur, respectively, five and eight times more often than the non-Aboriginal population in Canada. According to Health Canada (2010), that means that the annual suicide rates for young Aboriginal men are 126 per 100,000 population (compared to 24 per 100,000 for non-Aboriginal men) and for women 35 per 100,000 population (compared to 5 per 100,000 for non-Aboriginal women) each year. The 2013 Aboriginal Peoples in Canada: First Nations People, Métis, and Inuit National Household Survey tells us that approximately 1,400,685 people identify as having an Aboriginal identity – that means that the annual suicide numbers for the First Nations, Métis, and Inuit population in Canada are 1764 (men) and 490 (women).

The social costs of the current Eurocentric-based education system have been astronomical as evidenced by well-documented issues, such as suicide, chronic underachievement, and the high dropout rates of Aboriginal children. In 1996 only 12 percent of Aboriginal youth completed high school (Royal Commission on Aboriginal Peoples [RCAP], 1996). In the 2002–3 school year only 29 percent of the small group of Aboriginal students who made it into grade 12 actually graduated (Mendelson, 2008). The Assembly of First Nations (AFN) 2011 report entitled *First Nation Elementary and Secondary Education: A Discussion Guide* tells us that in 2006, 61 percent of First Nations youth had not completed high school versus 13 percent of the non-Aboriginal population. According to data provided by Indigenous and Northern Affairs Canada ([INAC], 2005) in its report entitled *Elementary/Secondary Education Enrolment Statistics 96–97 to 04–05*, the rate of First Nation graduation from high school was 36 percent for 2004–5, 30 percent for 2005–6, 32 percent for 2006–7, 34 percent for 2007–8, and 36 percent for 2008–9. These trends continue and statistics reveal that the current system of education is failing Aboriginal children.

While a few bi-cultural and bilingual or multilingual schools in Ontario privilege Indigenous thought and Aboriginal children, the predominant system is a provincial, Eurocentrically biased one designed to benefit and privilege mainstream students. Exceptions include First

Nations School operated through the Toronto District School Board; Ahkwesáhsne Freedom School run by the Ahkwesáhsne Mohawk Board of Education, an independent school board that oversees three schools (one in Ontario and two in Quebec); and Kawenni:io, a full immersion private school for kindergarten through to grade 12, and Gai Hon Nya Ni – the Amos Key, Jr. E-Learning Institute, both of which are located on Six Nations of the Grand River Territory. Some other interesting exceptions are coming out of the Nunavut Department of Education, the Yukon Education Reform Project, and Toronto's Africentric-focus schools. The United Nations Educational, Scientific and Cultural Organization (UNESCO, 2003) states that language choice (relatedly, I would add philosophies and knowledges) within formal institutions, such as an education system, provides the language with power and prestige. Article 14 of the United Nations Declaration on the Rights of Indigenous Peoples provides for access to and control over an education system that is culturally and linguistically aligned. Linguistic identity is a powerful driving force connecting a culture-sharing group to its past and providing a foundation for balanced, healthy communities. Indigenous languages provide the context for understanding ancestral knowledges and inform ways of relating and being in the world. Language and culture are inseparable and integral components of each other and, therefore, provide the basis for considering an Indigenous philosophy of education that (re)centres Indigenous thought. Although some themes are shared across many Indigenous culture-sharing groups, these epistemologies or knowledge systems are ecologically grounded and highly contextualized.

Iethi'nihsténha Ohwentsia'kékha as an Indigenous philosophy of education has significance for all teachers and students – particularly those seeking to become teachers; it is not just an *Indigenous thing.* Understanding the contemporary and historical relationships with Land and the ways Indigenous peoples continue to exist in respectful relationship to Land, one another, and indeed to all relations (animate and inanimate/human and non-human) is the key to success for all students as participants in their own place, as well as in the wider global community. It is important in building good and equitable relationships to bring teachers and students together as culturally located individuals who have the knowledge and abilities to bring relevant understandings of Land and self-in-relationship into their pedagogies and practices in respectful and appropriate ways – always being mindful of cultural contexts and protocols.

Outlining the Vision

To reduce hegemonic ideologies that serve to perpetuate dominant Western practices within education, an Indigenous philosophy of education must take seriously the diverse ecological, epistemic, historical, and contemporary realities of Indigenous communities as the basis for its central tenets. It has become clear to me that philosophical approaches to Indigenous education must underpin administration and infrastructure; networks and relations of power; the ways knowledge is constructed and legitimized within the dominating epistemology; policies, pedagogies, and classroom practices; and the complex issues regarding language, literacies, and evaluative strategies. Indigenous scholars (academic and community, national and international) agree that Indigenous world views, values, traditions, and spiritual practices are held in and communicated through language, particularly the ways language is used. Kawagley (2006) said it well when he stated: "The Yupiaq language holds within it the Yupiaq world view ... Yupiaq youth should be taught their language, values, traditions, and culture in the classrooms" (p. 86).

Any identification and articulation of an Indigenous philosophy of education must also have a related and inextricable statement about the complex and emotionally charged issues that inform conversations about Indigenous languages. Linguistics has classified Indigenous languages as polysynthetic: words can be built on and put together using base verbs. These base verbs are words that have sound but no independent meanings; one has to add words to the base verb to create sense and meaning. Indigenous scholars and community language experts agree that Indigenous languages across Turtle Island are verb-oriented and that this orientation has a profound and strong influence on Indigenous thought. The notion that the structure of verb-oriented languages informs thought has been contested by many linguists who argue that the concept is too closely connected to the controversial Sapir-Whorf hypothesis, which will be further explored in Section 4. A dialogue can productively be opened relating to the complex issues of language (which also draws on some aspects of linguistics), such as the ways Indigenous languages are intimately connected to the natural world and how those interconnected relationships inform Indigenous philosophies and constructions of self-in-relationship. Language and language use form the basis for understanding Indigenous thought, which includes storied connections to land, as well as constructions of identity and community.

Ethical Spaces

This book forms ethical spaces by creating opportunities for discussions concerning Indigenous and dominant Western thought, as well as by acknowledging and critically examining the tensions and contradictions of conducting this work within academia. The academy is a system long established in dominant Western thought and those academics and scholars who set themselves up as gatekeepers of the construction and legitimization of knowledges both within and outside academia. Ethics is an abstract concept and the manner in which it is understood and interpreted is vastly diverse and continues to shift across time and space. The concept of ethical spaces draws from the work of Willie Ermine, and in this context I find it useful to borrow his definition of ethics as the "capacity to know what harms or enhances the well-being of sentient creatures" (Ermine, 2007, p. 195), characterized by the notion of spaces as sacred. To that I would add that ethics is more than simply knowing; it is the enactment of and engaging with that knowing in a good[1] way that enhances and supports the well-being of others. The ways that the space is engaged creates either a sacred or an oppressive space. Sacred spaces seek to balance individual and collective moral considerations within contemporary multicultural and global contexts.

Ethical space is the space between two disparate world views – in this case Indigenous and dominant Western philosophical worlds. Initially this space is a construction of difference and "diversity between human communities" (Ermine, 2007, p. 194), each with its own distinct world views and philosophical foundations. Ermine writes that within these shifting and turbulent spaces created by cultural positioning are the ethical spaces. According to Ermine ethical space is instantly created when two sets of intentions are poised to confront each other. It is the unstated deep thoughts (conscious and unconscious); highly charged feelings, interests, and assumptions; and, I would add, values, beliefs, and meaning-makings that fill up the space and inform how the two world views engage with the space and each other. They also inform the ways these challenges, tensions, and contradictions are taken up in cross-cultural engagement, particularly what are, at times, conflicting and shifting feelings, interests, intentions, perspectives, and constructions of self, that work towards bringing forward a new consciousness or at the very least a shift in paradigms.

The spaces I want to engage in with in this book are complex and multilayered. Acknowledging and engaging the ethical, sacred, and

contested spaces between social, political, and historical consciousness will serve to disrupt colonial relations embedded in the current
system of education and inform Land-centred approaches to pedagogies. It will also open spaces between the two distinct but egalitarian
world views (Indigenous and dominant Western) that will unmask the
tensions, challenges, and contradictions that I have experienced while
doing this work within academia. Failure to critically engage the spaces
between the two world views leaves behind lost opportunities for creating shared understandings and genuine reconciliations; and leaves a
chasm filled with taken-for-granted biases and assumptions, perceived
and very real offences, and fractured relationships. This book opens
opportunities to actively engage those spaces.

As Ermine (2005) said, the confrontation of the two distinct world
views instantaneously creates ethical space – seemingly involuntarily –
perhaps accidently. I agree; however, I also believe we can create these
spaces purposefully and meaningfully. This work is one example of the
ways these spaces might be *created*. Ermine writes that ethical space
is "triggered by dialogue [that] sets the parameters for an agreement
to interact modeled on ethical and honourable principles" (p. 2) and
further, that this "dialogue is concerned with providing a space for
exploring" (p. 1) philosophies and knowledges. Ermine also writes that
ethical space is a neutral place where power relations cease to exist and
the ensuing dialogue provides a way for confronting and resolving the
conflict. As such, dialoguing is "itself an ethical act" (p. 4). In my view
the ethical space between two disparate world views is not neutral nor
do power relations cease to exist – they are engaged; however, I do
agree that dialogue provides a way to confront issues and intentions
and has the potential to resolve conflicts. The spaces created as two
disparate world views are positioned for engagement is based on and
filled with conflicting intentions and hidden values, beliefs, perceptions
of the *other*, and constructions of self. In this way ethical space cannot
be neutral nor can power be erased; rather the space is made up of
various shifting tensions, challenges, and contradictions. An example
of this is found in Youngblood Henderson's (2008) account of his experiences on the United Nations Declaration on the Rights of Indigenous
Peoples Working Group, which comprised human rights experts from
around the globe. His story clearly demonstrates that power relations
did not cease to exist within the committee; in fact, he asserts that as the
working group endeavoured to work together to talk about and articulate concepts and issues concerning Eurocentric colonization, they

discovered that "cognitive imperialism"[2] (p. 42) was alive and well and still perpetuating oppression and the privileging of status and established power structures.

The engagement of dialogic ethical spaces opens opportunities for the creation and (re)creation of ways for understanding and interpreting realities and relationships. Paulo Freire (2003) writes that dialogue is an encounter between people and in this way is "an act of creation" (p. 89). It requires a belief in the human power to create and re-create. Dialogic ethical spaces can be opportunities for liberation, or in this context, Land-centred approaches (as outlined in Section 4). The late John Mohawk (1989) wrote that the Peacemaker put forward the philosophy that "all human beings possess the power of rational thought and that in the belief is to be found the power to create peace" (p. 219) and that "in order to negotiate [engage] with other human beings, we must believe in their rational nature" (p. 220). Ethical space is a construction of engagement. This engagement initiates the dialogue for exploring Land-centred philosophies and knowledges. Therefore, when we engage in dialogue, ethical spaces are opened.

The creation of ethical spaces is a journeying process that begins by making a conscious and at times uncomfortable decision to move into unfamiliar territory. Ethical spaces that occur through purposeful journeying directly lead us to shift previously held assumptions and paradigms. Thus, ethical spaces may be created both automatically *and* with purpose and intent, and as such, they are neither static nor fixed but are fluid, interconnected, and iterative spaces continually evolving and changing contextually as we journey. In this way ethical spaces serve to disrupt colonial relations that continue to inform cross- and intercultural interactions. During an interview, Alfred Metallic said that it is possible for knowledges to "co-exist [in Indigenous and academic communities] without having to compete for voice" (McLean, 2010, p. 3). This book engages those conceptual, textual, and theoretical spaces.

Circularity and Storying: A Conceptual Theoretical and Philosophical Framework

The theoretical and philosophical framework used in conceptualizing an Indigenous philosophy of education and in developing this book was conceived when I came up against the limitations of dominant Western methods and frameworks that were unable to adequately address the tangled historical contemporary colonial relationships;

the privileging of community knowledges, interests, and needs; the appropriate adherences to cultural protocols; and the twisted web of tensions and resistances composing Indigenous inquiry. In the words of Homi Bhabha (1994), theorizing is born from struggle – the struggle to describe and rethink certain conditions, issues, or phenomena based on current methods without falling into forms of othering, categorizing, or deficit problematizing. Theorizing should be fluid, iterative, and responsive, developing deeper and richer understandings. I believe that Indigenous theoretical concepts can and often do serve as critical tools for social change in both research and education. Indigenous research methods, philosophical frameworks, and concept metaphors have foundations in some shared concepts, but they are also very context or place specific and relational. Circularity is one of those concepts shared by many Indigenous peoples around the world.

Circularity

Circularity has been used by many Indigenous peoples to contextualize teachings and teaching practices across diverse contexts, including use as a research method.[3] Black Elk, a famous Wichasha Wakan medicine and holy man of the Ogala Lakota Sioux, once said that "everything an Indian does is in a circle, and that is because the power of the world always works in circles" (in Neihardt, 2008, p. 155). Stewart-Harawira (2005), a Māori scholar and author, asserts that the iterative circle is a conceptual expression of Indigenous philosophies in that there is a "universal relational relationship expressed as a circle of interdependency involving all elements of existence" (p. 41). Fixico (2003), a Shawnee, Sac and Fox, Seminole, and Muscogee Creek professor at the University of Kansas argues that "Indian thinking is visual and circular in philosophy" (p. xii). Circularity is a sacred representation of wholeness and interconnectedness that brings all of creation together in a circle of interdependent relationships grounded in Land and under the Great Mystery. The Great Mystery is generally understood as a creative life force that finds expression through Land in all of its abstraction,[4] concrete connections to home lands/landscapes, fluidity, interrelatedness, and understandings of self-in-relationship. In other words, to draw from a particular Hodenosaunee oral teaching concerning the philosophy of circularity, we are all a part of the land beneath us, the sky above us, and all that surrounds us. Circularity allows for dynamic synergic movement that is culturally responsive and emergent. Therefore, use of the circle and of positioning concepts within circles provides a unifying concept that addresses the complex cultural and linguistic diversity of Indigenous peoples' experiences and lived realities promoting the holistic well-being of community.

Over 1000 years ago the Anishinaabe people etched petroglyphs into what are called Kinomagewapkong or "rocks that teach." These Kinomagewapkong are considered sacred by the Anishinaabe people and are located in Curve Lake First Nations territory (near Peterborough, Ontario). A circle teaching at that place tells us that no two people will experience the circle in the same way. However, if you journey around the circle (if you theorize) in deep and thoughtful ways, you will begin to see or understand something that was previously hidden. This iterative process takes each of us on a journey around the circle, with each cycle adding depth and richness to our understandings and conceptualizations. Although it may at first glance appear repetitive, particularly if one is unfamiliar with circularity, each cyclical journey adds dimension to the concepts as they are examined, explored, and connected across contexts.

Contemporary understandings of circularity are without a doubt grounded in ancient knowledges. In this context circularity as a method and organizing framework is based on hybrid connections between Hodenosaunee and Anishinaabe circle teachings, directional[5] teachings and four sacred medicine teachings,[6] as well as the connectivity of four interrelated elements: vision, relationships, knowledge, and action. The concepts of vision, relationships, knowledge, and action can be found in Dr John Hodson's 2002 model for curriculum development designed for an Aboriginal adult education program. After my introduction I then built on the original concepts of vision, relationship, knowledge, and action by reconceptualizing these elements into circle work as an organizing framework for other forms of inquiry. I then incorporated the ancient four sacred directions and four sacred medicine teachings into the circle framework, adding depth and dimension in the ways one might journey and theorize through the elements of the circle.

Circularity is not represented as fixed but as a conceptualization of the interconnectedness of relationships, as well as synergistic and organic movement or journeying within the circle in both spiritual and natural worlds. Circularity as a theoretical framework allows for a research or curricular design that is culturally and epistemically responsive and emergent according to shared themes and place-specific epistemologies. As a method or organizing framework, circularity (as can be seen

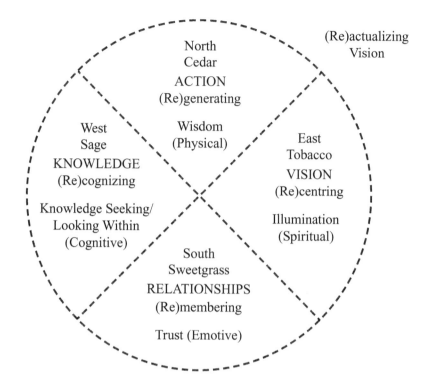

in the figure above) allows the educator or researcher to organize elements or ideas within a circle that is grounded in place-specific epistemologies, in this context Hodenosaunee and Anishinaabe epistemes.

Using circularity as a method and organizing framework, we begin our journey with Vision as shown in the figure. In both Hodenosaunee and Anishinaabe epistemologies, we enter the circle through the spiritual eastern door of illumination represented by the sacred medicine tobacco. Visioning can be seen to be the act of anticipating something that will or may come to be. It can also be used in the sense of envisioning, which is to imagine or conceive the possible or to be able to picture mentally some future event(s).

While in both Hodenosaunee and Anishinaabe traditions journeying through the circle follows the path of the sun beginning in the east, each tradition follows a different path around the circle. According to Hodenosaunee traditions, ceremonies, and dances, circles move counter-clockwise, denoting the "power of life and birth" (Porter, 2008, p. 53) that goes back to the most fundamental teaching in Hodenosaunee philosophy – Sky Woman and the Creation Story. Anishinaabe teachings tell us that the Seven Grandfathers demonstrated that each of the four directions offers specific powers: illumination, trust, knowledge seeking, and wisdom. These powers correspond with the four aspects of being: spiritual, emotional, cognitive, and physical. Anishinaabe teachings tell us that the Seven Grandfathers showed the people that the powers and corresponding aspects of being represented in the four directions are found through journeying clockwise around the circle. In both Hodenosaunee and Anishinaabe teachings, journeying around the circle reminds us that everything is connected, intertwined, and has a purpose. This understanding brings fullness, balance, and harmony to ourselves, to self-in-relationship, to everything we do, and to everywhere we journey.

As I am using hybrid connections between Hodenosaunee and Anishinaabe directional and medicine teachings we will, within the context of this conceptualization and in keeping with the original model, journey as my Anishinaabe brothers and sisters, clockwise through the circle to the emotive southern door of Trust in an examination of the relationship and responsibility we have to the vision represented by the sacred medicine sweetgrass. These relationships can also be evidenced by the connections, associations, and conditions of being related, of kinship ties, or of particular kinds of connections that exist between unrelated people who have dealings with each other. We proceed to the cognitive western door of Knowledge Seeking/Looking Within represented by the sacred medicine sage. The western door is the place from which we develop our collective and personal knowledge. It implies an acquaintance with facts, truths, or principles about the creation, use, or dissemination of special knowledge. We come full circle to the northern or physical door of Wisdom represented by the sacred medicine cedar. This is where vision is actualized – Action in this process is constant, consistent, dynamic, and sustainable. This iterative process leads to a revisioning that continues to develop relationships, creating and building new and very old knowledges, and thereby establishing additional courses of action that can be measured to reassess the initial visioning, and on and on the process continues. Circularity is a shared concept among many Indigenous peoples on Turtle Island and across the great waters and therefore is able to provide a decolonizing framework for (re)centring and privileging Indigenous thought while unmasking, resisting, and (de)centring colonial social and systemic relations of power. Colonial relations are acknowledged but decentred and Indigenous thought privileged and (re)centred. The idea of decolonization as an end result has met resistance among some Indigenous scholars because it fails to consider all the complexities and nuances of sense and meaning making inherent in the concept and is perceived as continuing to centralize and privilege colonial relations rather than Indigenous knowledges.

Decolonization: A Needle in My Brain

The term *decolonization* has always been like a needle in my brain – the sharp pain of the concept is embedded deep within the recesses of both my conscious and my unconscious thought. Decolonization is an abstract noun that carries in its interpretative basket many perspectives. While colonization practices have been a reoccurring and shifting part of human history, Loomba (2005) writes that modern understandings of colonization came into practice during the industrialization era with the movement of Europeans into permanent settlements and the organization of formal colonies in other lands. The term *colonize* originates from the Latin word *colonus*, referring to "a tiller of the soil or farmer" and in essence was used to refer to the "un-forming and re-forming" (p. 8) of another place into an economically and politically dependent relationship with the colonizing nation. Loomba writes that "colonialism can be defined as the conquest and control of other people's lands and goods" (p. 8). I, as do Loomba (2005) and Smith (2012), argue that colonialism is more layered and complex than the extraction of goods and resources from conquered lands – it (re)frames the conquered by drawing the colonized into complex and intricate social, economic, and political relationships with the colonizers, exploiting and commodifying both human and natural resources. Colonization and decolonization erases the histories and stories of the people living in the conquered lands by focusing colonial discourses and relations of power on the colonizers.

The notion of decolonizing is an active process whereby a colonized group attempts to return to a pre-colonial state of independence and sovereignty. Sovereignty is generally understood to be an independent autonomous nation state having full authority and power to govern itself – in the case of Canada, it would be a sovereign state within a sovereign state, both having equal power and rights. Contrary to the belief held by some, Indigenous sovereignty, as noted by Grande (2004), does not mean opposing democracy but rather that Indigenous sovereignty is democracy in action.

Decolonizing is a complex and multilayered process of eliminating colonial influences by freeing a colonized group of its colonial status. Smith (2012) writes that decolonizing is "a process that engages with colonialism at multiple levels" (p. 21). There are two concepts at play: decolonizing as the active process, and decolonization as an end result of the process of decolonizing. Freedom from colonial status may be granted by the colonizers and be reflected in their withdrawal from the colonized territory. Decolonization may also be accomplished by the colonizers remaining in the colonized territory but granting the colonized group sovereignty and the right and freedom to economically and politically govern themselves; in other words, the creation of a nation state within a nation state. Last, decolonization can be achieved through active resistance, and at times violent revolution, leading to the forcible removal of the colonizers. In the first two scenarios the decolonizing process is based on relations of power and privilege and the granting of freedom and status by the colonizing forces. In these instances the colonized are considered dominated bodies awaiting their fate. In the last scenario relations of power are resisted, engaged, and exercised. One of the many inherent dangers of this process are that the oppressed, in their active, socially just, and at times violent expressions of resistance, risk, in turn, becoming the oppressors (Freire, 2003).

Each of these decolonizing practices merely serves to re-engage and recentre colonial relations, as well as reinstalling and re-enforcing colonial practices. Alfred (2005) argues that "whatever the specific means or rationale, violent, legalist, and economic revolutions have never been successful in producing peaceful coexistence between peoples; in fact, they always reproduce the exact set of power relations they seek to change, rearranging only the outward face of power" (p. 22). Smith (2012) writes that decolonization in contemporary understandings "is recognized as a long-term process involving the bureaucratic, cultural, linguistic and psychological divesting of colonial power" (p. 101). Alfred (2005) and Kuokkanen (2007) both assert that decolonization refers to the "present struggle for political, intellectual, economic and cultural self-determination" (Kuokkanen, 2007, p. 143). In this way decolonizing is at the heart of social and political sovereignty. Yet decolonizing, while desired in principle, is a process that, by its very nature, is continually (re)centring colonial relations – the hamster caught in a never-ending wheel of repetition and replication.

The current context of colonialism is that the histories and contemporary realities of Indigenous peoples and colonial settlers within Canada, and indeed across Turtle Island, are now inextricably connected. We are all living together on this land – no one is leaving; no one is returning to their country of origin. This option is not feasible or desirable. Colonial relations are further complicated by the "enormous cultural and racial differences within each of these categories [colonizers and colonized] as well as cross-overs between them" (Loomba, 2005, p. 91). Further, Loomba writes that to put forward any single understanding or definition of decolonization is to erase the differences and complexities contained within that term. In addition I want to echo the caution of Tuck and Yang (2012) that "decolonization is not a swappable term for other things we want to do to improve our societies and schools" (p. 3); it is not a metaphor; it is not a figure of speech or a symbolic representation of something else. Decolonizing is an unsettling process of shifting and unravelling the tangled colonial relations of power and privilege. Relations of power and privilege and the networks that sustain them are always striving to maintain status quo and recentre whiteness. Whiteness is not about racial profiling based on identity and skin colour but instead relates to whiteness as a structural–cultural positioning of relations of power and privilege. It is not about *who* has whiteness but about *how* whiteness is perpetuated and maintained through networks and relations of power and privilege within and across societies – and in this case, within educational contexts.

To assert that we are in the process of decolonizing (as a process) or decolonized (as an end result) is to put forward the notion that we are, in effect, moving towards or already in a postcolonial context – that colonialism is now or will become "finished business" (Smith, 2012, p. 101). Can one ever claim postcolonial status when colonial relations of power and privilege continue to govern every aspect of the social, economic, and political lives of Indigenous peoples? Absolutely not! Smith quotes Bobbi Sykes in stating that "post-colonial can only mean one thing: the colonizers have left" (p. 101). We, each of us, remain inextricably woven in complex and shifting relationships. Kovach (2009a) emphatically states that there is nothing post about colonialism; it has simply been transformed and adapted to contemporary contexts. Lee Maracle reminds us in her 1990 text *Bobbi Lee, Indian Rebel* that the images of razor wire at Kanehsatake are a visible expression and tangible representation that we do not live in a postcolonial reality. As well, the circumstances surrounding the death of Dudley George at Ipperwash in 1995 or even

more recently Gary McHale's dogged presence at the Caledonia recla-
mation site, restirring unrest, augmenting already strained relations and
controversy, are also manifestations of current colonial relations. Similarly, Nock and Haig-Brown (2006) argue that "too little has changed for
us to claim that Canada is now in postcolonial times" (p. 7). Kuokkanen
(2007) writes that "colonialism continues to be the reality – we cannot
argue that Indigenous nations came from the current crisis intact. As
a result of colonialism, contamination is our reality today – to pretend
our pasts survived untouched by colonialism is a dangerous thing"
(pp. xv, 25). I agree with Alfred (2005) that we cannot allow the ideologies of colonialism to become *the* story of our existence – it is a discourse
that continues to centre colonial relations of power and privilege that
hinder our ability to move forward by continually reinforcing victim-
izing constructs of reality. However, I would also say that none of us
who reside within Turtle Island or indeed any colonized land can erase
colonial relations from our narratives – they are inextricably woven into
our stories of struggle, resistance, assertions of sovereignty, and the rec-
lamation of inherent rights embedded in Land.

The term *decolonizing* has been useful for Indigenous people nationally and internationally in negotiating, working through, and articulating ancient and contemporary deeply rooted rights based on
self-in-relationship to Land that have existed since time immemorial
and still persist. However, decolonizing as a conceptual tool also serves
to reinforce dichotomous and oppositional relationships. The colonized
continue to be depersonalized, victimized, and objectified, disappearing in a sea of anonymous collectivity with such phrases as "they are
all tree huggers and shamans" or sadly, the all-too-common statements
that "they are never going to succeed"; "they are all drunks, poor, and
bad parents"; "they are all just going to continue to live on welfare" (to
name but a few). Colonizers also disappear into collective anonymity
by declaring "we didn't have anything to do with what happened";
"why should we have to feel bad or apologize – I didn't do anything";
"it wasn't us – we didn't do it" (again, just to name a few). Wilson
(2008) writes that the process of decolonizing requires "developing a
critical consciousness about the cause(s) of oppression, the distortion of
history, our [Indigenous peoples'] own collaboration, and the degrees
to which we have internalized colonialist ideas and practices" (p. 71).
We, all of us, must develop a critical discourse that explores the ways
colonial relations continue to be perpetuated and maintained through
networks and relations of power and privilege. Circularity can provide

one context for going beyond identifying and centring colonial relations to promote change and transformative practices

Iethi'nihsténha Ohwentsia'kékha: Land

The concept of circularity is underpinned by a core theoretical concept grounded in the philosophies of Iethi'nihsténha Ohwentsia'kékha (Land). Iethi'nihsténha Ohwentsia'kékha is a Kanien'kehá:ka[7] (Mohawk) word meaning "our Mother the Earth." It refers to the ways we honour and respect her as a sentient and conscious being, which is why I capitalize Land in this context. The concepts derived from Iethi'nihsténha Ohwentsia'kékha gesture to and take seriously all the responsibilities we have in our relationships to her and to each other, and they extend to all our relations (animate/inanimate). Iethi'nihsténha Ohwentsia'kékha includes the sky (cosmos), the earth (urban and rural), waterways (including oceans, rivers, lakes, coastal areas; as well as reservoirs, aqueducts, culverts, and drainage basins in urban centres), humans and non-humans – near and far.

Philosophy generally refers to the study of the fundamental nature of knowledge, reality, and existence, particularly as they relate to academic disciplines and systems of thought. More specifically, it is the study of the theoretical or conceptual basis of a branch of knowledge or experience that may act as a guiding principle. Starting from that very broad understanding, I will journey through the principles of Indigenous thought that identify, value, and articulate Iethi'nihsténha Ohwentsia'kékha (Land), circularity, iterativity, and understandings of self-in-relationship.

Land as a theoretical and philosophical concept comprises circularity, understandings of self-in-relationship, language, storying,[8] and journeying as a central model for interpretation and meaning making. As I said earlier, Thomas King (2003) writes that "the truth about stories is that that's all we are ... you can't understand the world without telling a story" (p. 32). Indigenous philosophical and linguistic paradigms naturally flow into storying. These stories are metaphoric, symbolic, spiritual, ceremonial, and grounded in understandings of Iethi'nihsténha Ohwentsia'kékha (Land). Stories are circular, iterative, and relational:

> Stories go in circles. They don't go in straight lines. It helps if you listen in circles because there are stories inside and between stories, and finding your way through them is easy and as hard as finding your way home.

Part of finding is getting lost, and when you are lost you start to open up and listen. (Tafoya, 1995, pp. 11, 12)

Storying

Storying is an essential and culturally appropriate component for building relationships between the reader/listener and the author/ storyteller, together with the ideas I engage with in this text. Anzaldúa (1999) asserts that stories are active and temporally grounded and are "enacted every time they are spoken aloud or read silently" (p. 89). Storying, then, is a key component of Iethi'nihsténha Ohwentsia'kékha (Land) as it serves to disrupt dominant Western writings, thoughts, and understandings concerning Indigenous knowledges and philosophies. Storying is relational and reciprocal in that it locates and connects the author/educator/researcher to the ideas presented, the reader, and Land in an interconnected, circular, and iterative journeying process. Jeannette Armstrong (1998), Okanagan writer, poet, social activist, and scholar, writes that her "elders say that it is land that holds all knowledge of life and death and is a constant teacher – It is constantly communicating … We survived and thrived by listening intently to its teachings – to its language – and then inventing human words to retell its stories to our succeeding generations" (p. 178).

Stories cannot be separated from the land that holds those stories or the interconnected relationships that formed them. Within Indigenous understandings storytelling is as important as the story itself. For me, a dynamic part of the process of this journey was allowing myself to become lost before I could open up and understand the ways Land has been informing this storied journey and the ways it may also inform an Indigenous philosophy of education.

Hodenosaunee and Anishinaabe four direction teachings tell us that the east is the place where we begin our journey from the spirit world to the physical world; as such, it represents new beginnings, illumination, and rebirth. Visioning lies at the eastern door of illumination and is represented by tobacco. Tobacco was the first plant given to the people in order for them to be able to communicate with the spirit world, and it initiates interactions with all the other plant spirits. Tobacco is a very strong and sacred medicine; thus it is always offered first. All else is done through the offering of tobacco, and therefore like tobacco, vision is the beginning of all the other processes; it is the fountainhead. This, then, is the place to begin our journey into Iethi'nihsténha Ohwentsia'kékha

(Land) as an Indigenous informed philosophy of education that (re)centres Indigenous knowledges and very old pedagogies.

The vision for this work centres on developing a particular Indigenous philosophy of education as wampum for (re)centring, (re)membering, (re)cognizing, and (re)generating the holistic well-being of our children (those who are here and those yet to come) and by extension communities – essentially (re)actualizing ancient knowledges and very old pedagogies in contemporary contexts. Land is the foundational principle of this vision:

> You say that I [Native person] use the land, and I reply, yes, it is true; but it is not the first truth. The first truth is that I love the land; I see that it is beautiful, I delight in it; I am alive in it. (Momaday, 1997, p. 40)

SECTION TWO

Relationships –
(Re)membering

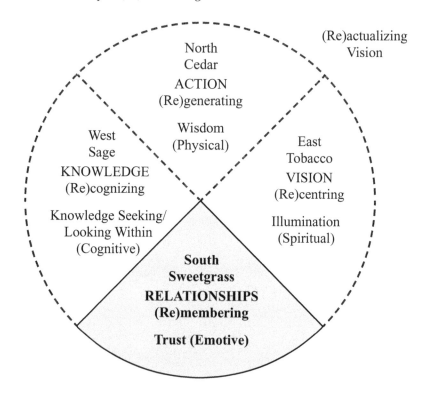

Section 1 focused on setting up the context for identifying and articulating a vision for an Indigenous wampum of education grounded in the philosophies of Land, specifically Iethi'nihsténha Ohwentsia'kékha (Land). I will continue journeying around the circle by now exploring what our individual and collective relationships and responsibilities are to that vision. Relationships lie at the southern door of our circle and are represented by sweetgrass, the sacred hair of Mother Earth. Its sweet aroma reminds people of the gentleness, nurturance, and loving kindness she has for the people.

In this section I explore some of the ways we may move from space to place and Land. I establish Iethi'nihsténha Ohwentsia'kékha (Land) as primary and central in legitimizing connections to very old pedagogies, as well as to learning processes and relations, by arguing that Land is a spiritually fluid, dynamic, and relational consciousness. Further, I examine (re)membered understandings of self-in-relationship, the ways identity was constructed traditionally, and the complexity of doing so in shifting contemporary landscapes. I argue that (re)membered understandings of self-in-relationship are critical in the processes of coming to know. One of the processes of coming to know focuses on (re)membering the ways identity is constructed, and I delve into the ways colonial relations continue to impact constructions of identity, particularly in the shifting contexts of twenty-first-century realities.

The concept of (re)membering as a form of action refers to the ways one is able to bring forward into the present a conscious awareness of past events, individuals, and knowledges. According to both the *Oxford English Dictionary* (OED, 2011) and the *Online Etymology Dictionary*, the prefix *re-* expresses fervent energy expressing "once more; afresh; anew"; the base word *member* is Latin for "mindful" or "calling to mind." The addition of *-ing* denotes progressive action, an active doing. In the context of this work, placing the *re-* in parentheses highlights an intense manifestation of being mindful or bringing knowledges forward in new contemporary ways. What is crucial to understandings of Iethi'nihsténha Ohwentsia'kékha (Land) as an Indigenous philosophy of education within shifting and contemporary contexts is that we must find new dynamic ways to (re)member our relationships to Land.

.

2 Iethi'nihsténha Ohwentsia'kékha: Space, Place, and Land

Land is a space that is somehow meaningfully organized and on the very point of speech, a kind of articulated thinking that fails to reach its ultimate translation in proposition or concepts, in messages ... the various landscapes, from frozen inland wastes to the river and the coast itself, speak multiple languages ... and emit a remarkable range of articulated messages.

(Kulchyski, 2005, p. 189)

Fully aware that there can be no single definitive understanding, declaration, or articulation of Land and the ways one may experience Land, I had many questions circling around in my thoughts as I worked through this particular juncture of my journey, such as, Where is Land, as an Indigenous philosophical and material construct, located or grounded? Is it located in space, in place, or is it something else altogether? Before I attempt to articulate any understandings of Land, it is important to begin by examining the complex ideologies relating to space and place, as well as to explore the some of the ways space and place may be connected to but are very specifically distinct from my conceptualizations of Iethi'nihsténha Ohwentsia'kékha (Land).

Journeying from Space to Place

Beginning from some general understandings, space is seen as a continuous area or expanse which is free, available, or unoccupied. I have heard it said, and I am sure I have even said it myself along this journey, that landscapes and places are located spatially and temporally, that is, grounded in space and time. It is important for me to point out here that the generally accepted assumptions are that space, in its formal context, is primary, absolute, infinite, and empty and that place making emerges from the vastness and existence of space. Lefebvre (1991) argues that "absolute space is a *non-place*" (p. 35). The OED, using dominant Western understandings, defines *place* as a particular position, point, or area in space – a linear and general perspective, particularly as it relates to time. The concepts of space arise out of the Eurocentric scientific assumption that space is neutral – a blank slate onto which culture and history can be written – that space requires the substance of culture and stories to render it placeful. Hence, and not surprisingly, was the belief that North America and its host people did not exist until they were *discovered* by European explorers and colonists – they had also proclaimed it tabula rasa – empty space, a blank slate – unstoried and theirs for the taking. Casey (1996) poses questions similar to the ones I posed; however, his queries focus on the existence of place: What comes first – where does place existence begin, with the chicken or the egg? When does space become place, where is it located, where is it grounded? At what point does it move from the impersonal and disconnected to the sacred, and I would add, to understandings of Land and self-in-relationship? Casey writes that according to dominant Western thought, the concept of space is primary, but for Native American people place is primary. The question, according to Casey, is not whom to believe but rather what to believe. Ancient philosophers, such as Archytas and Aristotle, together with more contemporary scholars, like Bachelard (1958/1994) and Casey, have all asserted that "place is prior to space ... that place is the first of all things" (Casey, 1996, p. 16) which is why we always find ourselves *in* places. Casey writes that space is empty and abstract, and place is concrete, sensed, and grounded in lived experiences and realities. Spatial scholars, such as Bachelard (1958/1994), Casey (1996), and Lefebvre (1991), assert that places "gather experiences and histories, even languages and thoughts ... and the trajectories of inanimate things" (Casey, 1996, pp. 24, 26). Feld's (1996) notion of inter-sensory perception allows a culture-sharing group to "turn over" the surface to look "underneath or inside" thereby revealing the subtleties, the "resonant depth" of meaning captured in place names, stories, songs, teachings (pp. 98, 99) – ancient knowledges.

(Re)membering Land

Ancient knowledges are (re)membered experiences forming deeply intimate and spiritual expressions of our connections to Land. Feld (1996) notes that "place is sensed, senses are places; as places make sense, senses make place" (p. 91). He asserts that experiencing and knowing place proceeds through "a complex interplay of the auditory and the visual" (p. 98). Bachelard (1958/1994) writes that "space that has been seized upon by the imagination cannot remain indifferent space … it has been lived in" (p. xxxvi) – it is embodied. One has to experience being in place in order to know they are in a particular place. Casey (1996) writes that we are never without "emplaced experiences … we are not only *in* places but *of* them" (p. 19). In other words we find our existence in the intimate and embodied expressions of place. Such knowledges are highly contextualized, soulful, (re)membered, and experienced. *Soulfulness* is deeply intense and emotional expressions of feeling; as such, place is storied, relational, and intimate. In this way we are in place as much as it is in us – every experience and expression of place is replete with multiple layers of memories each informing the other in diverse and entangled ways. These memories can be (re)membered through the (re)telling of stories and experiences of and in place. Space, then, is an empty generality; however, place is particular, it is storied, it is experienced. Iethi'nihsténha Ohwentsia'kékha (Land), in the context of this work, extends beyond the boundaries of place. Iethi'nihsténha Ohwentsia'kékha embodies principles, philosophies, and ontologies that transcend the material construct of place. With this understanding in mind, Land *is* spiritual, emotional, and relational; Land *is* experiential; Land *is* conscious – Land *is* a fundamental living being.

Indigenous people and their philosophies are informed by their spiritual, emotional, intellectual, and physical relationships with Iethi'nihsténha Ohwentsia'kékha (Land) and to their specific lands. For this reason Indigenous philosophies must also be considered within their ecological context. As human beings, each of us, whether we choose to acknowledge it or not, exist within interconnected and interdependent relationships to Land. Land is inextricably connected to storied place through place names. The self-identifying terms of culture-sharing groups express their intimate connections to their lands – that is how they continue to be identified to each other and to all their relations (human and non-human). Many scholars have written about the ways that Indigenous peoples' sense of being is grounded in place. Feld and

Basso (1996) in the introduction to their edited book, *Senses of Place*, state that "place is the most fundamental form of embodied experience – the site of a powerful fusion of self, space, and time" (p. 9). Places, according to Basso (1996), "animate the ideas and feelings of persons who attend to them, these same ideas and feelings animate the places on which attention has been bestowed" (p. 107). According to Deloria (1973) "American Indians hold their lands – places – as having the highest possible meaning, and all their statements are made with this reference point in mind" (p. 75). Deloria and Wildcat (2001) tell us that to be Indigenous means to have an intimate connection to places. Those connections to place are relational, dynamic, organic, in flux, and highly contextualized. While places can be construed as fluid, abstract, and at times diaphanous, they also contain enough substance to be sufficiently identified, articulated, and conceptualized. In this way space and time do not exist in isolation from one another but are contained *in* places.

Likewise, Land as sentient does not exist in isolation but rather finds expression within many layers of intimate and interconnected relationships. Building from the quotation at the beginning of this section, Kulchyski (2005) writes that land as a geographic space is "meaningfully organized and on the very point of speech, a kind of articulated thinking that fails to reach the ultimate translation in proposition or concepts, in messages" (p. 189). Kulchyski was referring to the ways Land communicates to us and the complexities and challenges of articulating the experiences of self-in-relationship to Land. Casey (1996) further articulates that "place is in first place with regard to its configurative arrangements, its landscape logic ... and that knowledge needs to be reconstrued as placial" (pp. 45, 46). That is, placial knowledge is embodied knowledge in that while some aspects of the materiality of land may be external to us, the ways we experience Land is shaped by who we are in relationship to the land. Embodied knowledges are culturally, spiritually, linguistically – intimately – connected to the place that holds the stories that are grounded in Land. Place and Land have both concrete and abstract properties that are at once storied, relational, and regional in that they do not exist in isolation and may be grouped together to inform the social and systemic norms, practices, and relations of power of a particular culture-sharing group. Laduke (1999) writes that as Indigenous people, "our leadership and direction emerge from the land up – our commitment and tenacity spring from our deep connection to the land" (p. 4). For Indigenous people land comes first, before all else.

The Philosophy of Land – Iethi'nihsténha Ohwentsia'kékha

Throughout this chapter I have explored some of the ways land and place have been addressed by many scholars as indistinguishable constructs, and while I acknowledge there are interconnectivities, I have also made clear distinctions between them. Place, in this work, refers to physical geographic space and is defined by everything that is included in that space – also referred to as landscape, ecology, or environment and in this context is denoted as land (lower case *l*). Connected but distinct, Land (capital *L*) expresses a duality[1] that refers not only to place as a physical geographic space but also to the underlying conceptual principles, philosophies, and ontologies of that space. These three concepts are connected but distinct. In this context principles refer to fundamental truths or propositions as a foundation for a system of belief or path of reasoning. Philosophy refers to the study of the fundamental nature of knowledge, reality, and existence (ways of knowing and being). This understanding of philosophy appears closely connected to what is generally understood as epistemology. Epistemology is the study of the nature of knowledge – including its presuppositions, its foundations, the ways of acquiring knowledge, and the limits of knowing. Ontology refers to a segment of metaphysics that considers the nature of being/becoming. Ontologies explore both what exists beyond experience and in what ways objects of experience compose the sole experience of reality as it relates to the nature of being/becoming.

Land as an Indigenous philosophical construct is both space (abstract) and place/land (concrete); it is also conceptual, experiential, relational, and embodied. Land is an expression of holism that embodies the four aspects of being: spiritual, emotive, cognitive, and physical. Many Indigenous and non-Indigenous authors explore the concepts of space, place, and land (lower-case *l*), as well as Indigenous knowledges, epistemologies, and philosophies; however, they have not connected these concepts to Land (capital *L*), particularly as they relate to Iethi'nihsténha Ohwentsia'kékha and the ways it is our first teacher – first as central and foundational, as in coming before all else. It appears that, when exploring place and land, many authors either collapse the two constructs or address one or the other without venturing beyond the physical and material aspects of land to explore the complexities of the fundamental being of Land. What is crucial in this work is an evolving understanding of the philosophical and ontological underpinnings of Iethi'nihsténha Ohwentsia'kékha (Land) and self-in-relationship as an Indigenous philosophical construct. This understanding is under-scored and embodied by capitalizing Land.

Building from the initial conceptualization in Chapter 1, understand-ing the ways land is our first teacher is a concept that originates in the early work of Dr Haig-Brown and community scholar Kaaren Dan-nenmann. Dr Celia Haig-Brown, a non-Indigenous author, researcher, scholar, and professor, was born into a family who taught her to respect the land. Haig-Brown has worked extensively with members of Indig-enous communities for over 30 years and they have worked unstint-ingly with her to refine her intimate connections to and understanding of Land. Kaaren Dannenmann is an Anishinaabe trapper and teacher from Namekosipiink (Big Trout Lake) near Red Lake, Ontario.

Land as first teacher is a contemporary concept derived from tra-ditional understandings of land based on ancient knowledges and very old pedagogies.[2] Place names are heard by those who use them as (re)membering the voices of their ancestors. Not only does place contain concrete form and structure (landscape), but the stories con-tained in place names also create a landscape that can be visualized with the mind, thereby transporting the individual to an "ancestral place-world" (Basso, 1996, p. 13) where time and space converge in place. Lefebvre (1991) tells us that when we speak of space, we must also simultaneously identify what occupies that space and articulate the ways it does so – space becoming placeful. Lefebvre writes that, connected but distinct, time is an articulation of what moves or changes within that space. Circularity determines that Indigenous concepts of space and time are not linear constructs moving along a continuum. Time is referred to only in a very general sense as one does not point to a specific point along that continuum. Stories and therefore time are circular and organic in nature.

Space, time, and place form complex, layered, and inextricable rela-tionships grounded and storied in Land. Storied (re)memberings of Land form spatial and temporal tracks left by our ancestors that can be *read* "with as much care as one reads the narratives of classical his-tory" (Kulchyski, 2005, p. 18). We may journey with storied connec-tions to land (lower-case "l") to generate sense and meaning making, as well as to perpetuate knowledge production and transmission that is grounded in Land. Storying may be seen as a crucial component of understanding one's place in the past in order *to be* in the present, communicating an "interrelationship between place [land] and Indig-enous identity" (Archibald, 2008, p. 74). Storied journeying may inform identity, representation, and the sense of home lands within the social, cultural, and physical landscape of a particular culture-sharing group. Kawagley (2006) and Kawagley, Norris-Tull, and Norris-Tull (1998) tell us that a spiritual landscape "exists within the physical landscape [that] urges us to come around to an understanding of ourselves" (Kawagley, 2006, pp. 7, 11). Further, world views or epistemologies are formed and informed from complex interactions enacted through respectful and reciprocal relationships between natural, spiritual, and human worlds. These epistemologies ground Indigenous educational realities in Land and the "sacredness of place" (Kawagley, 2006, p. 129).

Connections to Land are deeply intimate, relational, fluid, and spiritually dynamic. Indigenous education (including pedagogies and classroom practices) exists within a complex set of relationships where we engage with spiritual and natural worlds on a consistent daily basis. Pedagogy in this sense is grounded in organic relationships with Land that are constantly shifting and changing contextually and temporally. Land, then, is consistently informing pedagogy through storied relationships. These stories are etched into the essence of every rock, tree, animal, pathway, and waterway (whether in urban or rural/natural or built[3] environments) in relation to the Indigenous people who have existed on the land since time immemorial:

> Indigenous has to be understood ... in its original Latin it means, "born of the land" or "springs from the land" ... when you create something from an Indigenous perspective, you are creating it from that environment, from that land that it sits in. Indigenous peoples ... are shaped by the environment, the land, their relationship; their spiritual, emotional and physical relationship to that land. (Wilson, 2008, p. 88)

In essence our relationship with Iethi'nihsténha Ohwentsia'kékha (Land) is more deeply spiritual and intimate than first teacher. Land, which includes ancestral, historical, and present knowledge, as well as knowledge yet to be (re)cognized, comes first – it is the primary relationship, the one before all else.

To illustrate my point I will return to the story of the Manawatu River. The river was named by Haunui, a Māori ancestor, who had been pursuing his wife after she fled her home with another man. When Haunui arrived at the river he had to cross, he was filled with apprehension at the enormity of the task, and so Haunui called the river *Manuwatu* meaning "my heart stood still with apprehension."

This river is 180 kilometres long – its origin is in the mountain ranges in southern Te Matua-a-Māui (Hawke's Bay) and feeds into the Te Tai-o-Rehua (Tasman Sea) at Te Awahou (Foxton). The fertile flood-plains, as well as the river itself, were rich sources of food and made transportation between the two sides of the island less dangerous; the overland passes through the mountain ranges were treacherous, to say the least. This is also what made the area very attractive to European settlers. Since the land was covered in dense forest, the vast and very deep river ensured that large shipping vessels could travel up the river into the island for trade with the Māori, mostly for flax, which was important to the Europeans for making rope and clothing. The river was also teeming with large fish, which contributed to the development of fisheries for exportation. Te Awahou became a prominent and active port, leading to large settlements (farming, fisheries, and flax mills) and eventually towns and a city being built along the river. Over time, consistent flooding, erosion, and river movement, as well as human encroachment and interferences have shifted the direction and flow of the river. Not only is the river a fraction of the size it once was but it is also heavily polluted – so much so that at Te Awahou there are alerts during certain seasons that mean you cannot allow any part of your body to touch the water. You even have to wash off your boat after you take it into the water. One can certainly no longer eat anything caught in the river, a river that once nourished a people in so many ways that it was their taonga (a treasured thing).

The Māori people identify themselves through their intimate con-nections to their awa (waterways), maunga (mountains), iwi (tribes), and hapu (sub-tribes). The Māori who continue to exist in deep and intimate relationships with the land (re)member their stories and are working diligently towards restoring the Manawatu River and preserv-ing the estuaries with what plant and animal life remain. Piriharakeke, a particular part of the Manawatu River that once bypassed Te Awa-hou, literally means "the river that flax clings to." The significance of Piriharakeke is directly connected to the historical and contemporary importance of flax to the Māori people living along that part of the river. It is also the reason the Māori who live there are playing such a vital role in restoring that part of the river. They have a saying: *Ka Manawatu te awa, ka manawaori te iwi*, meaning when the heart of the river stands still in apprehension (in this case meaning the river is vibrant), the health of the people will be prevalent – that is, the vibrancy of the river is evi-dence of the health of the people. This philosophy directly connects the health of a people in deep and intimate relationships to their lands and waterways. Health in this instance is not just physical but also emotional, intellectual, and spiritual – (re)membering and restoring the balance and harmony between the people and their lands.

Another form of (re)membering Land is found in the Māori kapa haka dance and music performances. In my recent trip to Aotearoa (New Zealand) I had the privilege of attending the Pae Taiohi Regional High School Kapa Haka Competitions held in Te Papa-i-Oea (Palmerston North). *Kapa* refers to "standing in a row or rows" and *haka* literally means "to stir the air" or to dance. The kappa haka is the performance of contemporary (re)memberings of ancestral and contemporary knowledges and stories, which are sung in te reo Māori (Māori language). The participating Māori students in each performance set, represented by different secondary schools, sang songs and performed traditional dance routines (some with a contemporary flare) that demonstrated their connections to their ancestral knowledges and connections to their places. Some examples related to specific wildlife, their significance to Māori life, and the interactions between the Māori people and their lands. Another performance put the cosmos into context, describing the ways the stars relate to one another and how the people read and understand the stars and the cosmos. This performance has particular significance as it was performed during Matariki (eyes of God). Matariki is a Māori mid-winter celebration that typically begins around late May. Matariki is a collection of seven stars in the Pleiades star cluster that have important significance for navigation and the timing of the seasons, and, along with the rising of the new moon, it ushers in the start of the traditional new year for Māori. Some other groups in the competition performed the haka, which is a traditional posturing dance incorporating sharp rhythmic movements (slapping of arms, chest, and legs; stomping of feet), facial expressions (protruding tongue and eyes), and shouted vocal chants and chorales – all performed in unison and with precision. While it has generally been associated with aggressive posturing, such as the haka performed by the All Blacks – a New Zealand Rugby team – before each game, the haka is much more complex. The haka can be performed by both men and women[4] as an expression of a wide variety of emotions and spiritual energies. In the case of (re)membered understandings of Land and self-in-relationship, the haka performed by some of the groups in the competition were articulations of commanding political statements and expressions of resistance against government policies, agendas, and assimilationist practices. The kapa haka are very powerful reminders about and demonstrations of a people's relationship to their lands and connections to ancestral knowledges as well as their political stand as Māori here and now – in this time – on this land.

In the United States the Kiowa of southern Oklahoma are advocating to stop the commencement of mining on their sacred mountain, which is located on private property. One tribal historian has stated that "this is where we have always come. This is where our Elders used to come. The cedar gathered in this area has a unique scent different from any other cedar across North America" (Daffron, 2013). The mountain is a sacred and spiritual place to the Kiowa people where they (re)member their ancestors and ancient knowledges all the way back to their creation story. Even though it is privately owned, the owner has honoured a long-time verbal agreement allowing the Kiowa access to the mountain to perform their ceremonies and gather cedar without harassment. Mining activities will threaten the ecological well-being of the land, damage crops and wildlife, distribute harmful pollutants into the air, and kill the rare cedar trees that grow on the mountain. The Kiowa people (re)member their connections to their lands – they (re)member what it means to be Kiowa in deep and intimate relationship to their lands.

In Canada there are ongoing active resistances to the expansion of the Alberta pipeline by First Nations people, environmentalists, and various other individuals who stand alongside and support these movements. This pipeline moves Alberta crude oil from the tar sands to market, and the pipeline infrastructure is slated to expand across many First Nations communities across Canada. There have already been leaks, spills, and explosions in the pipeline over the years; with the expansion the potential for environmental damage is astronomical and would be devastating to the land and waterways, having far-reaching impacts on humans, domestic animals, wildlife, and crops. On 22 September 2016 more than 50 Indigenous First Nations from across Turtle Island signed a treaty alliance blocking several key pipeline oil sands expansions in their traditional territories – and more First Nations are expected to sign on. We have also had cross-country demonstrations against fracking, also known as hydraulic fracturing, in New Brunswick. Fracking is a process for extracting natural gas from shale rock that involves drilling deep into the earth and then injecting highly pressurized water and toxic chemicals into the well to fracture layers of shale rock and release trapped pockets of natural gas. Studies have proven that fracking and the resulting waste-water are devastating to the environment and waterways, while methane leaks pose serious threats to the stability of the land. Not only were First Nations people concerned about the environmental impacts of fracking, but they were also protesting the fact that the government violated treaty rights when they failed to consult with First Nations people concerning the fracking that was scheduled to take place on their traditional lands.

While this chapter provides some examples of the ways Indigenous peoples (re)member their sacred relationships with Land, I want to be clear that anyone can and should live in reflexive relationship to land (lower-case *l*); they often do so without ever understanding or acknowledging the fundamental being and philosophical nature of Land (capital *L*) or the intimate sacredness of the relationships Indigenous peoples have not only to their places but also to Land. Grande (2004) tells us that one of the key differences between dominant Western ideologies and Indigenous understandings of their places is that to Indigenous people their places are sacred, "signifying connections to family, tribe, and ancestors" (p. 72). Living in a deeply sacred and intimate relationship to Land requires respectful acknowledgment of whose traditional lands one is on, a commitment to seeking out and coming to an understanding of the stories and knowledges embedded in those lands, a conscious choosing to live in intimate, sacred, and storied relationships with those lands, not the least of which is an acknowledgment of the ways one is implicated in and informed by the networks and relations of power that compose the tangled colonial history of the lands.

I think that it is important to conclude this chapter by offering a cautionary note that as educators and learners we must refrain from turning Land into a romanticized utopia or an empty generality. To avoid this danger, Land must be central to any understanding or positioning of space, place, and time. Land is first before all else – therefore, the philosophy of Iethi'nihsténha Ohwentsia'kékha (Land) serves to (re)centre Land in its primacy and centrality in Indigenous knowledges, philosophies, relations and systems of power, and education. The concept of Land as our primary relationship draws on deeply intimate, sacred, and ancient knowledges, thereby centring, legitimizing, and grounding teaching and learning within the philosophy of Iethi'nihsténha Ohwentsia'kékha (Land) as the primary foundation of all our teachings.

3 Self-in-Relationship

The land has always taken care of our People – in accepting that we have always lived from our land, in accepting that the land has taken care of us, we also accept that the land is a gift given to us from the Creator. By acknowledging the land in this way, we affirm a relationship with all of its beings.

(Metallic, 2008, p. 62)

Embedded in the philosophical underpinnings of Iethi'nihsténha Ohwentsia'kékha (Land) are the principles of self-in-relationship, together with an understanding of the responsibilities one has to those relationships. In this chapter I explore (re)membered understandings of self-in-relationship and the ways (re)membering continues to be critical as colonial relationships continue to influence the ways individuals and community define themselves within contemporary contexts. Self-in-relationship is embodied, expressed, and grounded within the conceptual principles, philosophies, and ontological understandings of Land and may also be seen as one of the critical components of identity formation.

From an Indigenous perspective relationships are crucial to the survival and maintenance of every aspect of socio/political life whether spiritually, mentally, emotionally, or physically. Understandings of self-in-relationship is the place where we (re)member our collective and individual relationships with Land and creation, as well as our responsibilities to those relationships and to the vision as outlined in Chapter 1. As I said previously, the idea of (re)membering is being able to bring forward to our minds and (re)conceptualizing ancestral traditions, knowledges, and philosophies in new, dynamic, and contemporary ways, gesturing towards an active *doing*. Absolon and Willett (2005) write that in "re-membering ourselves we retrieve information about who we are" in relationship to our places and the words of our ancestors (p. 115). According to Haig-Brown (2005) the term *(re)member* "is an effort to capture the idea that such knowledge[s] must be put back together out of fragments held by individuals and communities who have had their traditional ways attacked as wrong for generations" (p. 90). Similarly, Momaday (1997) writes much earlier, "in as much as I am in the land, it is appropriate that I should affirm myself in the spirit of the land … The land, this land, is secure in racial memory … this trust is sacred" (p. 39). Racial memory is the idea that ancient knowledges, thought patterns, philosophies, and experiences are transmitted from generation to generation through various oral traditions, such as storying, ceremonies, and spiritual practices. The notion of racial memory is captured in the very essence of (re)membering – that is, bringing forward these ancient knowledges and philosophies in our memories and (re)constituting them into contemporary understandings and realities. These ancestral knowledges and philosophies are interwoven in understandings of self-in-relationship.

Interrelatedness (state of being related to all creation), interdependence (relationships in mutual dependency), and interconnectedness (connected reciprocally – a state of being that acknowledges a sense of oneness with all creation) are subtly distinct but intimately connected key concepts of self-in-relationship. Tadodaho Chief Leon Shenandoah states that "being human was to recognize the spiritual connection in all creation" (Wall, 2001, p. xi). It is generally understood that, regardless of the diverse complexities of contemporary Indigenous communities (urban and rural), conceptualizations of self-in-relationship are dynamically and fluidly threaded throughout social and political relationships, such as nations, clan systems, and familial and kinship ties that extend beyond bloodlines; traditional and elected forms of government; historical and contemporary treaties and alliances; and ecology[1] and cosmology.[2]

An example of this is found in the very powerful work of Arpege Taratoe, a graduate visual arts student with Te Pūtahi-a-Toi: School of Māori Art, Knowledge and Education at Massey University in Aotearoa (New Zealand). Her work moved me and I asked her if she would share with me her vision for the artistic piece she presented. She told me that her work on water was a response to the final assignment for Mata Oho Semester 1 Studio Paper. The students were asked to create a piece of art that connected to both the Treaty of Waitangi (Treaty) and a Māori sociopolitical movement. Most students naturally chose to create something connected to land as many of the issues surrounding the Treaty are about the unjust treatment of Māori land and the connections the people have to it. Arpege chose to focus her work on water – she indicated in our discussion that she had always felt this deep and intimate connection to water. For her what made water enticing as a medium was that it had uncontrollable elements to it – it could be calm or calming one moment and treacherous and awe-inspiring the next. Water reflects and bends light and, in its relentless fluidity, can shape the landscape.

The New Zealand government was in the process of selling its shares in major power companies to the public. This decision raised issues and concerns for iwi (tribes) not only because this places the major power companies in a position to be able to exert tremendous influence on waterways for the production of power, but also because those in the public sector who own shares are able to make a profit from the rivers. This is a direct violation of the Treaty, which stipulates that Māori retain rights to water and waterways. Water is taonga (sacred) for Māori – it is to be taken care of, treasured, and highly valued, not as a commodity but in relationship to it. The Māori do not want to "own" or "exploit" the waterways; they want acknowledgment of their inherent rights relating to water as a demonstration of respect for Māori historical and contemporary connections to their waterways.

Arpege stated that her work was a response to and a reflection of the ways Māori people feel about and engage with their waterways. Her intention was not to use her art as a platform for assault but to lead viewers to recognize the political injustice of the government's decision through emotion. She sought to invoke feelings by using sound and imagery to connect people to water in powerful ways. Arpege was not trying to generate pity for Māori but sought a sense of equality between the Māori people and the viewer. She hoped that the audience would connect with the piece and feel some of the emotions that Māori experience in their connections to their waterways. Arpege said that there is a saying among the people articulating the depth of the intimate relationships Māori have to their waterways: *As far as my people go we are the water and the water is us.* Water is whānau – it is an ancestor – it is family.

Arpege wanted the experience to be emotional and to have a presence. She chose to have the images playing in a loop on a large wall projector. The size of the projected image was a play on the physicality of the images being larger than the audience – thus to be somewhat intimidating or uncomfortable and to create a persuasive spatial presence. She chose Rhian Sheehan's "Standing in Silence #11" as the music to accompany the images. Opening the presentation Arpege used ink being dropped into water imagery as a way to represent that ink in pens is used to sign things, such as the Treaty. As the ink drops merge with the water they also represents colonial relationships and resulting land issues, including pollution of the waterways. The ways the ink dropped very slowly into the water also symbolizes a very slow process – like a melting pot. The sound of the drops was loud to represent the ways a judge slams down the gavel, securing a judgment – "that's it; there is to be no further word on the issues." Pākehā (non-Māori New Zealanders) interpret the Treaty as a contract – it is about who has legal rights over the use of the land – commodified and exploitive, whereas Māori see the Treaty as an expression of the intimate relationships they have to their lands – relational. Occasionally, powerful words flowed like a banner – refracted and distorted by their position behind the water. Arpege used the words to subtly add messages to coincide with the imagery.

Arpege's artistic representation of a people's deep and intimate relationships to their waterways is grounded in Te Aho Matua (Māori philosophies). The tears on an image of a woman in the water were accompanied by loud reverberations like the powerful rhythm of the grandfather drum – the heartbeat of Mother Earth. Tears are another form of water and this imagery represented the ways tears themselves are silent, but the emotions they communicate are loud, strong, and persistent.

The powerful symbolism in the imagery and sound relates to how our very existence depends on water: adult bodies are made up of about 60 percent water – for babies its 78 percent – we are born out of water from our mother's womb; our very first element is water. Water also has very important connections to Mother Earth – water is the lifeblood of Mother Earth – all life would cease to exist without water. In this way Indigenous people exist in deeply intimate and sacred relationships to Land and their places.

One can see that the deep structures of Indigenous philosophies conflict with dominant Western understandings about self-in-relationship. The core values embedded in Eurocentric thought concerning self-in-relationship are based in imperialism, capitalism, and expansionism,[3] each having core values of exploitation that serve to maintain unequal power relations across diverse sociocultural, sociopolitical, and socio-economic strata. Indigenous philosophies about self-in-relationship are grounded, reinforced, and transmitted through Land and expressed in values, beliefs, world views, and lived experiences; ceremonies, spirit names, and ancestral knowledges; sacred places, place names, and (re)membered stories; and understandings of the ways we exist in relationship to our own lived reality.

Indigenous thought is characterized by a very particular form of rational thought that is expressed in sacred manifestations of self-in-relationship. Both Sotsisowah (John Mohawk), Turtle Clan of the Seneca Nation, and Tadodaho Chief Leon Shenandoah of the Onondaga Nation, tell us that the Peacemaker, a powerful prophet sent by the Creator to the Hodenosaunee people, brought with him a prevailing spiritual message of hope, peace, power, and righteousness so that the people (re)member and (re)turn to living in good relations with one another, with creation, and with Land. The Peacemaker's message was that "all human beings possess the power of rational thought that is found in the power to create peace ... in order to negotiate with other human beings" (Mohawk, 1989, pp. 219–20) and walk the right path centred on a good mind. This premise formed the basis for Hodenosaunee political thought and systems of democratic processes grounded in Land and centred on the principles of self-in-relationship.

Seven Generational Thinking

One aspect of rational thought is found in what is generally referred to as seven generational thinking. Seven generational thinking is an articulation of self-in-relationship extending beyond the past or present well into the future. There is a Hodenosaunee oral teaching, which states that: *we are a part of everything that is beneath us, above us, and around us. Our past is our present, our present is our future, and our future is seven generations past and present.* Seven generational thinking as an understanding of interrelatedness transcends time and place wherein we, as Indigenous people, consider ourselves to literally be "walking upon the faces of those yet to come" (Laduke, 1999, 194) as we walk through this life and make decisions that can and will have long-term implications. This philosophical approach can have deep and lasting impacts on the ways we can all think about how we might choose to be in relationship with this world – particularly as global citizens. Both Hodenosaunee and Anishinaabe teachings tell us that it is crucial to conceptualize the implications of decisions seven generations into the future. Education is one of the areas reflecting the tangled and indeed tragic history of colonial relations having long-term implications for Indigenous people everywhere. I believe that we all, as educators and learners, must stop and ask ourselves what imprints the current dominant Western informed education system has left on those who have passed from this world, those who are here, and those yet to come.

Many national and international Indigenous scholars agree that learning is a relational act and that the process of coming to know is grounded in the principles of self-in-relationship. It follows then that teaching and learning are relational, reciprocal, and culturally located actions. Further, the understandings of Iethi'nihsténha Ohwentsia'kékha (Land) and self-in-relationship are foundational to Indigenous thought – Land is our primary relationship – it is first, before all else. Iethi'nihsténha Ohwentsia'kékha is at the very centre of the ways identity is formed/informed. (Re)membered understandings of self-in-relationship are key elements in coming to know ourselves and the ways we form an understanding of who each of us is as culturally located people in relationship to the First Nations, Métis, or Inuit people across Turtle Island (North America), as Onkwehonwe[4] and host people of this nation. It is crucial that we all consider and take seriously how we want to be in relationship to this world now and in the future:

> These are our forests, these are our ancestors. That inherited memory [(re)membered] is the essence of cultural restoration and the force that grows with each step toward the path – "the lifeway." (Laduke, 1999, pp. 5, 10)

4 "You're Not the Indian I Had in Mind"[1]

Identity is the essential core of who we are as individuals, the conscious experience of the self inside ... that identity is a state of soul – not of mind, not of citizenship.

(Anzaldúa, 1999, p. 84)

Constructions of identity for both individuals and culture-sharing groups are not bounded solely by what is conspicuous and visible; rather, they extend into lived experiences and understandings of self-in-relationship to Land that are forming and informing a conceptual framework of identity in situ. Here I explore some of the traditional ways identity was constructed, as well as the challenges of identity formation within the shifting realities and tensions embedded in contemporary landscapes. Colonial relations continue to transform the ways identity is constructed, understood, and legitimized. It is crucial to deconstruct and examine those various tensions and to look beyond blood and legislation to consider the ways Land informs constructions of the self, particularly for Indigenous people. This chapter asks some tough and risky questions in seeking to come to terms with identity in the twenty-first century.

In Situ

Many times constructions of identity for Native people across Turtle Island (North America) are perceived in relation to land within a rural or reserve framework. Reserve systems are colonial constructs designed to remove and contain Native peoples who were seen as an impediment to settler agriculture, ranching, and industrial expansion. According to the Canadian Indian Act the term *reserve* refers to a "tract of land, the legal title to which is vested in Her Majesty, that has been set apart by Her Majesty for the benefit of a band" (p. 3). This seemingly benign policy made it much easier to *legally* forcibly and coercively relocate Aboriginal people from their ancestral lands, maintain control, and enforce (many times violently) assimilationist policies and practices. It is important to mention that the development of reserve systems in Canada and the United States, while having many similarities, are notably different. Texts such as *Bury My Heart at Wounded Knee* and *Trail of Tears: The Story of the American Indian Removals* offer a heart-rending and provocative look at the violence of the forced removal, decimation, and relocation of Native people to reservations in the United States. The use of the term *reservation* is a United States designation – in Canada we use the term *reserved land* or *reserve*. In early Canadian history forceful militant relocations and blatant exterminations were not usual practices as these policies were very expensive, time consuming, and exceedingly controversial – lessons learned from the United States. The federal government used a more covert but nonetheless coercive and destructive approach to assimilation through education and proselytization.

What appears to be lost in the annals of history and contemporary understandings concerning what is and is not Native land and what is and is not an *authentic* Native identity is that Native people have continue to have deep intimate connections to Land in diverse urban and rural landscapes across all of Turtle Island. Waters (2004b) articulated her own growing and shifting understandings of self so beautifully: "Who I am now in the becoming of this place where my people walked and where they and I walk still as we voice ourselves into being" (p. 170). Contemporary realities dictate that we must take seriously the social context of the land on which we do our work in relation to the First Peoples of these lands. The point is that these understandings serve as an acknowledgment that *wherever* we live, work, and play we find ourselves on the land of the host peoples of this nation, whose identities are grounded in ancestral and contemporary lived experiences. These experiences are expressed in relation to Land that Aboriginal people have always occupied. In-mut-too-yah-lat-lat, also known as Chief Joseph of the Nez Perce nation, stated that "the earth and myself are of one mind. The measure of the land and the measure of our bodies are the same. Do not misunderstand me, but understand me fully with reference to my affection to the land" (as cited in Youngblood Henderson, 2000a, p. 260).

I want to draw attention to the unifying and shared understandings of Land in identity formation for Indigenous people nationally and internationally, which are in marked contrast to colonial reserve/reservation constructions of difference and alienation. Alienation in this context refers to the ways reserve/reservation constructs served – and in many ways still serve – to perpetuate colonialist agendas, policies, and practices for the separation, fragmentation, and distancing of Native people from what is fundamentally and inherently critical not only for identity formation but also for their humanity. By humanity I refer to the ways an individual or culture-sharing group constructs a sense of who they are in relation to their world – in this case what it means to be Indigenous. Intrinsic elements of alienation include but are certainly not limited to the complete removal of or restricted access to the most basic human rights of freedom, and relatedly, connections to Land and territories; kinship ties and the forced removal of children from familial and community connections; cultural practices; self-determination, as well as socio-economic and sociopolitical well-being and sustainability. Alienation continues to occur through the imposition of foreign educational and political practices, as well as through legislated and institutionalized constructions of identity. One need only to look at the issues surrounding the proposed First Nations Education Act that was put forward by Harper's Conservative government (the act has been tabled for now).

Historically, language, connections to lands, and sacred experiences and spiritual practices were clear indicators of identity and citizenship.[2] Identity is the intrinsic essence of our humanity – it is the conscious and spiritual expression of self-in-relationship. We internalize our construction of the self through storying, traditional teachings, and sacred experiences, as well as sense memories (spiritual, emotional, and physical recall) and connections to place. Identity is dynamic, relational, shifting, iterative, and emergent – it does not exist within a linear time/space continuum but rather is constructed and experienced in circular relationships to a world in flux. Place/land provides us with an understanding of who we are in relationship to our world that transcends temporal boundaries by providing an immediate circular connection to ancestors, providing an understanding of our past in relation to our present to conceptualize the future, and giving form to the moment of someone's birth. In other words, as landscapes change, evolve, and are storied through time so must the premise that drives our sense of identity. Kawagley (2006) profoundly states that "land urges us to come around to an understanding of ourselves" (p. 7). While language and citizenship have usually been seen as two of the most important and discernible ways to legitimize an individual's identity and standing within a community, I must also point out that within contemporary contexts it is equally important to consider the ways that identity is constructed in the narrow spaces between language, community, and sacred experiences.

As I said previously, identity is grounded in the lived experiences of people in relationship with Land and place. Identity is a complex construction in situ whether urban or rural – whether one remains in traditional lands, was born into or moved to an urban centre, or perhaps retains connections to both. Place is dynamic and emergent in which I, as a person of First Nations and mixed-blood European ancestry, who resides in my First Nations territory, and is an academic in a prominent dominant Western-informed university, carry within myself many shifting and at times conflicting, contradictory, and sometimes hidden identities. These identities converge in an understanding and acknowledgment of self-in-relationship that form who I am now – in this place in this time – and who I will become in relation to Land, where my ancestors made tracks layered upon tracks and where we continue to walk together, weaving our complex stories, making new and distinct footprints. The acknowledgment of these shifting understandings of identity and self-in-relationship opens opportunities for examining the ways Indigenous people who may or may not speak their original language, who live or work in urban centres, and who may or may not have access to what would traditionally be understood as sacred experiences take up issues of identity. It also considers what discourses persist and reinforce notions of identification.

Contemporary constructions of identity extend beyond the specificity of land consciousness to being grounded in the unifying and shared philosophies, principles, and ontologies of Land across urban and rural environments, as well as cross- and trans-nationally. Census data tell us that approximately half of Canada's Aboriginal population currently resides in urban centres. A 2011 report by Statistics Canada providing Aboriginal population projections into 2031 suggests that this trend will continue because the Aboriginal population is younger, more urbanized, and growing at a rate that is approximately 1.5 times faster than the general national average. This population is moving into urban centres at an increasing rate, seeking options that may not be available or are limited in their First Nations communities, such as access to higher education; better employment opportunities; and safe, adequate, or available housing. In the *Ęhse:gwé:ni* (*you will succeed*): *Words of Wisdom from Urban Aboriginal Youth* 2010 research report, when Aboriginal youth were asked whether they feel that urban Aboriginal youth struggle with their identity, replied with an unequivocal and unanimous "yes – we're all confused … if you say you're not, you're lying" (p. 22). They also expressed an overwhelming need to find the experience and answer for themselves what it means to be Native.

What Is This … Identity?

But what is this notion of identity? What is assumed when the word is casually applied? Starting from a very basic and general understanding, the etymology of the word is the circa late-sixteenth-century Latin *identitas*, referring to "the quality of being identical," which in turn stems from the early Latin *idem*, meaning "sameness." Gleason (1983) tells us that "*identity* is a new term, as well as being an elusive and ubiquitous one" (p. 910) having arisen to popular use sometime in the 1950s within the field of social science, particularly with regard to organized religion which was, at that particular time, seen as *the* mechanism by which one finds his/her place in society. The contradiction here is that in the process of attempting to create belonging, membership, and connectedness, identity fell into use in ways that constructed and imposed religious and social conformity, uniformity, and control. Its expression fostered divisiveness and dichotomous representations. Gleason writes that two core elements underpin the term identity: (1) it refers to the ways an individual or a group is known by the use of a name; and (2) it can also, and with greater complexity, refer to the unique characteristics and cultural features that make up the particular world view of a culture-sharing group. Gleason notes that by the 1960s the term *identity* had gained such currency and was infused "so widely and so loosely that to determine its provenance in every context would be impossible" (p. 918). Gleason concludes that ambiguity and confusion concerning possible interpretations and usage continue to be not only inevitable but also unavoidable. Dr Julia Coates, a Cherokee history professor and tribal councillor, stated that the concept of identity continues to remain a highly contentious, fuzzy, and shifting subject (Ridge, 2011, n.p.) – even after approximately 60 years of use. Despite the complex tensions, challenges, and contradictions, I believe that constructions of identity are and always have been an attempt to engage with the philosophical and ontological expressions of self-in-relationship – for all of us.

There are many ways to engage a dialogue regarding the complex and at times highly contested areas relating to Aboriginal identity. I will focus on three overarching themes that are threaded through the discourse concerning Aboriginal identity: traditional forms of identity relationships; racialized constructions of identity; and the contradictions related to the contemporary realities of mixed-blood and urban identities. The intention of this discussion is to purposefully, mindfully, and respectfully engage ethical space so we might explore the ways these discourses help to shape experiences and expressions of identity.

In traditional contexts identity was constructed around connections to land, clan membership, storying, spiritual practices, and roles and responsibilities to sociopolitical and kinship relationships. Identity then structures the values and beliefs that frame the ways an individual engages with his or her world. Dr Julia Coates stated, "300 years ago, there was little question who was Cherokee: If your mother was Cherokee, you were, too" (Ridge, 2011, n.p.). Issues of citizenship were defined through clan membership. According to Hodenosaunee philosophies, matrilineal clan membership roles and responsibilities were (re)implemented and (re)defined by the Peacemaker. An individual's clan and the fulfilment of the roles and responsibilities inherent in those relationships provided the fundamental elements of the ways identity was constructed. McCarthy (2010), Onondaga Nation, Beaver Clan, and assistant professor at the University of Buffalo, tells us that the Mohawk word *otara* for what is described in English as *clan* means "land, clay or earth" (p. 85) and when one asks what clan an individual belongs to, they are quite literally asking, "what is the outline or contour of your clay? Referring to the land you can access and the territory to which you belong … land relationships are the basis of understanding clans" (p. 85). In Aotearoa (New Zealand) the Māori similarly refer to themselves as tangata whenua (people of the land) to describe deep and intimate relationships to their lands, mountains, and waterways.

According to McCarthy clan membership is not just what or who you are; it is also about the ways you act on your responsibilities to that clan relationship. Similarly, Simpson (2011), an activist and scholar of Michi Saagig Nishnaabeg ancestry, writes that each of us live and become our identity and that we must do so in ways that move us towards "mino bimaadiziwin, the good life" (p. 13). She identifies the *good life* as a set of principles and philosophies that are grounded in language and culture that does not essentialize Nishnaabeg identity but instead allows for plurality within Nishnaabeg epistemes that are grounded in an in-depth knowledge of language, culture, and Nishnaabeg philosophies. Community acceptance was dependent on an individual's commitment to the expression of mino bimaadiziwin. Gregory Cajete, in Four Arrows, Cajete, and Lee (2010), says that identity as an "ideal of the highest thought is a generic term for a commonly held set of values and beliefs for guiding the alignment of mind, body, and spirit with high ethical and spiritual standards ... our beliefs indeed determine what we become" (pp. 56, 61). In this context identity, similar to Land, is above all a sacred and spiritual experiential construction.

Building from these traditional understandings, it is critical that I also acknowledge the many complex contemporary realities that, because of colonial disruptions, inform constructions of Aboriginal identity: reserve, rural, urban, or some combination thereof; full-blood or mixed-blood; status, non-status, and Bill C-31; language speakers, non-language speakers, and varying degrees of fluency; Traditional, Christian (in its broadest context), or some combination of the two; and many other shades of possibilities.

Colonial relations and interferences through legislation and assimilative policies and practices have shifted and distorted traditional constructions of identity in attempting to address the realities caused by funding restrictions, financial constraints, and political agendas. Concerns over funding and poor socio-economic conditions have overridden traditional understandings of Land and self-in-relationship. As stated earlier, identity has become a highly contested politically and economically driven topic for many rural and urban Aboriginal people and communities, leading to what Palmater (2011) identifies as "cultural trauma" (p. 57). Palmater writes that First Nations identity is primarily a construction of difference that needs to be protected for several reasons, including (1) protection under international law; (2) Indigenous peoples' special connection to this land that predates contact; (3) colonial relations that disrupted Indigenous sovereignty; and (4) Indigenous treaty relationships with Canada. To deny that Aboriginal people have an identity that is distinct within their own cultures and landscape is a particular form of racism. The crucial aspect of identity that is most often referred to is ancestry. Understanding our ancestry links us to our past and is critical for understanding how to be – now and in the future. Ancestry is an understanding that as an individual we are descended from a particular culture-sharing group, which links us to shared stories, ancestors, and lands, as well as to cultural practices, values, and beliefs. However, there are those that overstep traditional understandings of ancestral connections, blurring the boundaries between ancestral connections and blood quantum. Whereas ancestry focuses on shared familial and community kinship ties, blood quantum centres on notions of racial purity.

Politics of Purity

The idea of blood quantum originates with long-discredited biogenetic models, such as eugenics and phrenology. Eugenics, a branch of social philosophy that was developed in the nineteenth century, was seen as a way to improve the human race through selective breeding practices that encouraged the transmission of what were considered *desirable* characteristics – thereby achieving racial purity. Phrenology refers to the study of the shape and measurement of skulls as a determinant of mental acuity and character. These studies were used by government officials on Native Americans to determine who was and was not full-blooded for government registration purposes. Blood quantum came to be used as the criteria for determining identity in what I refer to as the *politics of purity*. Politics of purity as a method of determining identity and citizenship has both advocates and critics (with varying shades in between) and is fraught with many tensions and contradictions.

Those who are critical of applying blood quantum requirements to constructions of identity and membership of Indigeneity[3] state that when such a practice is adopted by Indigenous people it generates discourses that are racist, exclusionary, reductionist, stigmatizing, divisive, and fragmentary. It creates a form of objectified relatedness that calls into question racialized authenticity, purity, and contamination. Politics of purity reduces identity from deeply intimate, relational, and sacred connections to legislated, oppositional, and institutionalized constructions of difference. Strong and Van Winkle (1996) write that blood quantum remains a widely used, if contested, method for determining identity and membership among federally recognized nations in the United States. The levels of *blood* required for membership differ – while some nations in the United States do not ascribe to a minimum blood quantum for membership, others require a minimum of 25 percent (one-quarter).

Blood is generally, across many cultures and religions, considered the life essence; blood is sacred; it is the source of life; blood is (re)generative – without blood life ceases to exist. There is an ancient, unfathomable, and intimate relationship between life (existence) and blood. Proponents of blood quantum argue that individuals with less than 25 percent blood quantum claiming Native ancestry are perpetuating a "peculiar form of appropriation that lays claim not only to land, labour, and knowledge, but even to blood, the presumed (though colonially imposed) substantive basis of the colonized identity" (Strong & Van Winkle, 1996, p. 552).

In Canada blood quantum is generally disregarded and is not a term that has been written into legislation; however, current legislation does rely on degrees of separation. In other words, one generation of marrying out would equate to 50 percent blood quantum and two generations equates to 25 percent blood quantum, et cetera. The hegemonic discourses embedded within blood quantum generate fixed and rigid ideals concerning membership that erase all the nuances and shifting realities related to identity and belonging in the twenty-first century. One interesting contradiction in the discussions relating to issues of blood quantum is the ways individuals with low blood quantum (considered by advocates of blood quantum to be the oppressors) might also lay claim to being the oppressed – colonizers simultaneously claiming to be the colonized – the other. In this way the colonizers, through blood appropriation, may be naturalizing themselves and legitimizing claims to this land, its resources, and ancestral experiences. The appropriation of blood may also serve another form of insidious assimilationist agenda: the attempted erasure of Indigenous people from the consciousness of Land to accomplish the goal articulated by Duncan Campbell Scott during his tenure as superintendent of the Department of Indian Affairs in the early 1900s – essentially "to get rid of the Indian problem" (Titley, 1986, p. 50).

Advocates for blood quantum processes assert that with increasing federal financial constraints, bands cannot be held financially responsible for individuals who are not on their *list* of members. Blood quantum membership is seen as central to communities' struggles for sovereignty, resources (financial and natural), land claims, and claims to treaty rights. Another contradiction focuses on the ways Aboriginal communities, in resistance to federal legislation, such as the Indian Act, are drawing on those same colonially imposed ideologies about race and the politics of purity for determining identity and citizenship. However, blood purity is not a guarantee of active participation and community engagement – citizenship – and further, individuals with

Native ancestral heritage may be excluded under the politics of purity but would welcome opportunities to learn about their culture and ancestral knowledges, as well as to engage with community in active citizenship.

I find it disconcerting that legitimate community concerns relating to Indigeneity are not being addressed effectively or adequately and in an attempt to counter-respond some are, in fact, replicating and perpetuating colonial relations of determining membership. In considering the harmful but seemingly necessary colonial discourse regarding the politics of purity, it seems that we may be unavoidably left with what Spivak (1993) so eloquently articulated as a "useful yet semimournful position of the unavoidable usefulness of something that is dangerous" (p. 5). However, as I reflect on the words of Audre Lorde (1981), a Caribbean-American writer and political activist, "the master's tools will never dismantle the master's house" (p. 98), I question whether we have taken the time and asked the risky and tough questions. Have we journeyed beyond the boundaries of dominant Western impositions of colonial ideologies to find new ways of articulating identity that are grounded in very old knowledges? Thomas King (2003) writes that "we see race ... race is [both] a construction and an illusion. Never mind that it does not exist in either biology or theology ... the important thing is that we believe we can see it" (p. 44).

As a person of First Nations and mixed-European ancestry, I find having identity and membership defined solely on racialized constructs embedded in the politics of purity very disturbing and essentializing. Although I fully understand the reasons that communities may impose such restrictions, it is also a slippery slope that will ultimately serve to accomplish colonial agendas of assimilation and internal selective annihilation. It is both staunch traditionalism and the politics of purity as sole criteria for identity and membership that are problematic. Both may be restrictive, exclusionary, and raise questions concerning who is *real* or *authentic* enough to be First Nations, Métis, or Inuit (FNMI).

Many traditionalists assert that unless you speak the language fluently and actively participate in traditional cultural practices, you are excluded from being an authentic FNMI person. Please do not misunderstand me: I am fully committed to and passionate about issues around language use, maintenance, and preservation and assert that anyone who is in a position to teach or learn the language should do so and use it often and consistently in everyday social and political activities. I believe emphatically that language is critical to transmitting knowledges, stories, ceremonies, and cultural practices that are embedded in Land. I also believe that it is crucial to participate in and maintain traditional cultural ceremonial practices. However, language acquisition and degrees of fluency, depth of cultural knowledge, and the politics of purity should not be the *sole* markers of identity – but I do believe that they may be seen as benchmarks. Having said that, cultures and languages are not static – they evolve to meet the demands of innovations and contemporary mores, as do our continual and deepening understandings of those knowledges. Indigenous cultural practices and languages had evolved across millennia pre-contact would have continued to do so sans contact. Nevertheless, our current reality is that colonial relations continue to shift and disrupt languages and traditional cultural practices.

Identities, informed in great part by cultural practices and language use, are also organic, shifting and evolving to address contemporary realities. When I participated in an eight-week research internship in Aotearoa (New Zealand), I had an opportunity to talk with the Kaumātua (Māori Elders) in Tauranga, a northwestern coastal city, about these issues relating to identity across Turtle Island. The Kaumātua were silent for a few minutes, and then one spoke and said that in Aotearoa if an individual, regardless of appearance or degree of Māori ancestry, can trace his or her ancestors to the first waka (Māori canoes) that came across the great waters – if he or she can tell the story – then that person is Māori. For the Māori people identity is not tied to economics or politics of purity; however, it is strongly and intimately connected to understandings of Land, landscapes, self-in-relationship, and the responsibilities one has to those relationships – in fact, Māori refer to themselves as tangata whenua (people of the land).

Appearance is another racialized marker in the politics of purity for determining degrees of *Nativeness*. Individuals with multiple European lineages and diverse appearances are rarely if ever called on to justify their identity – for example, no one in North America says, "Prove to me that you're German. You don't look German. You don't act German or talk with a German accent. You cannot speak German. So you are not German enough. Where is your status card that proves you are German? How much German blood do you actually have? You have lost your status as a German because you married a non-German or your children can no longer claim German heritage because they only have 25 percent German blood"; however, nearly everyone has an opinion on politics of purity regarding Indigeneity. Race continues to be one of the most powerful indicators of identity and ethnicity and is particularly complex for urban and mixed-blood Native people. I believe that the inter-engagement between tribal and urban for the mixed-blood individual is fraught with many tangled and at times overlapping and conflicting tensions, challenges, and contradictions – not the least of which is resistance to internal and external stereotypes.

The youth that I interviewed in the *Ęhse:gwé:ni* (*you will succeed*): *Words of Wisdom from Urban Aboriginal Youth* research project indicated that there was nothing easy or simple about being urban Aboriginal or urban mixed-blood Aboriginal. They each said that they struggle daily with finding ways to conceptualize and express their *Nativeness*. The youth indicated that they feel excluded and marginalized for several reasons, including (1) the essentialized and racialized constructions of identity within many First Nations rural and urban communities; (2) the imposed federal policies on Aboriginal identity, such as status cards and the implications of Bill C-31: Amendment to the Indian Act; (3) the embodiment of these federal policies by First Nations communities through marginalization, which means little or no access to resources or traditional teachings; and (4) the internalization of racist practices and perceptions.

Identity-in-Relationship

Many community and academic scholars agree that the Indian Act and its implications have disrupted and displaced understandings and expressions of identity, particularly regarding relationality. Theresa McCarthy (2010), Onondaga Nation from Six Nations of the Grand River Territory, purports that these relationships and hence identity are tied to the clan system, which is an embodiment of language, ceremonies, and the Confederacy.[4] McCarthy writes that (re)asserting the clan-based Confederacy system can serve to *reconcile* Hodenosaunee people, regardless of where they reside or the degree of fluency (or lack thereof) of the language, with their identity, teachings, and ways of knowing and being in the world. Drawing on several common or shared understandings, McCarthy's choice of the word *reconcile* is an interesting one, implying that individuals need to be restored into friendly or right relations with the principles of the clan system, that they are settling a quarrel or need to be shown to be compatible with the clan system. The disruption of the clan system has indeed occurred because of colonial relations by way of assimilative and destructive policies, practices, and legislation; however, it would be more accurate to articulate the process of reconnecting Hodenosaunee people to the clan system as (re)membering rather than reconciling. To (re)member, as discussed in Chapter 2, is the action of being able to bring forward ancient knowledges from memory to the conscious mind. It follows that (re)membering is actively (re)conceptualizing those ancestral traditions, knowledges, and philosophies, such as the clan system, in new contemporary ways that can address the current complexities of Native people across Turtle Island.

(Re)centring the principles, philosophies, and ontologies of Land as primary (first) is one of the ways identity may remain intact. The clan system is one, albeit important, expression and embodiment of relationality, responsibility, reciprocity, and connections to land (lower-case *l*). McCarthy centralizes and argues for the primacy of the clan system with all of the various connections to language, ceremonies, and land. When Indigeneity is solely considered from the perspective of land (lower-case *l*) it serves, in many cases, to erase, marginalize, or exclude conceptualizations of identity for numerous Indigenous people, particularly urban and mixed-blood. Land (capital *L*), in which *all* Indigenous knowledges and pedagogies are embodied, comes first – Land is first before all other knowledges. It is from these understandings of Land that the Peacemaker gave birth to the Confederacy and the clan system.[5] It is Land that connects Indigenous people locally, nationally, and globally to deep and intimate understandings of self-in-relationship – the clan system is one interconnected and interdependent embodiment of self-in-relationship.

Regardless of positionality three main threads of thought regarding identity have risen out of this dialogue: (1) self-identification; (2) the roles, relationships, and responsibilities of citizenship; and (3) federally legislated membership and rights to access resources. Self-identification transcends arguments about blood quantum, legitimacy, and authenticity that are embedded in the politics of purity. Self-identity forms the essential core of who we are and how we position ourselves. As an individual of mixed blood, it is essential that I embrace all the elements that form my sense of self and being in this world creating a holistic, balanced understanding of myself-in-relationship. Self-in-relationship is not merely external but also a conscious embodiment and expression of the self within.

Self-identification may or may not be connected to the roles, relationships, and responsibilities of citizenship, regardless of whether one resides in a First Nations rural community or urban centre. Individuals may claim membership through self-identification and not take on active and effective citizenship but may attempt to claim the rights and privileges of that citizenship. Citizenship, found in clan membership and understandings of self-in-relationship, comes with certain responsibilities that guarantee being able to access the rights and privileges of citizenship. I would ask if one can truly identify (self or otherwise) without actively walking out the responsibilities of that citizenship? Supporters of blood quantum methods would certainly argue that if one attempted to self-identify outside the politics of purity, one could not. Appointments and adoptions are also another particular form of traditional membership that comes with specific civic responsibilities.

On 11 July 2011 the website of then prime minister of Canada Stephen Harper reported that he had been ceremonially named an honorary member of the Kainai Chieftainship by the Blood Tribe of Alberta. The honorary title was reportedly given to him as the highest ranking representative of Canada in response to the 2008 federal government apology. In his acceptance speech Harper indicated that it was a great privilege and honour to be named an honorary chief of Alberta's Blood Tribe. Further, he stated that the naming recognized the efforts that the government was making in investing in the future of Aboriginal peoples, and he would "*carry* his Blood name, Ninayh' poaksin (Chief Speaker), with great joy and pride" (McTighe, 2011; emphasis mine). Yet many First Nations communities continue to exist in third-world conditions – the implications of which are extreme poverty, lack of employment and educational opportunities, high-risk drinking water and sewage systems, substandard and at times dangerous housing conditions, and poor health and lack of accessible or adequate health care – all of which contribute to the overwhelming hopelessness and rising suicide rates. In his time in office after the naming, Prime Minister Harper never provided any indication that he intended to take seriously the roles, relationships, and responsibilities of his honorary citizenship to the Blood Tribe specifically or to FNMI peoples nationally.

While appointments and adoptions are one form of legitimate traditional tribal membership, genuine self-identification comes in a particular package that embodies the roles, relationships, and responsibilities inherent in understandings of self-in-relationship with that identity. There are a great many Aboriginal people living both in First Nations rural communities and in urban centres that embody that understanding and take seriously their roles, relationships, and responsibilities.

These individuals come from diverse linguistic, spiritual, and mixed-blood experiences, yet their commitment to citizenship and developing understandings of self-in-relationship is unquestionable and unwavering.

Having outlined self-identification and citizenship, it is important to point out the reality that, because of a variety of complex historical and contemporary reasons, many First Nations communities are unable to be self-sustaining and, therefore, must be fiscally responsible and accountable with their federal funding dollars – and most are. This creates an extra burden for financial restraint and the necessity of establishing rigid criteria for access to scarce and limited resource dollars. Many First Nations communities fear that allowing self-identification as a criterion for membership and the rights that come with citizenship would open the door for wider access to what are already strained resources and services. As noted earlier, the questions then become: Do the colonizers in some perverse form of appropriation become the colonized? In so doing should they be entitled to any rights and access of citizenship of the colonized? I would also ask, with great trepidation, are we able to have such dichotomous designations or distinctions anymore? Are distinctions, such as colonizer and colonized, appropriate in current contexts? Loomba (2005) asserts that any dichotomous oppositional relationships between colonizers and colonized are further complicated by the "enormous cultural and racial differences within each of these categories as well as cross-overs between them" (p. 91).

The inherent contradiction is that these constructions of difference, as lines drawn in the sand, are crucial in upholding the fiduciary and constitutional accountability of the federal government in historical and contemporary treaty agreements and legislation. Prime Minister Harper stated emphatically and with great aplomb in a speech at the close of the September 2009 G20 Summit that Canada has no history of colonialism. Ironically this statement was made before the leaders of the world 15 months after the June 2008 federal government apology was issued by the same prime minister who, as discussed earlier, also accepted an honorary chieftainship from the Blood Nation. First Nations communities are increasingly and legitimately concerned with maintaining those hard lines in the sand and keeping those constructions of difference in place to protect treaty rights and their constitutional identity as distinct peoples. It is also an interesting contradiction that First Nations communities, to protect federal treaty rights and for lack of any other currently discernible options, are using the very exclusionary tactics put in place by the federal government to use against Aboriginal people.

So many imposed constructions of identity are based on complex and interwoven historical and contemporary relations that we must carefully and respectfully untie the knots and peel back every layer and examine each construct. However, I want to point out that while it is necessary to deconstruct concepts and notions of identity and (re)membered understandings of self-in-relationship, I must be exceedingly careful that I stop before leaving nothing but ash in the wake of a burning desire for clarity within a tangled and combustive web of colonial relations. It has become very clear to me in examining the various tensions, complexities, and contested terrain relating to concepts of identity that identity is fluid. Identity shifts and transforms, and may be highly contextualized. Recognizing that no definitive definition can prescriptively outline what identity is and is not without being discriminatory, exclusionary, or otherwise marginalizing, we can, however, have landmarks that can act as indicators for identity. As Indigenous people we need to move beyond dichotomous and oppositional positionings towards meaningful and respectful relations with one another as the host and original people of this nation.

We began this journey looking to explore what our individual and collective relationships are to the vision for an Indigenous philosophy of education based on Land. Aboriginal people who, for a variety of reasons, either move from First Nations rural communities into cities and urban centres or are second- and third-generation urban Aboriginal people become "scattered like beads off a necklace and put back together in new patterns, new strings" (Erdrich, 1999, p. 220) in which new forms of identity, as well as connections to Land and self-in-relationship, must, quite literally, be (re)cognized. The philosophical principles of Land, self-in-relationship, identity, and epistemology in relation to the contemporary rural and urban contexts become (re)cognized in new, fresh, and exciting ways. Alfred (2008) states that survival of Aboriginal people in the twenty-first century depends on "finding new ways to love the land" (p. 10); in essence we need to find different ways of (re)membering and (re)cognizing identity and meaning making from contemporary rural, urban, and mixed-blood landscapes. While Aboriginal identity must be acknowledged as a construction of difference, it is important that we (re)member that it is also a construction of shared histories and territories, as well as of familial, kinship, and communal ties. These shared characteristics are grounded in the (re)membered and (re)cognized principles, philosophies, and ontologies expressed in and through Iethi'nihsténha Ohwentsia'kékha (Land):

> We do not worship nature we are a part of it. Indigenous people under-
> stand the land ... as a relationship made manifest ... in concrete rather
> than romanticized terms ... [and they] continue to recognize their ties to
> the land in various ways. (Kuokkanen, 2007, pp. 33, 42)

Knowledge – (Re)cognizing

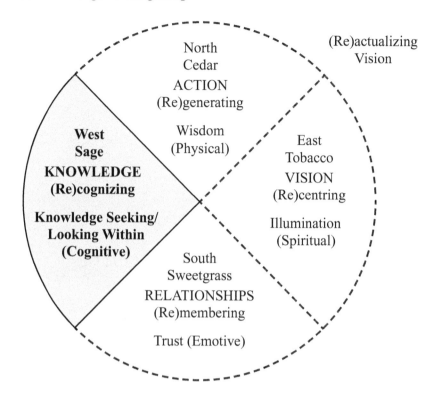

In Section 2 we examined what our individual and collective relationships and responsibilities are for the vision for an Indigenous philosophy of education. This section focuses on the ways we can develop individual and collective knowledges associated with that vision. As we continue our journey through the circle, knowledge is located at the western door of looking within or introspection and is guided by the sacred medicine sage. Sage is used in sacred fires to prepare people for ceremonies and teachings by calming and releasing what may be troubling or confusing the mind, restoring balance among the various aspects of being (mind, body, spirit, and emotion), and removing negative energies. Nii Gaani Aki Innini (Dave Courchene), Anishinaabe Wisdom Keeper, tells us that the fire, as a spiritual element of life, acts as a doorway into sacred and spiritual experiences – ceremony. Fire is one of the steps required for securing a vision from the Great Spirit – and in the words of Nii Gaani Aki Innini, "once individual vision is secured, it will lead to a collective vision that will bring peace into this world and a greater respect for all Life" (n.p.).[1]

This section brings forward and ignites those sacred fires: contemporary (re)memberings of ancient knowledges and very old pedagogies by exploring the complex circular and interrelated concepts informing Indigenous philosophies. The phrase *very old pedagogies* is defined as an acknowledgment and an honouring of the art and science embedded in traditional Indigenous teaching practices. In Relations of Privilege – Relations of Power I explore aspects of architecture and the ways spaces are inhabited and made placeful. I conclude with an examination of the ways these inhabited architectural spaces, along with networks and relations of power, continue to influence education, together with connections to Indigenous philosophies grounded in understandings of Iethi'nihsténha Ohwentsia'kékha (Land). Land and Circularity: An Indigenous Philosophical Approach to Thought is an exploration into rationality, particularly in relationship to Iethi'nihsténha Ohwentsia'kékha and understandings of self-in-relationship and circularity. This section opens opportunities for exploring collaborative, collective, and individual knowledge building in which we may (re)cognize, literally come to know again, very old knowledges in contemporary contexts.

5 Sacred Fires: Contemporary (Re)memberings of Ancient Knowledges and Very Old Pedagogies

As long as you remember what you have seen, then nothing is gone. As long as you remember, it is part of this story we have together. *Remember*, she said, *remember* everything.

(Silko, 1977, pp. 231, 235)

Traditional knowledges are living knowledges that evolve with the circular, fluid, and organic characteristics of Indigenous philosophies experienced through Iethi'nihsténha Ohwentsia'kékha (Land). Traditional knowledges continue to be transmitted through storying and ancestral teachings; shared values and beliefs; and Land-centred activities, reflections, and observations – they are woven out of individual and collective experiences. Kawagley (2006) tells us that Indigenous people could (re)cognize and adapt to an ever-changing landscape through "their ability to reconstruct and continuously modify their worldviews, so that *new* Native traditions" (p. 9) could evolve to meet contemporary realities.

The sacred fires of this chapter focus on the ways (re)membered ancient knowledges may be understood and (re)cognized within contemporary realities, bringing us closer to the vision for an Indigenous philosophy of education based on Iethi'nihsténha Ohwentsia'kékha. Ancient knowledges are able to be (re)cognized within contemporary contexts because these knowledges are living knowledges – they exist and are relevant now, in this time; they are not relics of some forgotten past. Hodenosaunee philosophers[1] tell us that traditional knowledge is based on storying and ancestral teachings grounded in Land, the ideology of rational thought, and the principles of the Peacemaker, which are confirmed as shared stories in the writings of many Indigenous authors across Turtle Island.[2]

Storying through (re)membered and (re)cognized knowledges is one of the ways that oral traditions may serve to disrupt dominant Western conceptualizations and (re)tellings of the tangled histories of colonial relations. Oral traditions and stories are alive and well, authenticating histories and teachings so that in the absence of text, those oral traditions continue to retain those knowledges. I want to be clear about my use of the term *authentic*. In this context *authentic* refers to how traditional knowledges are transmitted in ways that are emotionally and relationally appropriate, significantly relevant, purposefully, and mindfully respectful, as well as ethically responsible. Storied traditional knowledges make our spaces placeful, contextualize historical events, and are a vehicle for passing on our oral traditions and ancient knowledges. The sharing and creation of knowledges has always been and continues to be a social and relational activity because each individual or culture-sharing group adds their own lived experiences and understandings to oral and textual processes.

Indigenous philosophies are an acknowledgment that Land carries the storied footprints or tracks of our ancestors through (re)membering and (re)cognizing oral traditions, ancient knowledges, and very old pedagogies. As I stated in the Introduction, we speak and write from the position of who we are in relation to what we know. Ancient knowledges are the full range of all the values and beliefs that philosophically underpin an individual's own culture-sharing group. For Indigenous people these knowledges are grounded in Land and experienced as self-in-relationship that are as alive and relevant as they ever were and are passed on or communicated through shared common values and beliefs, storied place names, sacred experiences, and traditional teachings. Indigenous peoples' intimate and storied connections to their landscapes are also representations of the ways they perceive themselves in relationship to their lands. Symbolic reservoirs, such as language and land, may be used as vehicles to transmit knowledges and to establish and maintain social and moral values. These ancient knowledges existed pre-contact and remain on and in the land. Therefore, these knowledges while embedded in ancestral consciousness are also (re)cognized within contemporary realities.

Iethi'nihsténha Ohwentsia'kékha (Land) is a (re)cognition that those ancient knowledges and stories are still significant and relevant today, despite the fact they may be buried beneath mounds of concrete and asphalt. Woodworth (2010), a Kanien'kehá:ka (Mohawk) from Six Nations, puts forward three premises that he asserts underlie the contextualization of Indigenous knowledges in urban centres: (1) that all things revolve cyclically, (2) that the ancestors look over the people, and (3) that "spirits of place are defined as those who embrace the knowing held in the land" (p. 32). Building on those understandings, I would say that Woodworth's premises are also foundational to the (re)cognition of Indigenous knowledges not only in urban contexts but also across diverse cultural and geographic *Land*scapes. Considering this, it is my belief that the (re)cognition of Indigenous knowledges is based on the following three understandings: (1) circularity, including iterativity and reciprocity, (2) interconnected and interdependent understandings of self-in-relationship, and (3) philosophies of Iethi'nihsténha Ohwentsia'kékha (Land) that serve to ground traditional knowledges and the (re)cognizing of these ancestral knowledges and very old pedagogies within contemporary contexts.

However, in spite of the (re)cognized importance and relevance, Indigenous knowledges have been, and in many ways (some subtle and others more openly) continue to be, devalued, delegitimized, and decentred from what is considered *worthwhile* knowledge by scholars and educators who embrace a dominant Western imperialistic world view. These scholars and educators position Indigenous knowledges as quaint, mythical, exotic, and irrelevant in contemporary contexts. For this reason some Indigenous scholars, such as Youngblood Henderson (2009), reject the use of the term *culture* for *world view* because he considers the term *culture* a concept that fragments and compartmentalizes Indigenous world views into spurious (and I would add stereotypical) images and ideas. The term *culture* can also erase the complex and rich diversity among Indigenous people nationally and internationally, and negate the distinctiveness of intimate and storied connections to place. While the specificity of place is hugely significant, the term *world view* opens up opportunities to consider some of the shared philosophical footings that are grounded in Land and understandings of self-in-relationship.

A World View?

Themes of relationality, circularity, spirituality, and consciousness of Land provide the unifying context of shared world views among Indigenous people throughout Turtle Island and indeed across the great waters. The notion of one singular world view is steeped in dominant Eurocentric imperial and colonial ideologies and is framed within discourses based on privilege and power. Dominant Western privilege ensures that

those individuals or groups of individuals who are fixed into that particular world view are largely unaware of what they are unaware of.
Many scholars in various disciplines have written that dominant Western world views lean towards hierarchical, binarial, linear, alienating,
and contentious perspectives. Wilshire (2006), however, makes an interesting distinction between dominant Western "Euro-American thinkers
and their strictly European ancestor-thinkers" (p. 264). It is his argument,
and one that I think has strong merit, that Euro-American thought has
been greatly influenced by the Indigenous people of Turtle Island. One
example is the well-documented connections between Hodenosaunee
political thought and the democratic processes of both Canadian and
American government systems. The second is the *somewhat* less exploitive and more romanticized perspectives on notions of land and relationships to land. Wilshire goes on to draw on some of the connections
between Black Elk's notion of *The Great Hoop of the World* and Emerson's
Nature. However, the distinctions between the two works lie in understanding the sacredness of land. Wilshire writes that what is generally
understood to be a world view would be more aptly articulated as the
ways a culture-sharing group is intimately connected to their environment. I believe this reluctance in articulating or ascribing the spiritual,
relational, and sentient nature of Land is one of the greatest distinctions
between dominant Western and Indigenous thought. It is this understanding of Land that is at the core of Indigenous thought.

Iethi'nihsténha Ohwentsia'kékha as an Indigenous philosophy is a
complete knowledge system that has its own logic based on a particular
form of rational thought. Dr Erica-Irene Daes, special rapporteur to the
United Nations, summarized it well when she stated, "the heritage of
an [I]ndigenous people is not merely a collection of objects, stories, and
ceremonies, but a complete knowledge system with its own concepts of
epistemology, philosophy, and scientific and logical validity" (cited in
Youngblood Henderson, 2000a, p. 261).

Indigenous world views are generally founded on two related but
distinct circular and iterative concepts: (1) Land as an external system
in flux, and (2) the principles of self-in-relationship that are an expression of creation. Together these two concepts reinforce and maintain the
values and beliefs relating to circularity and that all things in the natural world are alive, dynamic, interconnected, and interdependent. For
this reason centring Indigenous thought (de)centres dominant Western imperialism. The acquisition and enacting of Indigenous knowledges are grounded in Iethi'nihsténha Ohwentsia'kékha (Land) and are

premised on understandings of self-in-relationship. It, therefore, follows that education and educational processes based on the acquisition and use of Indigenous knowledges are also grounded in Iethi'nihsténha Ohwentsia'kékha (which includes the specificity of place), circularity, and understandings of self-in-relationship.

Enacting Knowledges

The concept of enacting knowledge via visioning, process, and action are conceptualized in the figure below as expressed through the circular elements of vision, relationships, knowledge, and action. Indigenous knowledges and languages are an expression of a world in flux. They express that reality through fluidity, movement, and relationality. Simpson (2008) writes that "we must act. We must live our knowledge … the first step to making something happen is often a dream or a vision" (pp. 74, 81). According to the principles of Indigenous philosophy, it is

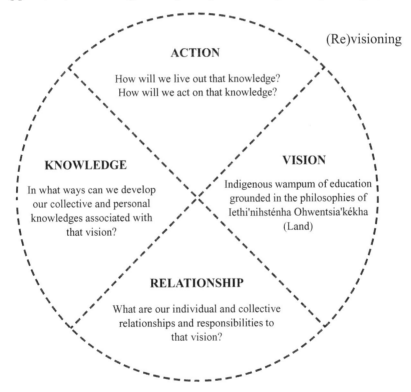

(Re)visioning

ACTION

How will we live out that knowledge?
How will we act on that knowledge?

KNOWLEDGE

In what ways can we develop
our collective and personal
knowledges associated with
that vision?

VISION

Indigenous wampum of education
grounded in the philosophies of
Iethi'nihsténha Ohwentsia'kékha
(Land)

RELATIONSHIP

What are our individual and collective
relationships and responsibilities to
that vision?

the process rather than the product that is valued and of paramount importance.

Note that the vision section in this figure is articulated by a statement while the other elements of the circle are represented by questions. While the genesis of visioning may entail questioning – when one enters this circle through the eastern door, one must have at least an initial, albeit fluid, articulation of the vision for journeying with the circle – it is this statement that will help inform the answers to the questions posed within each of the other elements of the circle. For example, we cannot address what the relationships are that connect us to the vision unless we have articulated, at least initially, what our vision for the journeying is. In this context journeying, as previously outlined, must be characterized by purposeful intent – otherwise it is nothing more than aimless wandering. It is this purposeful intention that is transformative, leading the journeyer towards shifting previously held assumptions and paradigms. Working through the questions posted in the action section will lead to (re)visioning in an iterative process, allowing for a deepening and richer connection and articulation of the initial vision. This process may and often does continue until the journeying and storying through the circle is completed – for some that is a short time; for others, it is a lifetime.

Land as Sacred

In attempting to identify and articulate a holistic vision for education grounded in an Indigenous philosophy of Iethi'nihsténha Ohwentsia'kékha we must consider the shared common values and beliefs about spirituality and the sacred. While specificity relating to spiritual and sacred experiences is highly contextual, the unifying concepts are grounded in Land and understandings of self-in-relationship. Stories, place names, and traditional ancestral teachings that ground the Indigenous person centre on the sacredness of land – land is sacred, spiritual, experiential, and expressive. Momaday (1997) so beautifully writes that "where words and place come together, there is the sacred" (p. 111) and that "to encounter the sacred is to be alive at the deepest centre of human existence" (p. 114). Therefore, learning in relation to Iethi'nihsténha Ohwentsia'kékha is to experience a sacred and intimate connection with self-in-relationship. Cajete (1999) refers to this sense of the sacred and intimate relationship as "spiritual ecology" (p. 3). These understandings of Land and self-in-relationship provide the philosophical basis for conceptualizing world views and our relationship and responsibilities to natural and built worlds, as well as the ways we identify with those values and beliefs. World views are inextricably threaded together with a sense of being and becoming in relationship to Iethi'nihsténha Ohwentsia'kékha. Indigenous people have always understood that intimate relationships with Land are crucial to their identity and indeed continued survival – "they [Indigenous peoples] and the place they lived were equal partners in life" (Cajete, 2000, p. 204). These understandings of Land remain as crucial today as they have always been.

Iethi'nihsténha Ohwentsia'kékha (Land), and the ways it is primary, central, sacred and deeply intimate is a well-grounded way to (re)conceptualize fundamental aspects of Indigenous thought and, relatedly, pedagogies and practices. I want to draw attention to the fact that the principles, philosophies, and ontologies of Iethi'nihsténha Ohwentsia'kékha are not only crucial but are pivotal in (re)membering and (re)cognizing understandings of ancient knowledges and very old pedagogies in contemporary contexts. I believe that Iethi'nihsténha Ohwentsia'kékha is a particular world view – one that connects all Indigenous people, indeed all people, who seek to acknowledge the primacy of Land as a (re)membering and (re)cognizing of ancient knowledges and understandings of self-in-relationship.

An extensive and growing body of scholarship outlines the ways Indigenous knowledges are critical for (re)generating our world. Indigenous knowledges are distinct knowledge systems in their own right, with internal consistencies, diversities, and ways of knowing and understanding natural and built worlds. In using the term *natural*, I am referring to what has not been constructed, caused, or influenced by humankind; and *built* refers to something constructed or made either by nature or humankind. While these two terms may be connected in that natural worlds often contain built environments, they also may be distinct when referring to spaces that have been constructed by human hands. These two terms are not necessarily used oppositionally but rather, unless otherwise noted, to ensure that both contexts are acknowledged. Indigenous knowledges arising from and existing within both natural and built worlds must be recognized as distinct knowledge systems that are on par with dominant Western thought.

Within the current system of education, Indigenous knowledges are relegated to contexts of specific racialized courses or within aspects of multi- or cross-cultural education. Indigenous knowledges provide a vehicle for acknowledging colonial relationships while exposing the hidden social/political/cultural agendas buried within the curriculum. Cajete (1999) writes that Indigenous people continually live a dual or splintered existence in which they are constantly forced to adapt themselves to a "social, political, and cultural system that is not their own" (p. 16). While it is generally agreed that education, as it currently exists, is problematic and a site of resistance, it is also seen as crucial to the survival and participation of Indigenous peoples as active and egalitarian global citizens. If that is so, and I believe it is, then we must shift our thinking from what is dominantly accepted as the *right* way of schooling our children to focusing on examining the networks and relations of power, as well as the assumptions, embedded in the *hidden* curriculum in schools. We must, in effect, seek a new way of thinking about how we *do* education. The question to be asked is, in what ways can Indigenous knowledges inform a philosophy of education and the process of schooling?

The notions of coming to know, coming to understand, or coming to awareness are embedded in ancient knowledges and very old pedagogies that may be (re)cognized in contemporary educational contexts. Cajete writes that "understanding the depth of relationships and the significance of participation in all aspects of life are the keys to traditional American Indian education and these understandings form the foundation of the beliefs about the nature of knowledge" (p. 205). Traditional Indigenous understanding of education is that children are like flowers, slowly unfolding, petal by petal, opening up to the morning sun and releasing their fragrance, which makes the world a better place – it is a sacred and intimate process of coming to know, understand, or find awareness. Learning through the philosophies of Iethi'nihsténha Ohwentsia'kékha entails a journeying with purposeful, mindful, and spiritual intent – seeking knowledge and understanding.

Centring Land disrupts and (de)centres dominant Western taken-for-granted assumptions and complacency currently embedded in and informing the ways Indigenous children are experiencing schooling, as well as pre-service teacher education and in-service professional development. One of the tasks of Indigenous education is to (re)cognize Indigenous ways of knowing that will lead to greater liberty in thought while also (re)storing balance and harmony in the natural and built worlds. Cajete (1999) asserts emphatically that his responsibility as an Indigenous educator is to heal and reconcile the "cultural and ecological split … Healing the split is not a task for Indian people only.

It is also the task of others who consider themselves people of place ... Today everyone must *look to the mountain"* (pp. 17, 18 – emphasis in original). The ultimate struggle is how we not only (re)cognize but also (re)generate new relationships between both knowledge systems, not only for Indigenous scholars but for all scholars who seek and are skilled enough to introduce and bring together two distinct knowledge systems into their pedagogies and practices while engaging the tensions, challenges, and resistances embedded in relations and systems of power and privilege that persist in the various spaces we inhabit.

6 Relations of Privilege – Relations of Power

Power is the living energy that inhabits and or composes the universe ... all of the connections or relations that form the immediate environment of that small world each of us inhabits.

(Deloria & Wildcat, 2001, p. 140)

Building from the discussions on spaces in Chapter 2, this chapter focuses on the ways spaces are constructed and used and on connections to networks and relations of power. I begin by examining architecture from the context of two particular spatial theorists whose work focuses on the ways spaces are inhabited and made placeful. From there I move to exploring a particular Foucaudian perspective on architectural spaces and connections to networks and relations of power. I conclude with an examination of the ways these inhabited architectural spaces, along with networks and relations of power, continue to influence education, together with connections to Indigenous philosophies grounded in understandings of Iethi'nihsténha Ohwentsia'kékha (Land).

Inhabiting Spaces

Spaces, as has been discussed, are empty and abstract, whereas place is concrete. Place is particular: it is geographically specific; it may be storied; it is always (re)membered; and it can be (re)cognized. Both Bachelard (1958/1994) and Lefebvre (1991), as well-known spatial theorists, focus on the ways spaces are produced that embody architectural spaces. Architecture in the context of Bachelard's work refers to the consciousness of embodied memories within constructed and natural structures that form types of homes and even the spaces within those homes through a phenomenological perspective. The study of human consciousness or awareness, particularly as it relates to direct experiences and the ways we understand those experiences, is known as *phenomenology*. Here, phenomenology refers to the consciousness of direct experiences in relation to our connections with spaces and, further, that these spaces, after captured within the essence of our creative mind, cease to remain indifferent or abstract and instead become intimately inhabited. To inhabit is an active process of occupying or living in and there are many ways one might inhabit spaces.

By inhabiting spaces – by being present in those spaces, to occupy those spaces, to story those spaces, to (re)member and (re)cognize those spaces – they become place*ful*. While Bachelard's work does not extend to land but rather is restricted to architectural or manmade spaces, it is my position that placefulness is not something independent from Land but exists *within* the context of Iethi'nihsténha Ohwentsia'kékha (Land). Land, as discussed in Chapter 2, reaches beyond the specificity, concreteness, and material geography of land and the making of place or placefulness. Land is more than the diaphanousness of inhabited memories; Land is spiritual, emotional, and relational; Land is experiential, (re)membered, and storied; Land is sentient.

Inhabited spaces while always intimate are never neutral. Lefebvre's (1991) work focuses on sociological and architectural interactions in the construction and appropriation of spaces, particularly in relation to urbanism. Sociological interaction refers to the study of individuals, social interactions, behavioural patterns, and underlying assumptions, particularly in shared spaces. Architectural interaction considers the ways built environments interact with and respond to natural environmental factors. Urbanism focuses on the study of urban centres, particularly with regard to the impacts of economic, political, geographic, and social characteristics, as they relate to the sustainability of built environments. Urbanism, colonization, and globalization, in the development of a capitalist world economy, draw on and perpetuate colonial relations and systems of power and privilege, thereby creating tensions and resistances regarding contested places – the ideology of manifest destiny. Manifest destiny is an expression of the belief in the inherent right and morality of expansionism of a particular people group at the expense of other culture-sharing groups, who are perceived as inferior. The ideology of manifest destiny continues to be fuelled by a sense of entitled racial and religious superiority maintained through networks and relations of power and privilege.

However, Bachelard (1958/1994) and Lefebvre's (1991) work is limited by their lack of exploration of the ways networks and relations of power and privilege impact and inform concepts of inhabiting intimate and shared spaces. Bachelard and Lefebvre focus more on the ways we experience *places* rather than challenging or addressing specific issues, tensions, and resistances relating to contested spaces (the empty abstract generality, as well as those being made placeful) in particular land and educational spaces. Land and education continue to be sites of tension and resistance in relationships between Canada as a whole and the host peoples of this nation, who, as I have stated elsewhere, have always existed on this land. Traditionally, education has been an area of strength for Indigenous people. In using the term *traditional*, I am referring to the ways ancient knowledges and very old pedagogies grounded in the principles and philosophies of Iethi'nihsténha Ohwentsia'kékha (Land) are experienced spiritually, emotionally, cognitively, and physically. Colonial relations have disrupted traditional pedagogies, imposing dominant Western systems of power and privilege into learning processes.

Privilege and Power

The notion of privilege is not connected to social, educational, or economic status. Individuals who, as a birthright, belong to the dominant privileged group may come from diverse social, educational, and economic status. What they share is that, by virtue of their birth, they have unlimited access to all the rights and privileges of that citizenship. Many authors who write about and deconstruct issues of race refer to privilege as *white privilege*. I contend that the term *white privilege* is too restrictive in that it racializes the concept of privilege, erases the nuances in other forms of privilege, and reflexively creates tensions and resistances that shut down effective dialogue. I prefer the term *dominant privilege* because it encompasses the ideology of privilege across a dominant group of individuals regardless of ablebodiness, class, gender, race, or sexuality. *Dominant* does not necessarily refer to demography; it does, however, refer to a group who occupy a position of assumed or presumed authority through complex networks and relations of power. The interactions between these networks of relations of power allow that power and control to be perpetuated.

Dominant privilege systems and relations of power are intentionally created and maintained in complex ways to ensure that individuals who are born into these systems remain oblivious to the privileges and power they access daily so that these systems remain unchallenged and unchanged. Individuals belonging to the dominant privilege system are taught that their hegemonic ideals, values, beliefs, and systems are benign, neutral, and normative, and further that they exist to serve the greater good of every facet of society – they are positioned with the *best of intentions* and are never to be questioned or challenged. To do so is to risk being labelled as deviant and undesirable – a troublemaker. These systems of privilege perpetuate the myth of meritocracy – that all are able to succeed *if they would only be more like us; if they would only just pull themselves up by their bootstraps and try harder.* Privilege provides protection and confidence in courses of action and entitlement. Critical race and anti-race theorists assert that only those who are privileged possess the freedom to criticize, affect change, or otherwise engage the very systems that confer the privilege to do so. In reality privilege consists of unearned advantages, as well as power and control – even the *right* to speak out against these systems and relations of power comes from a place of dominant privilege. This control may be exercised blatantly, covertly, insidiously, or unconsciously but always violently. Silencing, ignorance, erasure, denial, deflection, assimilationism, and colour blindness can all, in many ways, be as harmful, debilitating, and dehumanizing as overt acts of control, such as segregation, genocide, and physical assault. Power, according to McIntosh (1988), as a direct companion of privilege appears like strength, as something to be desired and obtained. McIntosh also writes that power is something that can be held by individuals to exert control over others.

While McIntosh's (1988) arguments are initially useful, her claims of absolutes have inherent limitations. In particular, her consideration of power does not go deep enough. McIntosh fails to grasp the complexities of the ways power operates, thereby perpetuating victimization and dichotomous representations of us versus them. Her analogy of unpacking a knapsack of privileges is helpful in initially examining the unconscious aspects and accessibility of privilege. However, McIntosh compartmentalizes power as something that can be possessed and wielded by an individual apart from networks and relations[1] of power. Possession is an ambiguous term that is often confused with ownership. One can possess something without being the owner, and someone can own something without being in possession of it. An owner does not relinquish ownership simply by virtue of not being in possession of an object. I will focus on two aspects of possession that are most relevant to this discussion: actual and constructive. In actual possession an individual has immediate physical contact and control of an object; in constructive possession individuals have both knowledge of and the ability to control an object without having physical contact with that object. Power is an energy that moves and operates through relations of power. Power is not an object that can be possessed or controlled by any individual(s). As well, no individual can have absolute control of power.

I have found Foucault's conceptualization of power very useful for exploring some of the ways power operates. Foucault (1988) writes that any individual who is chained and beaten "is subject to force being exerted over him, not power" (p. 83). Foucault (1977) asserts that power is not held by individuals but moves through networks and interconnected relations of power. Power, according to Foucault, may be "taken as a right, which one is able to possess like a commodity ... and is conceived primarily in terms of the role it plays in the simultaneous maintenance of the relations of production and class domination" (p. 88). Foucault rejects the absolute repressive nature of power, arguing that power "risks becoming oppression only whenever it over-extends itself beyond the rules of right which organize and delimit it" (pp. 89, 96). Foucault does not necessarily see the overextension of power relations as abusive but as an inevitable perpetuation of the mechanisms of power within the systems that have become normalized within society. The mechanisms of power are *the rules of right* that establish the parameters of power together with the *effects of truth* that (re)produce and transmit power. The mechanisms in interconnected and interdependent relationships form the foundation for power to operate.

Power relations cannot be exercised without discourses of truth, which, in turn, establish the rules of right that inform the parameters of power. The dominant power structures form and inform the triad of relations of power, rules of right, and effects of truth. Foucault (1977) writes that the effects of truths are "the ensemble of rules according to which the true and the false are separated and specific effects of power are attached to the *true*" (p. 132). Therefore conflict arises not from taking sides regarding truths and fallacies but rather from the sociopolitical positioning of truths within the relations of power. Power is engaged and operates via interconnected networks and relations, and individuals move along the threads that connect networks so that regardless of status (privilege or otherwise) – everyone is at once a recipient of and a vehicle for power.

Power is constantly moving, shifting, changing, and evolving – it is experienced in some way by every individual. Resistances are an exercise of power – a power that is resisting the exercise of power by dominant privilege. I use the word *is* because power is active in the present. In this way power and the exercise of power are not the exclusive domain of the dominant, privileged group within a society. Foucault (1977) points out that the mechanisms of power are "accompanied by ideological productions … for the formation and accumulation of knowledge" (p. 102). Ideology generally refers to the study of systems of ideas and sets of beliefs that constitute a group of individuals.

In Education

Dominant Western education and related ideologies continue to be a major system and mechanism for the exercise of dominant power and privilege. According to Meyer (1977), dominant Western education is organized into formalized and prescriptive "networks of socializing experiences" (p. 55), which ideologically prepare students for appropriate and effective citizenship. Meyer asserts that dominant Western education continues to be a central site of privilege, power, domination, and control for the expansion of nationalistic culture and ideals. Philosophy, as noted earlier, refers to the study of ways of knowing and being or what I consider epistemologies. Many scholars collapse epistemological and ideological concepts; however, while these two terms are connected they are in fact distinct. Epistemologies (philosophies) refer to the study of the nature of knowledge, including presuppositions, foundations, and ways of acquiring knowledge, and an acknowledgment of the limits of knowing. Ideology is a branch of knowledge that considers systems of ideas or set beliefs that encompass the ways a culture-sharing group senses, perceives, understands, and comes to know their reality – their world view. Thus, philosophies are informed by ideological foundations. In Indigenous philosophies these ideological underpinnings are relational, spiritual, and highly contextualized. Further, these sacred relationships and contexts are grounded in understandings of the centrality and primacy of Iethi'nihsténha Ohwentsia'kékha (Land).

Given the vast diversity of Eurocentrically informed philosophies, particularly within the field of education, historically and contemporarily it is extremely challenging if not impossible to arrive at one definitive understanding of what constitutes a dominant Western philosophy of education. The waters become murky and boundaries blurred when dominant Western philosophers generally cannot even agree on what the primary philosophical goal of education should be: personal development or citizenship education (and whether this discourse in itself creates a false dichotomy); education or enculturation; moral or character education; culturally specific programming in education; culturally focused schools or systems; legislative rights to education; social justice and advocacy education; teacher education, praxis, or education for indoctrination; or reproducing power, privilege, elitism, and class structure within education. The study of education generally focuses on curriculum, practice, policy, and training. Philosophy, as indicated earlier, includes the study of ideologies. Therefore, I believe that a philosophy of education must include a study of the ideological bedrock of education as it relates to training, practice, policy, and curriculum.

There are many educational theorists and philosophers from whom we can draw concepts of dominant Western-informed philosophies of education that continue to influence education today. Providing a comprehensive examination of the theorists and philosophers would be too voluminous and extend well beyond the scope of this book. Rather, the following discussion provides an overview of select historical influences and intellectual traditions that continue to inform contemporary dominant Western educational philosophies and resulting ideologies. The purpose of introducing some of the concepts embedded in the work of the following theorists is to gesture to the normalizing and influencing factors of dominant Western thought on current educational practices and the ways these philosophies of education are in direct opposition to Indigenous thought. I look first at the educational philosophies of British philosopher and educator John Locke, move onto the influences of behaviourist and developmental theorists Jean Piaget and B.F. Skinner, and conclude with a look at Michel Foucault's work concerning education.

Locke is generally considered one of the greatest educational philosophers and theorist in Europe during the seventeenth century. Locke (2010), in his text entitled *Some Thoughts Concerning Education*, writes that children are in need of "judgment, restraint and discipline. Children should look upon their Parents as their Lords, their absolute Governors. Fear and awe ought to give you the first power over their minds" (pp. 27, 28). Locke advised parents to use the corporal punishment on their children. Locke, with his focus on punishment and discipline, followed Aristotle's philosophy of morality, virtue, and habits that he believed existed in every child's nature. Education, for Locke, would serve the state in creating effective citizens.

Locke rejected Plato and Descartes's doctrines of dialectical methods and what he saw as pointless ideas. He believed that all humans are not created equal and firmly believed in the power of education to mould children and prepare them to take their place in society. In 1697 Locke was deeply involved with initiatives throughout the United Kingdom to establish workhouse schools for impoverished children that focused heavily on church attendance and trade-specific training. Even after his death in 1704, Locke's work continued to dominate English and French perspectives on parenting and education throughout the eighteenth and nineteenth centuries and in many ways continues to inform contemporary dominant Western education. In my view Locke's work in implementing workhouse schools, while not directly traceable, was one of the major influencing factors in the conceptualization and philosophical foundations for the creation of industrial/residential schools for Native people throughout Canada and the United States (mid-1800s to 1990s). However, having said that, the more direct impetus for the implementation of the residential school system in Canada came from legislation, such as the 1857 Gradual Civilization Act, 1869 Gradual Enfranchisement Act, and the 1876 Indian Act.

There are also the twentieth-century behaviourists and developmental theorists, such as Piaget (Swiss, 1896–1980) and Skinner (American, 1904–90), whose work focuses primarily on child development. Their contribution to philosophical issues in dominant Western educational contexts, while exceedingly complex, bears mention.

Piaget's theories of cognitive development focus on the various identifiable stages of intellectual development of the autonomous child – how children acquire, construct, use, and integrate knowledge. We can see his influence in the development of current education practices when we consider the ways children are grouped into grades and provided with *developmentally appropriate experiences*, with the assumption that all children will be ready to acquire and integrate knowledge and skills at the same time based on age and presumed stage of development.

Skinner's work, as a psychologist and social philosopher, focuses on what he termed radical behaviourism. Skinner's work on behaviourism focused on rewards and punishments to modify behaviour – creating an association between punishment and avoidance. We can see the influence of Skinner's philosophical concepts on education when he states that it is desirable to seek to "abolish the autonomous inner man and that his abolition has long been overdue" (Skinner, 1971, p. 200). We can see his influence reinforced in classrooms where children were seated in rows, with feet flat on the floor, robotic demeanors, raising hands to request permission to ask or answer questions, or to request permission to go to the bathroom. Any deviation from *acceptable* behaviours would result in swift punishment. Locke, Piaget, and Skinner's dominant Western philosophical approaches to and influences on education are in direct opposition to Indigenous philosophies.

It has become clear to me that dominant Western-informed philosophies concerning education, pedagogy, and practices continue to be focused on education for appropriate and effective citizenship, the perpetuation and maintenance of the networks and relations of power, hidden agendas of assimilation, and perceptions of cultural deficiencies. Foucault (1995), a French philosopher and social theorist, focused on the ways power moved in and through various systems, including education. In his text *Discipline and Punish: The Birth of the Prison*, first published in 1975, Foucault asserts that with the advent of factories and eighteenth-century industrialization, education became another homogenous articulation of factory production of individuals – and little has changed since. Schools have become vehicles for networks and relations of power that dominate and legitimize (or illegitimize) knowledge production; pre-determine and homogenize success and failure; define boundaries of inclusion and exclusion; and allocate access to resources, knowledge, and opportunities. According to Foucault (1995) this form of power produces and controls what constitutes acceptable realities, the determination of truths, individuals as objects – docile bodies – and the production and distribution of knowledge.

Education, in my view, is central to relations of power for a dominant group and is the place from which all other networks are interconnected. Foucault (1995) identified schools as one of the six main seats of power and control over the body (the army, government, penal system, church, and hospital being the other five). Docile bodies of students are seen as objects and targets of power for a dominant Western education system. Foucault asserts that a body is docile in that it "may be subjected, used, transformed and improved" (p. 136). It is this concept of docility that continues to be a subject of great interest, particularly to philosophers and educators. Docility is different from slavery in that slavery is based on appropriation, objectification, and ownership of a body. Appropriation refers to taking something without permission or consent and making it one's own. Ownership is the act of purchasing something for one's own use and implies relationships between people and things based on notions of power and control. In relation to the ideology underpinning slavery, concepts of appropriation and ownership represent power and control over bodies as objects of commodity and are connected to states of being and perceived inferior societal status. Docility, on the other hand, considers ways to mould and shape the mind and body for effective democratic citizenship – not unlike Locke's and Skinner's philosophies of education. Docility assumes a social status that supports egalitarian participation in democratic processes.

Docility, in educational contexts, gestures to the belief that students are easily taught and controlled, obedient, and very submissive. One of the main ways of exercising power and control over docile bodies is through the liberal use of discipline and, at times, various forms of punishment – to control by aversion. Discipline refers to the deliberate and rigorous training of docile bodies to conform to specific rules of behaviour, such as one would find in the military, religious institutions, prisons – and yes school settings. Many dominant Western-informed philosophers and theorists, such as Locke, Piaget, and Skinner, assert that discipline (including the use of punitive measures) and control are key in creating and normalizing *moral* and docile citizens. Foucault asserts that the discipline, power, and control of docile bodies require the enclosure, partitioning, classification, and pervasive unceasing surveillance of individuals within functional and productive space. Functional refers to having a specific purpose that is practical and useful but not necessarily visually pleasing. Productive relates to issues of productivity and commodification.

Panopticism

Foucault's conceptualization of Bentham's panopticon as an architecture of surveillance is a very interesting construct and way of considering the invisibility and insidiousness of the normalizing of networks of relations of power and control, particularly regarding docile bodies. The panopticon is an instrument of optimum surveillance, discipline, and power and control originally designed by Jeremy Bentham in 1791 for the penal system and subsequently adapted by Foucault for his examination of the network of relations of power across various discipline societies. The term *panopticon* originates from the Greek words *pan-*, meaning "all," and *-optikos*, referring to "sight or the act of seeing." While specially designed for the penal system, it continues to serve equally well for hospitals, psychiatric institutions, day care facilities, and educational institutions (including former residential and industrial schools). Foucault (1995) writes that the design of the panopticon provides for an unseen observer to watch all the internees of any institution (including students in a school) where consistent and uninterrupted surveillance was deemed necessary. The general architecture is designed around a central observatory (usually symbolized as a high tower). Buildings, which are divided into individual cells similar to honeycombs, are built around the tower. Each of the cells contains windows facing both the outside world and the tower that backlight the occupant(s) in each cell. This backlighting highlights the individuals while isolating them from the background; the occupants are further isolated from each another by walls. The tower allows for a constant and uninterrupted view of the backlit internees and the buildings as a whole (a form of exhibition). The structure is designed in such a way that the inmates or students in the institution are unable, at any given time, to ascertain when or if they are being observed.

It was/is assumed that internees/students would presume they are constantly being monitored – the *all-seeing eye*, if you will. The concept of the *all-seeing eye* has had many general and religious applications throughout history. The central or overarching hypothesis is that the eye (whoever or whatever that may symbolize) is all knowing, all seeing, and ever present. The premise of the panopticon is that individuals will behave in ways deemed appropriate to avoid judgment and punishment. The panopticon, according to Foucault, was an instrument of surveillance and an effective laboratory for testing the power of the mind over the body. Foucault defined the applications of his conception of panopticism as the spatial arrangement of docile bodies in relation to each other; the organizational positioning, ranking, or classification of docile bodies; the determination of the characteristics of relations of power; the definition of modes and interventions of power. Panopticism refers to the architectural philosophy and ideology of the panopticon. The goal of panopticism is "to strengthen social forces, increase production, develop the economy, spread education, raise morality, and to increase and multiply its populations" (p. 208). For its efficiency, power relations operating in and through the panopticon must have the illusion of permanence, be extensive, and be perceived to be everywhere at all times – always watching – always present – while remaining unseen.

Panopticism is a state of being and present in the form of built environments. As a state of being, the panopticon embodies an unconscious consciousness within its intimate and experienced architecture. This unconscious consciousness is perpetuated and normalized through the exercise of power, control, and discipline. The panopticon is also architecturally present in the ways spaces are structured, organized, and inhabited through intimate and unconscious experiences; as well, the panopticon is present in the interaction between docile bodies and architecture. The architecture of the panopticon remains a construct for surveillance in disciplinary societies, such as schools, military, hospitals, governments, places of worship, and the penal system. The architecture of the panopticon operates by moulding and manipulating those who reside within its walls, to exercise power and control over bodies in order to *know* them – to *transform* them. Panopticism opens opportunities for examining the ways dominant Western education continues to be structured, organized, and administered philosophically, architecturally, and in practice, as well as the relations and networks of power that inform curriculum, pedagogies, and teacher training.

Panopticism in educational contexts works to perpetuate power and control to develop what are considered fully functioning citizens. Foucault (1995) writes that "strict discipline is an art of correct training that makes individuals; it is the specific technique of a power that regards individuals as objects and instruments of its omnipotent and suspicious exercise of power" (p. 170). The Foucaudian concept of discipline is a two tiered approach of gratification and punishment, where the administration of rewards outweighs the use of punitive measures. Students are controlled by aversion. The focus of aversion in Foucaudian philosophy is not solely on the avoidance of punitive measures; rather, the focus is on the avoidance of punitive measures by seeking the rewards. Unlike behaviourists Locke, Piaget, or Skinner, Foucault, in his writings, opposes the hierarchized surveillance and normalizing judgments concerning behaviour and attainments being categorized as inherently either *good* or *evil*. Such judgments were, and in many ways still are, prevalent in dominant Western thought, particularly as they relate to education.

Concepts of good and evil are, in fact, word baskets filled with many constructions, understandings, and interpretations and as such are not helpful as descriptors in determining behavioural and educational outcomes. The term *evil* was generally understood across dominant European contexts to denote extreme expressions of disapproval, dislike, or disparagement. In particular, the Anglo-Saxons used the term to describe something or someone who was bad, cruel, unskilled, or defective. In the late eighteenth century the meaning was understood in reference to extreme moral wickedness. Conversely, *good* originates from the word *God* or *God-like* and later included biblical connotations. Good or goodness (as a quality or state of being) represents something or someone who is virtuous, desirable, and valid – in other words possessing the right desirable qualities – and is associated with notions of suitability, adequateness, and belonging. In fifteenth-century dominant European contexts, it was a term associated with well-behaved children. Foucault reasoned that judgments about good and evil behaviours were essentially sociopolitical struggles over constructions of truth and, relatedly, determinations of rightness and wrongness. Foucault writes that there is no single autonomous construction of truth. Rather, understandings of truths move and find legitimacy through networks and relations of power. These concepts have become universalized, normalized, perpetuated, and maintained through hidden dominant Western educational discourses and are communicated through a variety of systemic, structural, and administrative mechanisms. According to dominant Western thought, *well-behaved* children were seen as *good/right* and *ill-behaved* children as *evil/wrong*, particularly in school and religious environments – sometimes these were the same. This dominant Western dichotomous and oppositional understanding of behaviour fails to consider the wide range of behaviours between the two opposing values. It stands in direct contrast to Indigenous philosophical concepts of learning grounded in Iethi'nihsténha Ohwentsia'kékha, where Land is the school – the school is Land – where behaviours are not oppositionally good or evil or right or wrong but are seen as integral aspects of learning. In other words in Indigenous learning contexts, one does not interfere with the learning experience and behaviours or related natural consequences, and emotional responses are perceived as neither positive nor negative nor good nor bad but instead as valuable sources for learning and critical reflection.

The school, as a built environment, continues to evolve from the concepts of Panopticism and architectural interaction. The panopticon is designed for maximum efficiency in trivial, intrusive, but always intense observation – monitored classrooms, hallways, stairwells; open dining halls and half doors in toilet stalls. Architectural interactions refers to the ways spaces are designed with a specific purpose, how individuals interact with and make use of the form and function of built environments, and the ways architecture influences relationships with self and others within those environments.

Because of architectural interactions, teaching relationships, pedagogies, and classroom practices also became characterized by networks of surveillance, power, and control. Student helpers, prefects, and tutors were selected by teachers from among the *good* students. These helpers were at once vehicles and recipients of power, control, and surveillance, providing practical assistance to teachers and administrative staff by distributing supplies and delivering messages between classroom and administration. Student helpers as observers scrutinized and reported any deviant behaviour, and as teaching assistants they tutored less capable students. The students who were not selected as the *good* helpers developed complex passive and active relations of resistance that opposed dominant relations of power and control.

What Foucault's work and this book establish is that power is inherently relational and systemic in nature. These systems continue to be developed and implemented by individuals to protect, perpetuate, and maintain the established relations of power both within the system itself and through individuals who are interconnected within the system. Power is an agreed upon relationship between individuals within systems that are woven together by threads of power, control, and discipline. With Foucault, I believe that these systems, by their very nature, create tensions, challenges, and resistances that work to oppose absolute power and control. These resistances can take on various shades of passive or active forms within the relations of power and privilege. Power is never exercised outside the relations of power because individuals are always in continual relationship to power. Foucault (1995) suggests that while "individuals are vehicles of power they are not its point of application" (p. 98). These discussions about the exercise of power and relations of power are complex and multifaceted. While recognizing the impossibility of any final declaration of meaning or single conceptualization or articulation about the ways relations of power are engaged, I do not believe that power is ever completely absent nor do I hold that power is ever absolute. Haig-Brown (1988) writes that "people rarely comply fully and easily" (p. 98) with oppressive forms of power and control. Foucault (1988) adds that "as soon as there is a power relation, there is a possibility of resistance" (p. 123).

Relations of resistance are themselves relations of power. Foucault (1995) suggests that "power is neither given, nor exchanged, nor recovered, but rather exercised, and that it only exists in action … power is above all a relation of force" (p. 89). While McIntosh writes that power can only be exercised through privilege, I believe that power exists in many forms and is always relational and fluid. At the same time, privilege always connects one to power. The exercise of power is not exclusive to positions of privilege; however, privilege can only be accessed and exercised by those who are in positions of dominant privilege. Therefore, privilege cannot be transferred or distributed to or accessed by others outside the dominant group. Similarly power is neither transferred nor conferred[2] – it is, however, accessed and exercised, challenged, and resisted through action, fluid movement, and the need to balance the tensions inherent in power through its perpetuation and resistances by both docile and aware bodies.

I would suggest that docility need not be a permanent state of consciousness, that is, the ways one is or may be unaware and unresponsive to one's environment. There is always the possibility that a docile body can (re)generate – become aware and responsive – a coming to know again. Power, as stated earlier, is an agreed on relationship. Consider the power that a teacher holds within the classroom – she/he has power over grading, evaluation, curriculum, course content, classroom management, and practices. However, such power while a reality is also an illusion of absolutes. The only power an educator really has is to share knowledge. For example, if all the students in a classroom made a collective decision of resistance and walked out of the classroom, the teacher would become a recipient, rather than a vehicle, of power. Students, through relations of resistance, are no longer docile bodies but aware, responsive, and active participants. In a much larger scale, at Kanehsatake in 1990, Ipperwash in 1995, and Caledonia in 2006, the 2012 First Nations Summit with Prime Minister Harper, and in 2013–14 the collective response of First Nations people across Canada to the proposed First Nations Education Act, docile bodies (re)generated and took a stand for social and moral justice. On a national level we have the Idle No More movement and in a global context, consider the events that have taken place in the early twenty-first century in Egypt, Libya, Ukraine, and Syria. Docile bodies have awoken en masse to resist and topple oppressive dictatorships in networks of relations of power across countries.

Indigeneity

Indigenous philosophies concerning power are based on notions of self-in-relationship and the understanding that we are grounded in interconnected relationships with the enduring energies that exist throughout all of creation. These energies are present regardless of whether we choose to acknowledge or understand the interactions of self-in-relationship. Deloria and Wildcat (2001) write that power is the "living energy that inhabits and or composes the universe … all of the connections or relations that form the immediate environment of that small world each of us inhabits" (p. 140). Unlike dominant Western concepts of power that are human and systemically centred and focus on the ways power is circulated, the tensions, challenges, and resistances that exist within Indigenous concepts of power and self-in-relationship consistently seek to (re)balance and (re)harmonize the spiritual and natural energies inherent in self-in-relationship. Similar to Foucaudian understandings, individuals in Indigenous concepts of power are not the source of power but are vehicles and recipients through which power operates. The differences are in the ways power is circulated, used, and perpetuated to maintain balanced self-in-relationship within human and natural worlds. In Indigenous philosophies power is circulated through ceremony. These networks of relations of power and ceremonies are experienced through sacred understandings of self-in-relationship that are grounded in Iethi'nihsténha Ohwentsia'kékha (Land). These relationships are fragile, but it is a fragility that represents "the intricacies of a continuing process, and with a strength inherent in spider webs" (Silko, 1977, p. 35).

7 Land and Circularity: An Indigenous Philosophical Approach to Thought

> You have noticed that everything an Indian does is in a circle, and that is because the power of the world always works in circles, and everything tries to be round ... all our power came to us from the sacred hoop of the nation, and so long as the hoop was unbroken, the people flourished. The flowering tree was the living centre of the hoop, and the circle of the four quarters nourished it ... This knowledge came to us from the outer world. Everything the power of the world does is done in a circle. The sky is round and I have heard that the earth is round like a ball, and so are all the stars. The wind in its greatest power whirls. Birds make their nests in circles for theirs is the same religion as ours. The sun comes forth and goes down again in a circle. The moon does the same and both are round. Even the seasons form a great circle in their changing, and always come back again to where they were. The life of a man is a circle from childhood to childhood, and so it is in everything where power moves.
>
> (Black Elk in Neihardt, 2008, pp. 155–6)

In Chapter 6 I discussed some of the influences on dominant Western thought in relation to education and educational practices. In this chapter I will explore rationality particularly in relationship to Iethi'nihsténha Ohwentsia'kékha (Land), understandings of self-in-relationship, and circularity. Indigenous philosophies will be positioned as interconnected paradigms and ways of knowing that need to be considered in ways that are equal to but distinct from dominant Western thought. Sarris (1993), Coast Miwok/Pomo, writes that these different voices are "capable of communicating with and informing one another" (p. 7). This chapter is not intended to be an in-depth analysis of dominant Western philosophies, to generate contrasts and comparisons, or to defend the legitimacy of Indigenous philosophies juxtaposed with dominant Western philosophies; it is, however, intended to contextualize both Indigenous and dominant Western patterns of philosophical thought. I will use the discussion to explore the ways two epistemically diverse forms of thought might communicate and inform each other cross-culturally.

Dominant Western Approaches

The journey of what has come to be understood as dominant Western thought has been marked by many complex tensions, challenges, and resistances. Killion (2006) tells us that the genesis of dominant Western thought developed from Greek/Hellenistic, French, German, British, and various other dominant Western philosophies that shifted and changed throughout the late antiquity, medieval, renaissance, enlightenment, and modern eras. The word *philosophy* originates from both Latin and Greek *philosophia*, which is literally translated as "love of knowledge, wisdom" – but whose knowledge? Whose wisdom? Anthony Quinton in Honderich (1995) articulates philosophy as

> Rationally critical thinking, of a more or less systematic kind about the general nature of the world (metaphysics or theory of existence), the justification of belief (epistemology or theory of knowledge), and the conduct of life (ethics or theory of value). (p. 666)

The problem with dominant Western understandings of philosophy is the inherent and embedded perception that there is only one prevailing and legitimate conceptualization of what is rational, epistemically correct, and ethical. While having an appearance of critical thought, Stewart-Harawira (2005) writes that dominant Western philosophical traditions have historically failed to examine their own embedded and taken-for-granted assumptions, meaning making, and interpretations. There are Indigenous and non-Indigenous philosophers and scholars who critically engage the underlying assumptions of Eurocentric philosophical traditions that claim this lack of critical consciousness and self-reflection remains as prevalent as it ever was – particularly in academic fields of study steeped in Western traditions. Cajete (2000) writes that these dominant Western philosophies deny the balance, unity, and holistic aspects of being to maintain and perpetuate the rationalistic Newtonian-Cartesian scientific paradigm. Kuhn (1962) explains that dominant Western paradigms are influenced by scientific theories or discourses that value, support, and legitimize rationalization and directly observable and measurable outcomes. In so doing, these philosophical paradigms, particularly those that developed out of the enlightenment era, have required that natural and spiritual worlds be denied, rationalized, and objectified in the interests of dominant Western imperialism and capitalistic agendas. Two enlightenment thinkers were particularly influential in what is considered modern Western philosophies.

Isaac Newton was a physicist, mathematician, astronomer, theologian, and philosopher. He is generally considered by dominant Western science to be one of the most influential people in history. Newtonian theories focus on scientific concepts of universal gravitation, the three laws of motion, and optics. His theories dominated the scientific and philosophical communities for over three centuries. Gribbin (2002) states that Newtonian theories described a form of reality grounded in the hard sciences and that his conceptualization of the universe was based in rationalized laws that became influential in enlightenment philosophies. René Descartes (Latin: Renatus Cartesius – *Cartesian*) preceded Newton and was himself immensely influential and is considered the *father* of modern philosophy and rationalism. Rationalism stems from the belief that perceptions of reality begin in the human mind in that solid reason is the only source of knowledge. Descartes, even though he professed to be a devout Roman Catholic, rejected spirituality, the existence of God, and any ideologies that could, on any level, be doubted or reasoned away. Descartes rejected the ancient and well-respected philosophies of Aquinas, Aristotle, and Plato, and micro-dissected every philosophical thought and ideology, every sense and feeling, even the reality of his own body, until he finally arrived at a presupposition that was, in his mind, undeniable. Descartes rationalized that his own existence was solely evidenced by the very fact that he did doubt and question – "I am thinking therefore I exist" (Descartes, 1637/2006, p. 28). Descartes theorized that the mental, physical, and spiritual aspects of human beings were separate and distinct, and that philosophies and philosophical debates should be compartmentalized in the rational and logical mind apart from the other aspects of humanity (physical and spiritual). Emotionality never entered into his speculation because, according to Descartes, it could not be trusted – it could not be rationalized.

The work of Descartes's philosophies were subsequently carried out by Newton and other scientists – "the concepts of an idea, of mathematical laws of nature ... are so fundamental to modern con-sciousness that it is hard not to regard them as part of the natural property of the human mind" (Shorto, 2008, pp. 78, 79). Newtonian-Cartesian rationalism continues to exist, has permeated disciplines beyond science and math, and continues to be one way that science and math scholars judge the legitimacy of knowledge production and the works of other scholars across all disciplines (including those outside the hard sciences). Each new generation of scientists and philosophers builds on the existing logic and rationality that link back to Newton and Descartes.

Newton-Cartesian rationalism in all its rigidity and focused intellec-tualism resists or erases the importance of the other aspects of being. This mechanistic rationalism continues to form the basis on which sub-jects, such as math, sciences, and language arts, are taught in schools from the earliest grades and throughout students' academic careers and indeed beyond into the workforce. Newton-Cartesian rationalism provides a framework through which self is understood in very par-ticular fragmented ways in relation to natural and built worlds. Fur-ther, the perpetuation of Newton-Cartesian rationalism has provided the basis for the industrialization and marketization of knowledge since the seventeenth century. In many cases the texts and evaluative strat-egies that continue to be used in contemporary educational practices have not changed greatly throughout the years, relying on antiquated foundations of Newton-Cartesian rationalism. Morgan (2003) writes that Newton-Cartesian rationalism informs contemporary educational processes through curricular underpinning around core concepts of universality, objectivity, false dichotomies, and insulated categoriza-tions, maintaining perceptions of a mechanistic and fragmented nature of reality. Mechanism is a belief that all the elements making up reality – anyone's reality, which includes living beings – are not intimately con-nected until, when combined, they form a whole. Newton-Cartesian rationalism reduces education and learning processes to a series of factors or elements leading towards a universally predetermined out-come – all else is deemed irrelevant. I, like Foucault, would also say that Newton-Cartesian rationalism expressed through curriculum and classroom practices is a tacit example of what is actually supporting the mechanization of educational practices. Newton-Cartesian rationalism is maintained and perpetuated through the networks and relations of power embedded in education, which finds expression in the ways we *do* education.

Returning to the Newton-Cartesian mechanized compartmentalization of thought in the realm of the rational and logical mind, Tran (2001) offers a cautionary note that the relationship between rationality and logic is intricately complex; therefore, we must be consistently conscious of the limits of knowing in any attempt to define the nature and relationship of these two concepts. Spivak (1993) much earlier also noted that critical or rational thought as a philosophical principle must always be mindful of the limits of knowing. Hallett (2009) writes that all logic is reason but not all reason is logical and that logic forms the structure in defining what is understood to be sense. Sense, in this context, generally refers to rational approaches contextually and problematically. Simply put, rationality "rationalizes or formalizes human activities" (Tran, 2001, p. 253). If, as Hallett discloses, logic is a map, then rationality is how one reads, understands, and follows the map. I would say that every culture-sharing group has their own understandings and structures of logic and rationality.

Indigenous Approaches

The mechanistic rationalism embedded in Newton-Cartesian rationalism is in opposition to the organic fluidity inherent in Indigenous philosophies. However, the notion of rational thought is not exclusive to dominant Western philosophies, nor is it a foreign concept in Indigenous thought. I believe that what constitutes rational thought according to Indigenous philosophies is distinct from, but just as valid as, the rationality found in dominant Western paradigms.[1] Indigenous philosophies extend beyond the boundaries of a rationality that is compartmentalized within the intellect to one that is grounded in the sacred understandings of Land, circularity, and self-in-relationship. Dominant Western rationality aligns with the Cartesian notion that *I* am thinking and therefore *I* exist whereas Indigenous rationality considers self to be in-relationship – *we* exist together here in this place and therefore *I* belong – I find my place in the world. Indigenous philosophies do not consider the individual distinct and separate from connected and interdependent relationships to Land and to the energies that exist within all creation (human/non-human, animate/inanimate). The energies inherent in these relationships are "locked deep in blood memory" (Silko, 1977, p. 220).

To dispel any myths that Indigenous philosophies are historic, quaint, romantic, and void of rational thought, I refer to the work of Sotsisowah

(John Mohawk), Hodenosaunee philosopher and scholar from the Seneca nation. Mohawk (1989) writes that ancient Hodenosaunee people had constructed political and social philosophies based on deep rational thought. These philosophies are grounded in the peace, power, and righteousness teachings of the Peacemaker[2] that led to the establishment of the League of Hodenosaunee Nations. The Peacemaker expounded that "all human beings possess the power of rational thought and that in the belief in rational thought is to be found the power to create peace" (p. 219). The Peacemaker elevated the concept of rational thought to a political, social, and indeed spiritual principle that has guided and informs everyday life and activities for the Hodenosaunee people. The Hodenosaunee creation story, which long predates the time of the Peacemaker, is alive with examples of a rational universe. In dominant Western patterns of thought nature is seen as wild, unpredictable, and irrational and thus something to be conquered and controlled. In Indigenous thought, human beings may be capable of irrational thought, behaviours, and imperfect understandings; however, the natural world has its own unique rationality and its own logic and order. The concept of rational thought that the Peacemaker instituted was grounded in Iethi'nihsténha Ohwentsia'kékha (Land), the sacred understandings of self-in-relationship, and the responsibilities we have to those relationships and to use our minds in *good* ways – that is what is meant when Indigenous people talk about having a *good mind*.

Indigenous peoples' relationships to natural and spiritual worlds are the greatest distinction between Indigenous and dominant Western thought. Many Hodenosaunee scholars concur that the foundational political and social philosophies based on rational thought set forth by the Peacemaker have informed the very bedrock of democracy in both Canada and the United States, and indeed in many Western democratic societies. These ancient philosophies remain as relevant today as they were for the Hodenosaunee people and the founding of the League of Nations. Laduke (1999) writes that the Hodenosaunee people expanded their influence and standing under the principles of the *Kaienarakowa* (the Great Law of Peace and the Good Mind). These philosophies enabled "the Hodenosaunee to become one of the most politically and philosophically influential peoples in history" (p. 227).

The concept of rational thought in Indigenous philosophies is not limited to the philosophies of the Hodenosaunee people. Cajete (2000), Tewa Pueblo; Deloria and Wildcat (2001), Sioux and Muscogee, respectively; and Stewart-Harawira (2005), Māori, write that Indigenous philosophies embody intimate relationships with Land, creation, and ecology, as well as enacting the responsibilities of those relationships. Stewart-Harawira refers to Indigenous philosophies as "relational ontologies involving consciousness of both the inner and outer realities of existence" (pp. 36, 37). Cajete (2000) asserts that Indigenous philosophies are "living ecological philosophies where the life-giving principles of the Earth nourishes and connects all life" (p. 59). Further, Cajete adds that "with our creative evolution of mind, we are reflections and participants of a greater universal whole. We are the Earth being conscious of itself" (p. 61). Cajete's concept of the creative evolution of mind intersects in multiple ways with the work of Sotsisowah (John Mohawk) and the Hodenosaunee philosophy of rational thought, specifically regarding analogous and metaphoric representations from natural and spiritual worlds, storying (as described in Chapter 1), as well as lessons about living a *good* life, walking the *good* road, and having a *good* mind. Cajete (2000) asserts there are tensions between the creative/metaphoric nature of the human mind and rationality that both complement and oppose one another. Cajete refers to the creative/ metaphoric mind as the "elder brother and the rational mind as the younger brother of human thinking" (p. 29). Albert Einstein, a theoretical physicist, much earlier also stated that that "the intuitive or metaphoric mind is a sacred gift and the rational mind is a faithful servant" (cited in Samples, 1976, p. 26). Samples claims that in modernity we have come to glorify the servant while disrespecting the gift. Youngblood Henderson (2000b) writes that Indigenous peoples have the right to reject dominant Western philosophies in order to assert a new Indigenous theory about thought.

I conclude there are four major aspects of Indigenous philosophies that are, for the most part, distinct from dominant Western ideologies: (1) principles, philosophies, and ontologies are embedded in Iethi'nihsténha Ohwentsia'kékha (Land); (2) understandings of self-in-relationship are central; (3) circularity in the natural and spiritual worlds is fundamental; and as discussed above, (4) rationality is based on an understanding that the rational mind is inseparable from the creative, spiritual, and metaphoric mind. Horne and McBeth (1998) write that Indigenous "philosophies of life are rooted in the lives of those doing the philosophizing" (p. 128). Similarly Erdrich (2004), in creative metaphoric prose, asserts that as the roots of trees are alive and run deep into the land, so are Indigenous concepts of and their relationship with Land.

In many instances survival of Indigenous peoples in what at times could be harsh and difficult landscapes was dependent on intimate and sacred connections to Land. This is no less a reality in today's rural/urban and natural/built environments. These sacred and intimate connections underpin the principles, philosophies, and ontologies of Iethi'nihsténha Ohwentsia'kékha (Land) and are expressions of ancient knowledges and very old pedagogies alive through storying, ceremonies, and social and political structures. Abram (2007) writes that landscapes are "alive with stories and that all things, animate and inanimate, have the power of speech" (n.p.). To live a storied existence is to exist within a world that is unconditionally "alive, awake, and aware" (n.p.). Silko (1977), Laguna Pueblo, writes that "everywhere he looked he saw a world made of stories ... it was a world alive, always changing and moving" (p. 95).

Indigenous philosophies are an acknowledgment of rationality that is not exclusive to human logic and reason and instead is grounded in the primacy and centrality of Iethi'nihsténha Ohwentsia'kékha (Land). Silko (1977) asserts that ceremonies have always been adapted to diverse contexts and "at one time, the ceremonies as they had been performed were enough for the way the world was then ... but the elements of this world have shifted and it has become necessary to make changes ... this growth keeps the ceremonies strong" (p. 126). Similarly, Porter (2008) writes that "if tradition does not bend or change it dies" (p. 9).

Just as landscapes are alive and in flux so are ceremonies. Ceremonies may shift and change contextually – they emerge and evolve and may be (re)cognized in modernity while retaining their original energies that emanate from deep within what Silko refers to as blood memory. These blood memories are engaged, expressed, and embodied through ceremony. Silko (1977) adds that these "new ceremonies were not like the old ones; but he [Betonie, the Elder] had never said they were not complete, only different" (pp. 233, 234). That does not mean that we can ignore or erase traditional protocols embedded in these ceremonies – they are in place for a reason. An example of this was storied to me by Kaaren Dannenmann, an Anishinaabe community scholar. One day she was out on the land with her young grandson to collect red willow branches. Taking anything from nature necessitates performing a ceremony to the element or animal asking for permission and an offering of thanks for the giving of life for our purposes. Kaaren asked her grandson to perform the ceremony. At each clump of willow her grandson performed the ceremony, and he indicated that the willows said they had not fulfilled their purpose on this earth and were not yet ready to give up their lives. Finally, her grandson came on another group of willows, and after performing the ceremony he turned to his grandmother (Kaaren) and said, "The willows want you to introduce yourself and tell them what purpose they are going to be used for." After Kaaren had made her introduction and told the willows her intentions, her grandson advised her that the willows are satisfied and "have agreed to give their lives to you for your purpose" (Dannenman, personal communication, November 10, 2011). The thanksgiving ceremony was performed on the collection and they returned home. This is one of the ways stories and ceremonies fit together "to become the story that is still being told ... and in the belly of this story the rituals and the ceremony are still growing" (Silko, 1977, pp. 2, 246). Ceremony remains the heart of life within both urban and rural communities.

Indigenous philosophies expressed through social and political structures are found in clan systems. Many Indigenous peoples follow various forms of clan systems, but the following discussion specifically focuses on Hodenosaunee clanology, with reference to other nations' clan systems. A clan generally refers to a group of close-knit and interrelated families with strong common interests, roles, and responsibilities. Clan systems are an embodiment of self-in-relationship grounded in solid kinship ties that extend beyond the boundaries of bloodlines. Porter (1993) writes that many thousands of years ago the Hodenosaunee population increased, extending beyond small and close-knit communities they once were – villages and families grew apart, losing love and respect for one another and becoming like strangers instead of acting like family. Rónikonhrowá:nen, a Hodenosaunee man who lived during that time, observed how the Creator had organized the natural world into water, air, and land with all of creation belonging in one of the three groups, each having its own role, responsibility, and characteristics. Rónikonhrowá:nen advised the people to follow the example of the natural world and organize themselves into manageable working groups. The Peacemaker, many hundreds of years later (re)generated the clan system and integrated it into the Gayanęhsra> go:wah (Great Law of Peace) and it "continues with a great vibrancy in all Hodenosaunee communities today" (p. 6). Porter explains that the clan system is fundamental to Hodenosaunee philosophy and that it provides an individual with an understanding of their place within ceremonial life.

Through the clan system one may derive a sense of being in relation to the world. It is similarly so with other Indigenous peoples globally who also follow clan systems. McCarthy (2010) argues that "having a clan isn't just about something you are, it's about things that you do and how these understandings and actions are situated in Hodeno-saunee teachings and cosmology" (p. 84). Indigenous scholars, such as Benton-Banai (1988), Ojibwa; Battiste and Youngblood Henderson (2000), Mi'Kmaq and Chickasaw/Cheyenne respectively; Deloria and Wildcat (2001), Sioux and Muscogee, respectively; Fixico (2003), Shawnee, Sac and Fox, Muscogee Creek, and Seminole, write that their respective clan systems came into being as political and social struc-tures from similar circumstances – self-in-relationship to natural and spiritual worlds. The principles, philosophies, and ontologies drawn from Iethi'nihsténha Ohwentsia'kékha (Land), circularity, and self-in-relationship birthed the clan systems of political and social structures which are seen as central and foundational to Indigenous philosophies. Essentially, Iethi'nihsténha Ohwentsia'kékha continues to be not only the first teacher but more than that, it is our primary relationship – the one before all others. Iethi'nihsténha Ohwentsia'kékha is primary and central to all aspects of sociopolitical structures and the spiritual well-being of communities.

Circularity is also an inherently important, interconnected, and relational aspect of Iethi'nihsténha Ohwentsia'kékha (Land). In Sec-tion 1 I wrote that Cajete (1994), Kawagley (2006), and Youngblood Henderson (2000a) assert that Aboriginal thought and identity are grounded in the land and therefore must be considered within their ecological context. In Section 2 I referred to ecology as an understand-ing of the ways living organisms relate to each other and to the natu-ral world. Tadodaho Chief Leon Shenandoah states that "there are no straight lines in nature. Life's not flat either. Our lives are circles. Everything comes back in circles ... There is no beginning, no end, you just go back to the beginning. There is a centre ... the centre is everywhere you journey through the circle" (Wall, 2001, p. 81). Black Elk, an Ogala Lakota Sioux, in Neihardt (2008), and Hampton (1995), of the Chicksaw Nation, purport that the power of circles lies in the six directional patterns "representing heaven, earth, east, south, west, and north. It implies circular movement in both natural and spiritual worlds" (Hampton, 1995, p. 6). Black Elk and Fixico (2009) assert that among the sacred elements contained within the centre of the circle is a drum.

The circularity of the drum for many Indigenous peoples represents the earth and the sounding of the drum is the pulse, the heartbeat of Mother Earth connecting all of creation in complex sacred and interdependent relationships. Circularity focuses on the complex connections or relationships within or between knowledges rather than the outcomes of linear thought where responses are sequentially compartmentalized into disconnected or fragmented stages. Fixico (2003) defines linear thought as the rationalization of "how something originates at point A, is affected by some force or influence and transforms into point B, to point C, and so forth" (p. 15). Circularity, according to Fixico is "the fundamental philosophy of traditional American Indians and it is integral to their belief system" (p. 57). In addition to the drum, Black Elk also saw at the centre of the circle a tree of life that was symbolic to the Sioux people's survival – as long as the circle remained unbroken and the tree flourished, so would the people. Cajete (2000) writes that many Native American stories refer to the "life-giving principle of the earth that nourishes and connects all life" (p. 58). Further, it is a symbol that is at the core of many Indigenous philosophical understandings of the interconnectedness of all life and "rootedness to the earth" (p. 58). In other words, the tree of life symbolizes the philosophical understandings of self-in-relationship with Iethi'nihsténha Ohwentsia'kékha (Land), which is, in essence, a living philosophy. Land, as the centre of circularity, is not simply the first teacher; it is our first primary relationship – the one that comes before all else. This relationship with Iethi'nihsténha Ohwentsia'kékha (Land) is deeply intimate and spiritual.

The notion of *first* in this context is not a linear construct but rather gestures to the primacy and centrality of Iethi'nihsténha Ohwentsia'kékha (Land) in learning processes and understandings of self-in-relationship. Circularity provides the movement in and around the centre. Iethi'nihsténha Ohwentsia'kékha and self-in-relationship are iterative processes in which each journey around the circle moves the journeyer to a higher ideological or philosophical state of consciousness. The deep structures of Indigenous thought about Land, self-in-relationship, and circularity disrupt dominant Western thought about how to be in relationship to the world.

I believe that all life is circular and grounded in the principles, philosophies, and ontologies of Iethi'nihsténha Ohwentsia'kékha (Land) and in my view this has implications for the ways we might move forward and (re)cognize education. Burkhart (2004) emphatically states that "in American Indian philosophy we must maintain our connectedness, we must maintain our relations, and never abandon them in search of understanding [or reason] but rather find understanding through them" (p. 25). In other words the process is equally, if not more, important than the result.

Action – (Re)generating

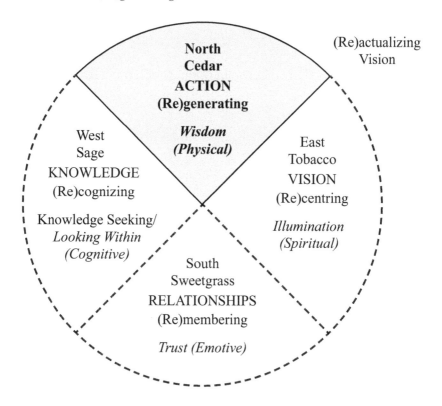

Section 3 looked at ways that complex circular and interrelated concepts informing Indigenous philosophies, ancient knowledges, and very old pedagogies informing the vision for this work can be (re)cognized in contemporary contexts. (Re)generation focuses on actualizing or making the vision a reality. In this section I discuss the ways Indigenous philosophies may be reconceptualized, reformed, and revived in contemporary and dynamic ways that consider the pathways through which Indigenous and dominant Western knowledges may coexist to form new distinctly sovereign relationships between knowledge systems. I explore the emotionally complex and highly charged issues relating to Indigenous languages as verb-oriented expressions and the ways this orientation influences and is influenced by Indigenous thought. I engage in a critical examination of understandings concerning decolonizing processes that serve to continue (re)centring colonial relations. I suggest Land-centred approaches that acknowledge but (de)centre colonial relations while privileging and (re)centring Indigenous thought and focus on the philosophies of Iethi'nihsténha Ohwentsia'kékha (Land). Last, I examine constructions of community as multilayered, fluid, and dynamic rather than fixed and static. I also explore the ways community is experienced in relation to urban/rural constructs and ancestral connections. Action, in this context, is a fluid, dynamic, and sustainable process where visioning is actualized and (re)visioned.

Continuing our journey through the circle, action, which rises out of the north, must be guided by wisdom and is represented by cedar, the medicine of restoration and healing, hence (re)generation. Therefore, action and (re)generation represent resistance to and (de) centring of colonial social and systemic relations of power and a (re) centring of Indigenous thought. Among many things, cedar crackles when placed in the fire with tobacco, the medicine representing visioning, thus calling the attention of the Creator to the offering. The outcome of action leads to a (re)generated and (re)actualized vision through a process that is dynamic, circular, and iterative. The etymology of *regeneration* originates circa 1300 from the Late Latin *regenerationem*, referring to a type of "being born again," from the Classic Latin *regenerates*, meaning to "make over, generate again," from *re-* meaning "again," together with *generare*, "to produce." In the mid-sixteenth century the term *regeneration* was used solely in reference to human/animal tissue; however in the late nineteenth century, with the advent of industrialization, marketization, and commodification, the term was expanded to include forests. Matlack (1997) writes that the concept of regeneration with regard to forestry was a response to industrialization and the increasingly expanding demands for land in the eighteenth century that led to large amounts of deforestation for various uses, including but not limited to land for agriculture, wood for fuel, the mining of natural resources, and the marketization and manufacturing of goods and services. The continued and growing need for land and resources contributed to entrenched resistances relating to reforestation – until very recently.

This understanding of regeneration in relation to the commodification of land as a renewable resource that can continually be used, abused, and exploited creates one of the greatest distinctions between dominant Western and Indigenous thought. Land, as I have written many times, is spiritual, (re)membered, and experienced – Land is fluid, circular, and relational – Land is consciousness – Land is sentient. And if Land is sentient, that is to say a conscious being that has the ability to sense, experience, and be aware, then capitalist concepts of ownership, appropriation, exploitation, and commodification of Land could be seen as another form of slavery. As discussed in Chapter 6, the ideology of slavery is based on appropriation, objectification, and ownership, specifically in relationship to a body. Further, it is a position that points to one way for gaining power and control over what is blindly or negligently perceived as inferior, as a something (an unspecified object) that can and should be exploited. This form of thought is directly oppositional with Indigenous philosophies of Land and understandings of self-in-relationship – Land is sacred – Land is spiritual – Land carries the very bones and words (in the form of language) of our ancestors through deep, intimate, ancient, and sacred knowledges together with very old pedagogies – Land also carries the promise of those yet to come. As Indigenous people we believe we exist in deeply intimate relationship with Land: we are birthed from the womb of the land and return to it when we die; it was our first environment, which is one reason our burial sites are considered sacred – burial grounds contain the bones of our ancestors, their knowledge, their words, their stories.

These sacred relationships are expressed in the Kanien'kehá:ka (Mohawk) word *Onkwehonwe* referring to the original or first people of the land and the intimate relationships we have to Iethi'nihsténha Ohwentsia'kékha and to each other arising out of the original instructions given to us by the Creator. Similarly, Māori identify themselves as whenua – people born of the land. Whenua is used in referring to both land and placenta – it is their whakapapa, the expression of their deep and intimate connections to their ancestors, lands, waterways, and mountains.

In relation to Indigenous philosophies (re)generating refers to the intensely spiritual process by which ancient knowledges and pedagogies are reconceptualized, reformed, and revived into different and contextually relevant ways. (Re)generating in Indigenous thought, like (re)membering and (re)cognizing, is grounded in understandings of Iethi'nihsténha Ohwentsia'kékha (Land), self-in-relationship, and sacred experiences. It is crucial that classroom practices and learning processes as they are currently epistemically located within dominant Western philosophies and practices be (re)generated to align with Indigenous values and beliefs regarding

educating children as whole beings – indeed, not only for Indigenous children but for all children. Iethi'nihsténha Ohwentsia'kékha,
according to Indigenous thought, is *"generative and regenerative on
its own schedule. From it experiences are born and to it human beings
(and other organisms) return for empowerment"* (Casey, 1996, p. 26;
emphasis mine).

8 Indigenous and Dominant Western Philosophies: A Bridge Too Far?

Even our bones nourish change, and even a people who … were saved for thousands of generations by a practical philosophy, even people such as we, the Anishinaabeg, can sometimes die, or change and become.

(Erdrich, 2004, p. 210)

The heart of many of the struggles relating to Indigenous education concerns constructions of difference between Indigenous and dominant Western knowledge systems. These constructions are positioned as hierarchical and oppositional, and Indigenous views are often positioned by Western thought as being less than dominant Western knowledge systems. This chapter focuses on some of the ways these two knowledge systems might coexist within and transform current contexts of education.

The phrase "a bridge too far" refers to the concept of overreaching and originated with the 1975 book and the 1977 movie of the same title. It is a historic (re)telling of the failed attempt to capture several bridges in Germany during WWII. The phrase is derived from a comment attributed to a British officer who, when queried about the success of the mission, states, "I always felt we tried to go a bridge too far" (Levine & Attenborough, 1977, n.p.). Its relevance here is that in conceptualizing some of the pathways through which Indigenous and dominant Western knowledge systems may be (re)generated to form new relationships between knowledge systems, I do not wish to overreach the bridges of connections and fail in my attempts to seek some pathways of understanding between the two philosophies. However, not attempting to reach those connections would be to perpetuate the perception of a completely dichotomous and oppositional relationship between Indigenous and dominant Western philosophies.

I want to be clear on this point. It continues to be my assertion that Indigenous and dominant Western philosophies are distinct and mutually sovereign ways of knowing and being. Nevertheless, there are connections or bridges of understanding that can serve as points of reference for commencing and forging new mutually egalitarian relationships and moving beyond oppositional colonial relationships, particularly as they relate to education. In addition, tremendous challenges must be faced in the struggle to build bridges whose ends are geometrically positioned precisely across from each other. The connections must not begin from and end in different locations and perspectives, becoming unstable and therefore unsafe or at times missing each other entirely. Education is one such site of resistance and struggle. While both Indigenous and dominant Western perspectives see education and learning processes as important, the processes, specific goals, and outcomes create disparity in that they are not positioned to connect or are missing altogether and that misalignment is often characterized or understood as being oppositional.

Education

Current ways of *doing* education are failing far too many students, particularly Indigenous students. Any Indigenous philosophy of education must include culturally aligned and holistic agendas based on spiritual infusion, local control, and parental responsibility. I, as do many Indigenous scholars, assert that the current system of education, and the ways individuals experience schooling, is designed to support and reproduce knowledge grounded in dominant Western thought. Grande (2004) writes that dominant Western patterns of behaviour and social organization are "embedded in the hidden curriculum" (p. 70) of educational structures to perpetuate and maintain the core values and world views that are foundational in marketized societies. These dominant systems of knowledge production have rarely, if ever, given any thought, beyond token gestures, to representing Indigenous ontologies and philosophies – effectively silencing, erasing, and invalidating Indigeneity within all aspects of educational processes. The school system as it currently exists is designed to serve the colonial agenda, thereby perpetuating and maintaining systems and relations of power through curricula and praxis. Education is a site where world views clash and collide fragmenting the principles of self-in-relationship. Kawagley writes, "There is a significant contrast between the [dominant] Western educational system and Native worldviews" (p. 33) in the following ways:

Dominant Western Perspective on Education

- Study, analysis, objectivity, and learned or memorized factual knowledge seek to predict and assert control over the forces of nature.
- An emphasis on the compartmentalization of knowledge (by disciplines) is often taken or used out of context and alienated from lived experiences.
- Little or no consideration is given to the ways the various compartments are interrelated within the whole.
- Competencies are based on predetermined notions of knowledge acquisition and assessment.
- Principles of exploitation and cognitive imperialism underpin education systems.

Indigenous Perspective on Education

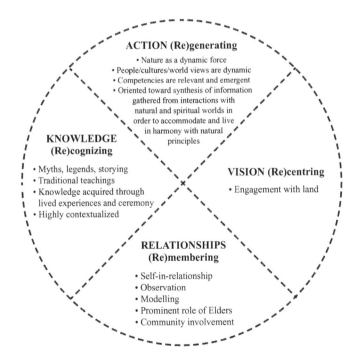

Placing Kawagley's elements of Indigenous education within the circular model[1] used throughout this book clearly shows the ways that Indigenous education engages with and is informed by understandings of land and self-in-relationship, that it is holistic in nature connecting knowledges across diverse contexts, and that assessments of competencies are relevant and appropriate. As well, the Indigenous world views of education are that it is always informed by the interactions between natural and spiritual worlds. The goal of education should be to enable Indigenous children, indeed all children, to have an education in which they can see themselves represented in positive ways, in which they can be happy and hopeful, and above all in which they can flourish. Sadly, Kawagley (2006) writes, "the schools have not given them the tools with which to achieve their aspirations" (pp. 85, 86). He argues that we need to move beyond the illusion of *Indian control of Indian education* and towards *implementation* of Indian control of Indian education, as defined by the National Indian Brotherhood (1972) policy paper, which is grounded in local control and parental responsibility.

Local control and parental responsibility are established through the development of local Indigenous education authorities and infrastructures having full control over finances; administrative and hiring practices; parental and Elder involvement; and development of culturally relevant pedagogies, learning environments, and classroom practices. These education authorities are to have jurisdiction for students across diverse community contexts, including urban and rural and on- and off-community schools. The illusion that Kawagley is referring to is one where there is merely a semblance of community control – paying lip service to the idea of local control. While there may be a few Native school board members, largely, educators and administrative staff are, for the most part, people outside the community, finances are controlled outside community, community interests and needs are largely ignored, and the system continues to reflect dominant Western educational ideals. Kawagley writes that what is required is a system of education that is Indigenous controlled, administered, and practised, effectively blending traditional and contemporary values. Kawagley promotes a "multidisciplinary, multi-sensory, holistic approach to education" (p. 98) where Indigenous philosophies, world views, and ways of knowing and being are the foundations of a dynamic approach to teaching and learning.

These Indigenous philosophical underpinnings enrich students spiritually, emotionally, intellectually, and physically, and are grounded in intimate and spiritual connections to place. Education grounded in the philosophy of Iethi'nihsténha Ohwentsia'kékha (Land) and expressed through the principles of self-in-relationship, (re)membered stories, and sacred experiences crosses curricular boundaries, interrelating and interconnecting knowledges across diverse subject areas: cultural studies, language arts, mathematics, social studies, audio and visual arts, and sciences. Indigenous education is immersed in spirituality, which, according to Akwesasne Notes (1978), is the highest form of social and political consciousness.

Education (formal and informal) is seen as a political and social construct embedded in any culture-sharing group. Infusing spirituality into an Indigenous philosophy of education ensures that it will become an inseparable aspect of all areas of education and learning processes. To that end, Porter (2008, 1993) maintains that spiritual, social, economic, and political dimensions of life are inextricably related and as such spirituality must be a value infused into any Indigenous philosophy of education. I believe that we must first identify what we want from our schooling system – what is our goal – and then we can create the vehicle that will guide the processes by which we will get there. All aspects of education should be reflected in the philosophy of the school and should be the guiding force behind pedagogy, classroom practices, assessments, measurements of success, and administrative practices. As such we need to be extremely mindful of how we choose to go about *doing* and *thinking* about education so that we do not perpetuate colonizing goals and agendas. One excellent example of this would be Te Aho Matua.

Te Aho Matua is generally translated to mean "Māori world view." Te Aho Matua is a Māori philosophy of education that, on 22 February 2008, was enacted into legislation as a supplement (Issue 32) to section 155A of the New Zealand Education Act 1989. Te Aho Matua has its roots in the Kohanga Reo (language nest)[2] movement dating back to the 1970s and 80s. In July 2013 I had an opportunity to talk with Mari Ropata-Te Hei, academic coordinator for Te Aho Tātairangi Māori immersion initial teacher education program, offered at Massey University in Palmerston North, New Zealand. Before taking up her position with Massey, Mari was the principal at Te Kura Kaupapa Māori O Te Rito, a Māori immersion school in Otaki (a town in the Kapiti Coastal district located on New Zealand's North Island) and is well experienced in the history, context, and use of Te Aho Matua in teaching and curriculum development. She shared these stories with me.

Te Aho Matua, in its original Māori form, was written in 1987 by a committee of 10 key individuals involved in the kura kappa Māori movement. The committee worked through ways to formulate Māori knowledge into a formal document that would change the ways Māori children were being taught. They wanted to get at the spiritual essence of what it means to be Māori. It was not about teaching subjects – it was about looking at how we should be philosophically practising our teaching. Te Aho Matua[3] is a living document that validates what it means to be Māori within a teaching and learning environment. Out of the development of Te Aho Matua in 1987 the first kura kaupapa Māori (Māori immersion school) was developed to address the needs of the children emerging out of the Kohanga Reo's. They now had a school in which to continue learning through te reo Māori (Māori language) and curriculum that was being developed through the principles and philosophies of what it means to be Māori.

Te Aho Matua became the foundational and guiding principles of every aspect of the kura kaupapa Māori. The goal was not to make Te Aho Matua fit into existing curriculum but to ensure Te Aho Matua was the central foundation for curriculum development. The six principles are as follows: (1) Te Ira Tangata relates to the nature of human kind (particularly as it relates to children); (2) Te Reo focuses on the advancement of language learning for students; (3) Ngā Iwi refers to the social networks that support and influence child development, that is, looking at students both from within their own iwi (tribal) perspective and in relation to other iwi nationally; (4) Te Ao relates to the development of children both in relation to their natural environment and from a global citizenship perspective, including understandings of their respective roles, relationships, and responsibilities to their world; (5) Ahuatanga Ako lists the principles of effective kura kaupapa Māori teaching practices that are considered vital to the success of the learning of children; this addresses teaching practices from a whānau perspective while also meeting the requirements of the national curriculum – in other words it goes beyond the national requirements; and (6) Te Tino Uaratanga articulates the overarching goals that the kura seeks to develop in Māori children, focusing on a holistic view of children as human beings in a global sense and also on what it means to Māori here and now – in this place.

Land-centred approaches to education provide ways to (de)centre colonial relations and (re)centre Indigenous interests and community needs, as well as legitimizing Indigenous knowledges in education. If we take seriously the decolonizing of education, then we must look towards strategies and practices grounded in Indigenous thought. Waters (2004a) asserts that dominant Western institutions, like education, have applied "non-understandings" concerning Indigenous peoples into Eurocentric constructs, thereby adopting a dualist or binarial world view, which is a form of *othering*. A dualist world view approaches education from a cognitive and physical perspective, often denying or erasing the emotional and spiritual elements of learning. Indigenous children, all children, have the right to an education that does not abuse, marginalize, or erase their understanding of who they are and how they are to be in relation to this world. Kovach (2009b) writes that education is a powerful tool and it can violate or it can transform. I, as do so many Indigenous scholars in the field of education, agree that education is a human process of interaction and as such it is relational, spiritual, dialectical, active, and reciprocal. Both educators and learners come into the learning environment as culturally located individuals who may be disparate or oppositional. Land-centred approaches to education and other forms of inquiry may open up opportunities for educators and students, regardless of cultural positioning, to effectively build bridges between various perspectives that acknowledge but (de)centre colonial relations and (re)centre Indigenous knowledges and pedagogies.

Educators, regardless of their cultural capital/positioning can, and some often do, make great efforts to include culturally relevant course content. However, many of these efforts are isolated in specific courses, such as social studies, history, and art. The effective teaching profile identified in Bishop and Berryman (2006) states that effective teachers "create culturally appropriate and responsive context for learning in their classrooms" (p. 273). According to Bishop and Berryman's effective teaching profile, culturally responsive teaching can be achieved in the following ways: (1) rejecting deficit theorizing related to Indigenous students; (2) being committed to professional development as a means of understanding how to bring about positive change in Indigenous student achievement; (3) demonstrating care for Indigenous students as culturally located individuals; (4) genuinely caring about the academic performance of Indigenous students in their classrooms; and (5) being able to create a healthy, safe, fun, interactive, and well-organized learning environment that consistently incorporates Indigenous knowledges and ways of being into pedagogy and classroom practices. Education, if done effectively, must integrate Indigenous and non-Indigenous histories, knowledges, philosophies, and texts into curriculum and classroom practices – across all subject areas. Te Aho Matua is an effective example of one way that might be done.

Integration refers to the bringing together of two forms of thoughts, ideas, individuals or groups of people in an egalitarian relationship based on mutual and equal partnerships and membership to bring balance and wholeness. The etymology of the term *integration* is as a verb – an active doing – originating circa the 1630s from the old Latin *integratus*, which translates to "putting together parts or elements and combining them into a whole." The challenge is to examine the ways this might be accomplished without (re)centring colonial relations while simultaneously acknowledging and respecting the value found in both knowledge systems.

Typically current scholarship and various historical and contemporary reports, including the National Indian Brotherhood (1972), the RCAP (1996), and the Task Force on Aboriginal Languages and Cultures (2005), support a system of Indigenous education that is autonomous, independent, and distinct from dominant Western education systems. Having said this, it is important to explicitly state that it is not my argument that Indigenous education be positioned in opposition to dominant Western education. Indigenous education can remain distinct and autonomous while balancing and incorporating some of the strengths and wisdom that can be found in dominant Western education. Indigenous education can be offered in ways that continue to centre and privilege Indigenous thought while keeping dominant Western knowledges in perspective. In Ontario this philosophy operates in the Ahkwesáhsne Freedom School (AFS) and in the focus schools of the Toronto District School Board (TDSB). The AFS is operated by the Ahkwesáhsne Mohawk Board of Education (AMBE), an independent school board operating in partnership with the Upper Canada District School Board. The focus schools operating under TDSB and AMBE mandates are not completely autonomous, but they do operate in ways that support the academic success of particular culture-sharing groups who, for a variety of reasons, are disadvantaged within the dominant Western school system. The TDSB currently has two types of focus schools: (1) Africentric schools and (2) First Nations School of Toronto (FNST).

For this discussion I will focus on publicly available information on the FNST[4] and the AFS.[5] FNST was developed by Cree Elder Vern Harper in 1977 as an alternative school and was originally called the Wandering Spirit Survival School.[6] The philosophy of the school was grounded in Ojibwa and Algonquin knowledges, understandings of self-in-relationship, sacredness, and circularity. The school believed in and operated on the principles of local control and parental responsibility. In 1983 the TDSB recognized the school as a Cultural Survival/ Native Way program rather than an alternative school. In 1989 the program was renamed First Nations School of Toronto. The school offers a tradition-based, Aboriginal-oriented curriculum that balances all the requirements set by the Parent Council, the TDSB, and the Ontario Ministry of Education. Students have the opportunity to learn about traditional Anishinaabe culture and heritage while acquiring the hands-on and technical skills necessary to be successful academically.

Another Indigenous focus school, the AFS, is located in Cornwall, Ontario, and falls under the AMBE. AMBE is an independent school board established to address the unique educational needs of the Mohawk people who reside in Ahkwesáhsne. AFS was established in 1979 by Mohawk parents concerned about the absence of cultural and linguistic services available in local public schools. The mandate of the school continues to be the revival and maintenance of the traditional Hodenosaunee culture and Mohawk language. The Mohawk language is one of the six language groups of the Hodenosaunee people. Those residing in the Ahkwesáhsne territory are from the Mohawk nation, hence their commitment to the Mohawk language and culture. AFS is a private school for pre-kindergarten through to grade 9. Pre-kindergarten through grade 6 are complete immersion; that is, all curriculum, in-class and outdoor activities, meals, and extracurricular activities are conducted through the Mohawk language. Grades 7 through 9 are transitional years in which English is integrated and students are taught in both Mohawk and English languages.

Focus schools have garnered both criticisms and praise for their alternative approaches to learning. The majority of the criticism comes from editorials and public responses readily available in the media. Such criticisms include (1) these schools are simply another form of segregation (moving back not forward); (2) they continue to promote rather than diminish or erase racialization; (3) they encourages individual to *withdraw* from rather than fit into the larger society; (4) they are only appropriate for one segment of the population and as such further perpetuate exclusion rather than inclusion (of course this criticism is a direct result of the power and privilege inherent in the dominant Western critique); (5) they are plagued by poor enrolment, attendance, and low achievement rates; (6) they have increased rather than decreased incidences of violence; (7) issues of racism can only be resolved by direct engagement, not withdrawal or self-segregation; and (8) inclusivity requires spaces where one can engage with alternative or opposing world views and constructions of difference. Supporters of the focus schools argue that (1) the schools address issues relating to underachievement, disengagement, and high failure and dropout rates; (2) students can see themselves represented in positive, meaningful, and relevant ways throughout the schools; and (3) genuine and respectful representation contributes to a sense of belonging within the school, reduces feelings of alienation and marginalization, and serves to eliminate stereotyping and racism.

Guswhenta – A Guiding Principle

In response to the critics, I point out that there are some similarities between the concepts forming the foundational principles of the focus schools and the sociopolitical principles of the Guswhenta (Two Row Wampum Treaty). This oral treaty initially established in 1613 set out the ways that the preceding Silver Covenant Treaty would be enacted.[7] The Silver Covenant Treaty is one of the earliest treaties between the Crown and the host people of this nation. The treaty, which was first an oral agreement then subsequently recorded on wampum, states that "the Red Man and the White Man would have but One Heart, One Head, One Eye and One Hand and the two parties would hold each end of the chain forever as long as the sun shines and waters flow" (Thomas, 1978, p. 9 – capitalization in original). The Guswhenta is considered the foundational principle on which all other agreements and interactions between the Hodenosaunee and the Federal government are based. The Guswhenta was recorded on a wampum belt and consists of two rows of purple wampum set against a background of white wampum. The purple rows of wampum represent a Hodenosaunee canoe (or government/political systems) and a dominant European ship (or government/political systems) with the understanding that neither of the two vessels would intermingle or interfere with each other but would coexist while remaining distinct, equal, and independent from each other. In contemporary times this treaty is still used to resolve issues relating to interactions between the two vessels. This very powerful treaty remains in full force and is as valid and relevant as the day it was created. Further, as a conceptual model the philosophical principles of the Guswhenta can be used to address the complexities of Indigenous education within the dominant

Western education system and the possibility for the coexistence of two knowledge systems.

The Guswhenta has always represented an agreed on moral code of non-interference. The implications and interpretations of this treaty have always been that an individual must be in one vessel or the other and that to straddle the vessels would result in disaster. This notion has been deeply connected to constructions of identity, politics, social interactions, and general ways of knowing and being in the world. The Guswhenta can also represents knowledge systems and the ways knowledges may or may not coexist within education. Dr Haig-Brown once told me that she inquired of an Elder if it was possible for Indigenous knowledges to inform the dominant Western knowledge system. The Elder advised that, while it was possible for individuals to *look* into the other vessel and perhaps even be influenced by each other, each one must remain in their own vessel.

At the time of this writing I was watching the America's Cup Race and was reminded of a discussion with a long-time friend and colleague who advised me that on a personal level he sees himself navigating the two knowledge systems on a catamaran. For him it is not about being in one vessel or the other or merely looking into the other vessel, he says that he straddles both knowledge systems and moves comfortably in both worlds – Indigenous and non-Indigenous. When I watched the America's Cup team members working together and moving seamlessly between both sides of the catamaran to maintain balance and achieve a common goal or purpose – the prize – while keeping the vessel from tipping over in rough waters and high winds; gaining speed and efficiency; and using the wind, water, and the construction of the vessel to their best advantage, I thought about how education can be similarly compared. A catamaran consists of two parallel hulls of equal size with a wide beam joining them, making it much more stable than single-hulled boats. The dual-hulled catamaran sits higher in the water and is much lighter, making the best use of the power of the wind to move efficiently.

Using this example for educational purposes within the context of the Guswhenta model, we can have two distinct but egalitarian knowledge systems coexisting and working together. Building a catamaran to bridge both knowledge systems would ensure stability and efficiency – both hulls (knowledge systems) would be distinct but equal and the wide beam would bridge the two. Teachers who are qualified to teach in this way, together with students, could move between the two knowledge systems as necessary without losing stability or effectiveness of learning and teaching practices. Cajete (2000) writes that such cross-cultural exchanges are not only beneficial but desirable, with the proviso that Indigenous knowledges are acknowledged as equal but distinct and should not be compared through a dominant Western lens. In this way each knowledge system remains in their own independent and sovereign vessel. Sovereignty is not something that can be given; it is something that is – you either are or are not. Grande (2004) argues that political sovereignty has important implications for Indigenous intellectualism. Similarly, Alfred (1999) in his earlier sociopolitical text writes that the key to avoiding potential *intellectual co-optation* is to maintain intellectual sovereignty and distinctiveness. Intellectual sovereignty relates directly back to the principles of the Guswhenta and the embodies ethics of non-interference that essentially mean that no individual, government, or institution should interfere with the rights, activities, and privileges of the other.

The Guswhenta perspective regarding the coexistence of two sovereign knowledges is indeed a construction of difference; however, the key to successfully coexisting is that one is cognizant and respectful of those differences. Constructions of difference are not to be construed as dichotomous or oppositional, which would only serve to erase the complexities of the two knowledges and fail to engage ethical spaces. I believe that it is this tendency to perceive constructions of difference as oppositional, hierarchical, and confrontational that is at the heart of many of the struggles concerning Indigenous education and creates the notion of a *bridge too far*. The coexistence of the two sovereign and independent knowledges can extend beyond and expand on the ways education is currently experienced. One crucial aspect of considering the ways Indigenous knowledges might successfully coexist within dominant Western education relates to the issue of language and the ways language constructs thought and thought informs language.

9 Indigenous Languages and Thought: A Verb-Oriented Reality

Language is one of the most important social practices through which we come to experience ourselves ... once we get beyond the idea of language as no more than a medium of communication, as a tool equally and neutrally available to all parties in cultural exchanges, then we can begin to examine language both as a practice of significance and also as a *site* for cultural struggle and as a *mechanism* which produces antagonistic relations between different social groups.

(Freire & Macedo, 1987, p. 153)

The discussion in this chapter will point to how language, its structure, and the ways it is used may inform how individuals perceive and interact with the world. This exploration into Indigenous languages as verb-oriented expressions is an important part of looking into the ways Iethi'nihsténha Ohwentsia'kékha (Land) as a philosophy is grounded in ancient knowledges and very old pedagogies that are contained in the language. I also examine some of the complex relationships between grammatical distinctions and the deep structures of thought. As well, I explore the ways I, as an individual who is First Nations and mixed-Euro ancestry and a non-speaker of my language, may think about and engage with the concepts of Indigenous thought.

Discussions concerning language issues, particularly as they relate to Indigenous languages, are intimate and emotionally charged, filled with many tensions, resistances, and varied perspectives. Some of the tensions are between mainstream institutions that do not support FNMI languages and Indigenous speakers. These tensions, particularly in education and employment sectors, concern the legitimacy and validity of speaking an Indigenous language. I have heard many people from my own community who do not believe that learning or having an Indigenous language is of any use – "it won't get us a job" – "it's useless in the 'real' world." These sentiments have been instilled and reinforced in FNMI people during the residential school era and are still played out in many areas of FNMI people's daily interactions. Other tensions arise among First Nations speakers themselves. Whether a person speaks the language is a very big determinant of who is seen an authentic "Native" person and who is not. I have also heard many arguments relating to degrees of fluency and dialectal influences. Still other tensions arise from the need to preserve the "high" or "original" language before it is lost, how to create new words to address current realities, the appropriateness of audio-recordings, and the dangers of decontextualizing the language and related teachings. Several community language experts once advised me that one of the goals of language preservation efforts on Six Nations is, while addressing current and shifting realities regarding language use, safeguarding the original or high language so that it can always be made available to future generations. In response to these tensions and resistances, many community language experts, Elders, and Knowledge Keepers have established rigid guidelines and limitations that ultimately question notions *authenticity* or *legitimacy* concerning identity and, relatedly, access to ancestral knowledge and philosophies, which do not always address the contemporary realities of many Indigenous peoples, including me.

However, in acknowledging and bringing forward these tensions, I want to be clear that I believe Indigenous languages are unequivocally crucial to the preservation and understanding of Indigenous philosophies and are essential in accessing and comprehending ancient knowledges and pedagogies. I agree with the many Indigenous scholars who argue that Indigenous thought and languages are inextricably connected. I believe that Iethi'nihsténha Ohwentsia'kékha (Land) is found within the relationships between the two. Nevertheless, language issues are deeply embedded in constructions of identity and notions of what constitutes authenticity; participation in ceremony and access to the various nuances of understanding embodied in Indigenous thought, and cultural, social, spiritual, and political sovereignty. This chapter explores some of those issues concerning language that continue to be complex, emotional, and multilayered. Freire and Macedo (1987) tell us that "nothing about society or language or culture or the human soul is simple" (p. xii) and that language and issues relating to language are complex, highly emotional, deeply personal, and value laden.

The reality is that many FNMI languages are at risk, and many of those individuals who are fluent in their language are coming to the end of their lifespan. Because of the influences of residential schools, the 60s scoop, and the criminalizing of ceremonial practices, many Indigenous people have been raised without their language and with limited or no access to language, ceremonies, and cultural teachings. Some come to realize their ancestry only as adults and struggle to understand their identity and to recapture their connections to community, knowledge, and cultural teachings. For these and many other reasons, while Indigenous languages are essential to understanding Indigenous thought, many Indigenous individuals have little to no access to their language and must come to understand Indigenous thought through cultural teachings and through understandings that are shared in a translated form in other languages, such as English. Some Indigenous people equate knowledge of Indigenous language and cultural grounding as *the* markers of authenticity and identity while others do not place as much emphasis on those markers.

Ontology of Language

Ontology refers to the study of the nature and state of being. Many speakers of their first language insist that language is an embodiment of being – language and thought are an inextricable and evolving part of who we are as Onkwehonwe (First Peoples). Languages as a form of communication have, throughout the ages, constantly evolved to meet the needs of shifting realities. In some cases and for a variety of reasons, some languages have ceased to exist altogether. Davis (2009) and Wurm (2001) tell us that of the approximately 7000 languages spoken in the world today, half are either in the process dying or disappearing altogether; they are dying at such an accelerated rate that they leave no one who can speak the language and pass on that knowledge. It has been said many times by Native scholars who write about Indigenous languages that our languages and cultures are place specific and are found nowhere else in the world – if they disappear, there is nowhere to go to (re)generate them. Similarly, Kuhn (1962) writes that no language is neutral or free from subjectivity but is pregnant with meaning and is the vehicle through which we make distinctions. How we interpret or understand those distinctions is related to the values embedded in the language used both to create the distinctions and to understand/interpret them. The relationship between language and thought is circular, iterative, and relational.

Languages are, for Indigenous people, deeply intimate and personal – they are spiritual and sacred connections to the ancestors, ancient knowledges, and very old pedagogies. Many Indigenous people argue that their languages are the keys to identity and understanding their place in the world. Battiste and Youngblood Henderson (2000) and Taylor and Wright (1989) write that the essence of language is not that it is solely a method of communication but rather powerfully gestures to the uniqueness of a particular culture-sharing group. Taiaiake Alfred (2005) recounts his interview with a well-established language teacher on Six Nations of the Grand River Territory who stated that "if we lose the language, we are no longer Onkwehonwe" (p. 251). Anzaldúa (1999) states that "ethnic identity is twin skin to linguistic identity – I am my language" (p. 81). Further, according to Davis (2009), "language … is not merely a set of grammatical rules or a vocabulary. It is a flash of the human spirit, the vehicle by which the soul of each particular culture comes into the material world" (p. 3). According to the Aboriginal Peoples Survey 2001 report, "language is often recognized as the essence of a culture … [and] is not only a means of communication, but a link which connects people with their past and grounds their social, emotional, and spiritual vitality" (Statistics Canada, 2003, p. 28). After extensive consultations with First Nations, Métis, and Inuit communities, the Task Force on Aboriginal Languages and Cultures (2005) determined that "languages are … more than just ordered systems of words. Culture animates language" (p. 58). Battiste and Youngblood Henderson (2000), Cajete (1994), Davis (2009), Grant (2004), Kovach (2009a), and Wurm (2001) agree that "language is a reflection of how we organize and perceive the world" (Cajete, 1994, p. 45) and "when you lose a language, you lose a culture, intellectual wealth, a work of art. It's like dropping a bomb on the Louvre" (Davis, 2009, p. 5; see also Wurm, 2001). This profound statement reverberates like the last beat sounded on a drum …

> What could be more lonely than to be enveloped in silence, to be the last of your people to speak your native tongue, to have no way to pass on the wisdom of your ancestors to anticipate the promise of descendants … in our lifetime half of the voices of humanity are being silenced. (Davis, 2009, pp. 3, 166)

Waters (2004a) states that language loss is a loss of "conceptual ontology; it is a loss of a way of being in the world, it is a loss of ways of relating in the world" (p. 106). These scholars are making the argument that languages are pivotal to Indigenous thought; language, in other words, is central to knowledges, philosophies, and systems of thought. In this way languages reflect a collective articulation of self-in-relationship. Feld (1996) asserts that Indigenous languages are the experiential processes of action "that invests places with memorable depths laminating living to language" (p. 113). The philosophy of Iethi'nihsténha Ohwentsia'kékha (Land) leads us to consider that "to inhabit a language is to inhabit a living universe and vice-versa" (Basso, 1996, p. 69; see also Porter, 2008, p. 152). Indigenous languages are living, deeply spiritual, and intimate languages expressing a relational and dynamic universe in flux – a reality that is constantly moving – and one that exists in understandings of self-in-relationship to that universe.

Various scholars have argued that many Indigenous languages, particularly those across Turtle Island, offer a very distinct grammatical structure that appears to inform communication and understandings in ways that are uniquely different from dominant Western languages – and one I believe is related to verb-orientation rather than noun-orientation as expressions of self-in-relationship. *Verb* is a linguistic or grammatical term referring to a large collection of words that indicate the doing of an action or express existence or state of being. The verb-orientation and the ways language is used are inextricably connected with thought. For my use in this discussion, *orientation* refers to the central positioning of verbs to express fluidity, relationality, and a reality in flux.

Verbology

Indigenous languages have been characterized by linguists as polysynthetic, which combines the prefix *poly-*, meaning "many, multiple, or very much," with *synthesis*, referring to "combining or bringing together." Polysynthetic was one of the classifications developed by Edward Sapir in his work with various Indigenous languages. Polysynthetic languages have also been referred to as *incorporating languages*. The verb-oriented structures of polysynthetic or incorporating languages are created by putting together many morphemes to form words that correspond to entire sentences in languages like English. A morpheme is the simplest or smallest unit of a language that cannot be further divided into smaller units of meaning. Indigenous languages are formed from root verbs to which affixes are added; these affixes provide information regarding tense, singularity, plurality, gender, and more complex grammatical information. Polysynthetic refers to the ways language is grammatically structured so that ideas are grouped together in ways that form a complete thought, idea, or expression with one word.

Community language expert and Knowledge Keeper Amos Key Jr., when queried about his or other Indigenous language experts' familiarity with and use of such terms as *polysynthetic* and *verb-orientation*, advised that while he had heard the term *polysynthetic* used to describe Indigenous languages, he uses the term *verb-based* since even the nouns in Indigenous languages are verb-oriented. He provided the example of the noun *police* or *policemen* to illustrate his point. In the Cayuga language *sha go di ye nahs*, which translates as *people/males who catch people* is the term used to describe police or policemen. The verb to catch is *yenah; sha* is the pronoun *they (males) go; di* who do something to others. Terms such as polysynthetic, incorporating, and verb-orientation have strong resonances with each other. Polysynthetic and incorporating are linguistic terms, whereas verb-oriented or verb-based are terms used by Indigenous language experts to describe their own languages and the ways those languages are intimately and inextricably interconnected with Indigenous philosophies. My use of the concept of verb-oriented expressions is to gesture not only to the ways Indigenous languages are grammatically structured to denote relationships, process, and an active doing but also to the ways that structure is informing the deeply intimate, spiritual, and dynamic aspects of Indigenous thought. Language informs the ways one thinks about, converses, and interacts with the world, and the ways one thinks about and interacts with the world informs the ways one speaks about that world. Many Indigenous scholars writing about language assert that Indigenous languages are verb-oriented in that they are relational, participatory, and fluid, and focus on human and non-human interactions.

Indigenous languages are expressions of deeply intimate and spiritual connections to Iethi'nihsténha Ohwentsia'kékha (Land) and understandings of self-in-relationship. Indigenous world views represent a deeply intimate and spiritual reality that is dynamic, experiential relational, in constant motion, and commonly described by Indigenous people as the Great Mystery. In verb-oriented languages the processes and relationships are emphasized rather than the subject. Alford (in Dellaflora, 2005) indicates that dominant Western languages are image based, that is, the sentences conjure up certain images, whereas Indigenous languages are kinesthetic – reflecting actual movement of reality. Armstrong (1998) writes that "language is a constant replay of tiny selected pieces of movement and action that solicit a larger active movement that are connected to you" (p. 190). Time, place, and creation are all made of interconnected and fluid waves of movement constantly stretching outward and inward. According to Battiste and Young-blood Henderson (2000), Indigenous knowledges expressed through language do "not describe reality; [they] describe the ever-changing insights about patterns or styles of the flux ... to experience its changing form, and to develop a relationship with the forces, thus creating harmony" (pp. 77, 79) and that Indigenous languages are not "a method to explain the forces or to change them, merely to contain them" (p. 79; Youngblood Henderson, 2000a, p. 262). Verb-oriented languages tend not to incorporate fixed or compartmentalized subjects, allowing for a more fluid, experiential, and relational understanding of wording that enables a speaker to create vocabulary in the moment that articulate varying shades of sense and meaning making. The categories that do exist within Indigenous languages exist within the context of self-in-relationship that is deeply spiritual and intimate and in constant flux.

Benjamin Whorf,[1] a linguistic anthropologist, is best known for his work relating to the Sapir-Whorf hypothesis. Whorf met Edward Sapir through a mutual acquaintance and began corresponding sometime in 1930. Eventually Whorf became one of Sapir's students at Yale University. It is important to note that Sapir was educated in and heavily influenced by the Humboldtian tradition developed in the early 1800s by Wilhelm von Humboldt at the University of Berlin. Pritchard (2004) writes that Humboldtian traditions are grounded in the following tenants: (1) unity and egalitarianism between educators and learners in learning processes and the pursuit of knowledge; (2) unity and equality in teaching and research practices; (3) a belief that all knowledges are held together by a unifying spirit of reason; and (4) freedom in the development of the inner self based on cultural and learning environments.

Sapir mentored Whorf throughout his academic career and, according to Lee (1996) and the late Dan Moonhawk Alford (in Dellaflora, 2005) greatly influenced his work on Athabaskan languages. Whorf was in the process of articulating the deep connections between language and thought until his failing health and premature death at the age of 44. Whorf premised that the grammatical structure of a language "contains a theory of the structure of the universe or *metaphysics*" (Duranti, 1997, p. 60) and provides the conceptual framework on which one develops an understanding of her or his world – in other words, the ways we speak is connected to the ways we understand and connect to our reality. Whorf challenged other Western notions of linguistics by stating that any change to a language also transforms our understanding of the universe and our ways of being in the world. Whorf posited that if there are variances among European languages, such as English, French, German, Russian, Latin, and Greek, that make communications challenging, if not impossible, then there must also be even greater divides between languages with completely different origins. This concept informs the development of Whorf's notion of linguistic relativity. Linguistic relativity is the "idea that culture, *through* language, affects the way we think, especially perhaps our classification of the experienced world" (Gumperz & Levinson, 1996a, p. 1). The concept of linguistic relativity suggests that language has a particular influencing factor on the ways individuals make sense of their world. Relativity is based on the understanding that nothing in the universe exists in isolation but instead exists in ever-changing and dynamic relationships.

What is also interesting is that in the late nineteenth and early twentieth centuries Albert Einstein, a theoretical physicist, spent a great deal of time engaging in deep conversations with Jost Winteler, also a Humboldtian trained linguist. Alford states that Winteler was an inspiration for Einstein's earlier ideas and often credited Winteler and his take on linguistic relativity with helping him formulate his own early thoughts on relativity. Alford explains that Einstein extrapolated from human languages to mathematical languages to build on and support his theories on relativity, and Whorf, realizing that Einstein took the theory of linguistic relativity and turned it into physical relativity, dedicated the rest of his life to reclaiming relativity for linguistics.

It is the layers and intersections of all these relationships that led to the development of linguistic relativity and what has, over time, become known as the Sapir-Whorf hypothesis. Linguistic relativity seeks to make strong connections between the grammatical structure of language and thought, as well as the ways they may work to inform each other. Taking the position that one does not exist in isolation from the world but in constant interconnected relationships, linguistic relativism tries to answer the question of whether language informs thought or thought informs language. Supporters of the Sapir-Whorf hypothesis indicate that an understanding of the linguistic structure of the Navajo language, one of the Athabaskan language families and the subject of Whorf's study, is essential for understanding Navajo thought. Whorf was just beginning to consider his hypothesis beyond the confines of the linguistic structure of language to the place where self is seen to be in relationship – to the sacred – to the cosmos – to the natural world. In fact Lee (1996) writes that in Whorf's Yale report he states that one of the "neglected phases of (linguistic) cultural anthropology is the study of the finer shades of meaning, and the values which are recognized as ideals" (p. 271). Whorf's work with the Navajo languages and investigation into understanding the connections between thought and language was creating a shift from unidirectional and linear approaches to ones that had more connections with Indigenous paradigms regarding language and thought.

During his investigative journey Whorf strived to create linkages between language and psycho-linguistics, such as the Gestalt principles, which underpin his notions of linguistic relativity. Generally, Gestalt is a psychological term that references a unified whole. It refers to theories of visual perception and is an attempt to describe the ways people organize visual elements into groups or unified wholes. Lee (1996) writes that Whorf's incorporation of Gestalt principles into his work created some of the deepest levels of thinking concerning patterns of perception and thought particularly about "isolates of experience and meaning" (p. xvi) and the ways these terms influenced his understanding of linguistic relativity. For Whorf, isolates of experience relate to the "perceptual data" (p. 126) generated through one's interaction with their environment, and *isolates of meaning* are the ways one interprets and makes meaning from that data. Whorf also experimented with connections pertaining to varying levels of consciousness where language use operates: Freud, Leary, and Bakhtin's dialogic.

Whorf's work makes some important contributions to my own thinking about language and thought, and I am drawing on aspects of the Sapir-Whorf Hypothesis together with the work of Bohm, whose concepts are more closely connected with Indigenous concepts concerning the relationships between language and thought, particularly in light of the fact that, as Dr Carrie Dyck so aptly stated, language is a necessary but not sufficient condition for determining thought. Gopnik (2014) similarly writes that "we are not captives of our tongues but we are citizens of our languages" (p. 39). In other words we act as citizens do – we are active and reciprocal participants in the relationships we have to our world and to our languages. Indigenous peoples' intimate and sacred interactions with their places shape the ways Indigenous languages are formed and expressed, both orally and in thought.

One of the core concepts in Indigenous thought is the understanding of interconnectedness and interdependence – that self exists within a holistic and sacred relationship to the universe and all creation, human/non-human and animate/inanimate. David Bohm (1980), an American physicist and philosopher, and a supporter of Whorf's work, addresses the concept of a holistic and interrelated universe. In so doing he concluded that modern science needed a new language with which to describe this deeper reality and more accurately communicate the findings of his research. Bohm and Peat – also a physicist – (1987) argue that this new language required new conceptualizations of order. Order in the their work refers to a universe in flux, that all matter in the universe (known and unknown) exists in dynamic, interconnected, and interrelated relationships and that nothing exists or is experienced in isolation. Bohm and Peat further write that the entire spectrum of an individual or indeed a culture-sharing group's philosophies, perceptions, and interactions are held and experienced within that order. This new order requires alternative ways of thinking, communicating, perceiving, and interpreting reality, as well as of engaging with and acting on that reality. Resistances arise when attempting to conceptualize knowledges considered radically new using an old order – in essence putting "new wine in old bottles" (Bohm and Peat, 1987, p. 96).

According to Indigenous paradigms, languages as the sacred holders of ancient knowledges, informs thought, and thought informs the ways we think about and use language. Language and thought exist in interconnected, layered, and circular relationships. Little Bear (in Dellaflora, 2005), states that Bohm believed that an enfolding universe is a conscious and continuous manifestation of the enfolding of past, present, and future. In this way the past has already manifested, the present is currently unfolding, and the future is inside each of us as yet unmanifested. Similarly, a particular Hodenosaunee oral teaching grounded in ancient knowledges states *our past is our present, our present is our tomorrow, and our tomorrows are the seven generations past and present.* Bohm (1980) asserted that thought is also a continual process of enfoldment and implications and therefore, "language is also an enfolded order and meaning is enfolded in the structure of the language and meaning enfolds into thought" (Bohm and Peat, 1987, p. 182). Among the various orders within the universe Bohm and Peat assert that there is also an "order of language" (p. 297). Several scholars working with Indigenous languages write that many dominant Western languages are strongly noun-oriented expressions in that nouns form the basis of communication within these languages – in fact, many times verbs are used and transformed into nouns. Languages that are noun-oriented give primacy to objectifying, classifying, and categorizing reality, leading to a large number of fixed concepts that are then grouped into rigid constructs of thought. Bohm (1980) writes that the noun-oriented language of modern science classifies and fragments the ways the world is perceived and experienced. Noun-oriented expressions are limited in their ability to express the interconnected, layered, and circular processes and relationships of the Great Mystery within a universe in constant flux.

Quantum physics is about understanding and describing energy, movement, process, relationality, and transformation that is exceedingly similar to the ways Indigenous languages and thought processes interpret and describe reality. Bohm (1980) out of frustration at what he felt were the limitations of the languages he was familiar with to be able to describe quantum theory, developed what he called the *Rheomode*. The Rheomode is, in essence, a language based on process and movement, which, for Bohm, was a new way of considering language. Bohm sought to experiment with the structure of languages that build on root verbs. His goal was not to create a new language per se but to observe the deeper connections between thought and language. Bohm began his study by acknowledging that certain unconscious assumptions hidden deep within the structures of thought and dominant Western language use perpetuate and maintain a fragmented reality. Bohm, in his experimentation with language structures, notes:

> One of the best ways of learning how one is conditioned by a habit (such as the common usage of language is, to a large extent) is to give careful and sustained attention to one's overall reaction when one *makes the test* of seeing what takes place when one is doing something significantly different from the automatic and accustomed function in an unending experimentation with language (and with thought). (p. 25)

Bohm begins with an understanding that language and meaning are processes in flux. He argues that if one were to transform the structure and meaning of sentences to reflect verb primacy, the root verb must first be separated from adjectives and nouns to structure sentences and build language based on these root verbs. This separation requires a rearrangement of words within sentences and system of guidelines for the ongoing development of new words to represent a world in flux.

Bohm offers a cautionary note that one must be consistently aware of transforming the verbs in the sentences and using them as nouns – as with gerunds.[2] In other words it is not simply a process whereby one may substitute verbs for nouns in the sentences and call them verb-oriented – rather, it is the ways those verbs are used to describe the world. Peat (2007) writes that one should not "ask what a word means, [rather] ask how it is used" (p. 69). Gee (2008) similarly writes that discourses are more than the "content of what you say ... but how you say it ... who you are and what you're doing while you say it" (p. 3). In other words, language becomes a highly contextualized and complex way to describe the ways one interacts with and is in relationship to the world.

Scollon and Scollon (1981) observed the primacy and emphasis of verbs in Athabaskan languages and, in fact, write that they are beginning to consider the early works of Sapir specifically in relation to his examination of various Athabaskan languages. Vermeulen (1998) writes that Sapir's work led not only to grammatical classifications, such as polysynthetic, but also to making some initial connections between linguistic structures and culture. Sapir, according to Vermeulen, believed that each language contained its own genius – that is, every language conforms to a particular logic and has the ability to express all the concepts and ideas it requires for sense and meaning making. Sapir also posited that languages were unique and that no two languages could or would express the reality in exactly the same way. Whorf, following Sapir's death, continued exploring and developing the concept of linguistic relativity. Both Sapir and Whorf believed that language, in relation to culture, is fluid, dynamic, and expressive. It appears that Sapir, and then Whorf, was looking to conceptualize language in ways that balance form and expression in its influence on thought.

While the discipline of linguistics is a manifestation of dominant Western thought, the notion that Indigenous languages are relational, expressive, spiritual, and verb-oriented is not *new* knowledge. Indigenous scholars and community experts on language and Indigenous thought have been formally and informally gathering, speaking, and writing about these very points for decades.[3] In the mid-1980s, after becoming familiar with and impressed by the work of Bohm and Peat regarding language and quantum physics, Leroy Little Bear (Blood Indian, Blackfoot nation) invited them to attend an extensive meeting on language in a Blackfoot community in Alberta. It was at this meeting that Bohm and Peat encountered Indigenous people speaking in the language that

Bohm had envisioned when he had created the Rheomode. Elders and language experts at the meeting advised Bohm and Peat that Indigenous languages, as verb-oriented expressions, are spiritual, process oriented, and an articulation of self-in-relationship with a world in flux. Indigenous languages carried many similarities for Bohm to his goal of developing the Rheomode. Both Bohm and Peat were excited and had several discussions with Little Bear; unfortunately Bohm died suddenly, before there could be any collaboration or further development of Bohm's work. One of the many connections for Little Bear, Bohm, and Peat was looking at the ways languages informed thought. Following Alford, Bohm, Little Bear, and Peat, I say that there is a circular and interconnected relationship between language, thought, and reality. The ways Indigenous languages are structured has a direct influence on Indigenous thought – Indigenous thought informs the ways language is used – thought and language are intimately connected in the ways we think about and understand self-in-relationship in our world.

To lose a language or to change its structure is to lose or alter all the thought and knowledges embedded in the language. For this reason one cannot separate Indigenous thought from Indigenous languages. The interconnection of the two creates Indigenous philosophies. Having said this, and to avoid romanticizing Indigenous thought or putting forward a utopian or an exclusionary perspective on Indigenous philosophies and the connections to language, it is important to take seriously contemporary realities and to consider the implications for ways an Indigenous English speaker may or may not be able to take hold of Indigenous thought.

I strongly believe that Indigenous languages are crucial and central to any discussions relating to Land and Indigenous knowledges. I have always been a passionate advocate for Indigenous language learning, maintenance, preservation, and revitalization and that it is one critical aspect of identity formation. While Youngblood Henderson (2000a) opens an interesting point of consideration when he asserts that Indigenous people can experience a degree of their culture through English, but they cannot comprehend the breathtaking depth, nuances, and intimacy of Indigenous thought, so "they end up living a translated life" (p. 264). Jojola (2004), on the other hand, argues that while language and community participation may be concrete ways of determining the depth of an individual's connection to his or her identity, they are also limited in determining the ways an individual defines his or her sense of what it means to belong to community.

I am a person of First Nations ancestry who, at this moment, is a non-speaker of my Indigenous language – and as current literature highlights I am not alone. In what ways do I go about discovering, developing, and maintaining Indigenous thought patterns and under-standings of Land, circularity, and self-in-relationship?

"This Is Not a Pipe"[4]

I did not delve into thinking about the ways language informs thought until I began exploring the ways land and understandings of self-in-relationship inform my teaching practices and course development. In looking back I can see that my first steps in the journey into Indigenous thought began when Dr John Hodson introduced one particular circle model as a way to conceptualize curriculum development. Since that initial encounter, circle work as a conceptual framework has evolved in my thinking as a deeper and more complex model for developing curriculum and various forms of inquiry and now is completely inte-grated in my thought processes. I use the term *circularity* to describe a particular form of circular and fluid logic that informs the conceptual framework for the ways I organize my thoughts and engage in deep thinking and conceptualize and do research; it also informs my teach-ing philosophy and practices, curriculum development, and indeed even this book – through circularity the world makes sense to me. As previously mentioned I did not grow up knowing my First Nations ancestry or being immersed in the Mohawk language, yet the journey towards circularity as a form of thought felt like I had found my way home.

In my earlier work concerning the varied and complex relationships between education, educational practices, and language, I have found that the roots of all those tensions, challenges, and resistances relating to the complex and hotly debated issues about language have their foundations in constructions of identity. I have explored issues of iden-tity elsewhere in this book, but this is critical and worth repeating here: constructions of identity are intimately connected to issues of language and as such we must also address the impact of languages and identity for non-speakers. I am reminded of the story in Basso (1996) where a Navajo Elder was performing a coming of age ceremony for a young Navajo woman. The Elder was performing the ceremony in English as the young woman was a non-speaker. The Elder was upset at the limi-tations of performing the ceremony in English not because the young woman was a non-speaker or because he had to use English; rather, his frustrations arose from deep within himself as he struggled with the limitations of communicating verb-oriented expressions of Navajo knowledge in English – a noun-oriented language. He was fearful there was so much that he could not tell her about her role as a young woman in the community because the concepts were simply not available nor could they be translated and articulated in English.

Engaging with Indigenous philosophies as a non-speaker is to immerse oneself in a translated and somewhat blurred version of Indigenous thought that fails to capture the totality of the complex nuances and meaning making that would be communicated through the language. The etymology of *translate* originates from the Latin *translates*, literally meaning "carried over," which acts as a past participle of *transferre*, referring to "bringing over or carrying over." *Translate* comes from two words: the prefix *trans-*, meaning "to go beyond," was originally a present participle of the verb *trare-*, meaning "to cross," and *+latus*, meaning "to carry or be born across." The term *translation*, whether referring to language, biochemistry, physics, or mathematics, refers to movement, process, and action. Peat (2005) writes that translating Indigenous languages is more than moving between two different languages; it is about shifting between two disparate world views. This form of translation results in what Archibald (2008) calls "weak translations shaped to fit a [dominant] Western literate form" (p. 7), where the substance and subtle shades and nuances of meaning are lost. Indigenous languages and thought exist in interconnected and circular relationships. Therefore, translations of thought from one particular distinct world view to another pose similar challenges.

Iethi'nihsténha Ohwentsia'kékha (Land) is a particular philosophy grounded in ancient knowledges and very old pedagogies that are held within Indigenous languages as verb-oriented expressions. It follows then that translating Indigenous thought contained in the language is also an attempt at translating a *profoundly different world view*. It has been said by many Indigenous and non-Indigenous scholars that a translation cannot be compared with or be equal to the original – it is but a two-dimensional image of the original. Spivak (1993), in articulating the politics of translation, writes that "there is no real translation only a simple miming of the responsibility to the trace of the other in the self" (pp. 180, 181). This reminds me of Foucault's (1982) *This Is Not a Pipe*. In his examination of two separate images of what appears to be the same pipe, Foucault concludes that one cannot point to either image and state *this is a pipe*. One can only say with any degree of certainty that the image is one interpretation or translation of a pipe – "the life of interpretation [and I would add translation] is to believe that there are only interpretations [translations]" (p. 12). As a person of First Nations and mixed-race European ancestry, as well as being a non-speaker who is engaging with the concepts of Indigenous thought, I am painfully aware that I walk the path of interpretation and translation. I can only say with any degree of certainty that this text is my interpretation of Indigenous thought in relation to Iethi'nihsténha Ohwentsia'kékha (Land), circularity, and understandings of self-in-relationship. Further, I am prudently, painfully, and purposefully "making the road by walking" (Horton & Freire, 1990, p. 6, 7).

As I engage with this work I am always aware that, as a non-speaker, some crucial aspects of Indigenous thought are going to elude me. I am also very much aware that I am engaging Indigenous thought as a verb-oriented expression through English, a noun-oriented expression, and as such I am always engaging and negotiating the shifting and at times conflicting world views within my own thinking. This is not to say that this work cannot be done meaningfully or respectfully; however it does take conscious effort to acknowledge ancient knowledges and very old pedagogies in their original context while moving towards (re)cognizing these ancient knowledges in contemporary realities.

Rather than being constrained and frozen by efforts to respectfully and mindfully interpret and at times translate Indigenous thought, I see this as one tentative step in the long process of (re)cognizing ancient knowledges to address the contemporary realities of Indigenous peoples. As I have indicated elsewhere the boundaries of Indigenous thought evolve to meet the needs of the people at every point in time – they are living philosophies in a constant state of flux while moving towards achieving balance and harmony – they live and exist within Iethi'nihsténha Ohwentsia'kékha (Land). Before this work I would have stated that these are some of the ways decolonizing thought can (de)centre colonial relations and privilege Indigenous philosophies. However, I now emphatically assert that focusing solely on the concept of decolonizing only serves to (re)centre colonial relationships. I would suggest that perhaps Land-centred approaches might work better as a concept for (re)centring, (re)membering, and (re)generating Indigenous thought. Land-centred approaches acknowledge colonial relations but do not centralize or place emphasis on those relationships.

Land-Centred Approaches

An Indigenous philosophy of education must seriously consider the implications of colonial relations. Because of positionality and privilege, it is entirely possible for non-Indigenous people to be completely oblivious to the historical and contemporary implications of colonial relations. However, for Indigenous peoples it is highly unlikely that they would be unaware of colonial relations, particularly as they relate to the historical impacts and the contemporary insidious implications of those relations. With this in mind I turn to exploring the ways to articulate practices that serve to centrally position and privilege Indigenous thought without (re)centring colonial relations. Kovach (2009a) urges each of us to push beyond merely identifying the impacts of colonial relations to promote change and argues for tribal-centred approaches to any forms of Indigenous inquiry. Tribal-centred approaches, outlined earlier, refer to place-specific ways of knowing, understanding, and interacting with the world. Alfred (2008) profoundly and simply queries, "What is colonization if not the separation of our people from the land?" (pp. 9, 10). Colonization indeed separated Indigenous people from self-in-relationship to their specific lands, and to (re)centre Indigenous thought we as Indigenous people must, first, (re)generate our understandings of our connections to Iethi'nihsténha Ohwentsia'kékha (Land).

Whether any of us chooses to acknowledge it or not, each of us lives in deep and profound relationship to Iethi'nihsténha Ohwentsia'kékha. We feel Land's rhythms. We experience joy and peace when the warmth of spring awakens the earth after her long winter sleep, we gasp at the magnificence of fall's adornment of the maple and birch trees, and we laugh when we see children playing in the first snow fall or experience the awesome hush as the snow crunches while we are walking under a full winter moon. Many of us feed and shelter birds through the scarcity and harshness of winter and plant flowers in pots, boxes, and gardens to attract butterflies, bees, and hummingbirds in the spring. I remember well the rhyme that was taught to me as a child, which inevitably always proves true: red sun in the morning, sailor give warning; red sun at night, sailor's delight. I know individuals who plant the four sacred medicines in large pots on their balconies in the city. I, as do many people, love to be woken in the morning to birds singing and rejoicing as brother sun rises to fulfil his duty once again and to fall asleep to the sounds of the night frogs croaking and crickets chirping as grandmother moon watches over me. In Aotearoa (New Zealand) the melodic sounds of the native birds welcoming the morning with all their hearts is a very different sound from home, and I was once again reminded how far (and yet not so far) from my land I really was. I also have seen people near and far (as do I) stop what they are doing and lift their eyes in awe to the cry of the eagle or its little brother, hawk, as it flies over them. These relationships transcend and are sustained beyond the boundaries of built or natural environments. Kulchyski (2005) writes that "nature retains its power within each of our bodies. One cannot be closer or further away from that which is within us" (p. 18).

I have written many times that Iethi'nihsténha Ohwentsia'kékha (Land) (re)centres and privileges Indigenous knowledges, philosophies, relations, and systems of power, which include education and various forms of inquiry. I argue, then, not solely for decolonizing approaches but rather for Land-centred approaches to education and various forms of inquiry, particularly as they relate to Indigenous people in urban and rural communities. Land-centred approaches provide the context for privileging Indigenous thought and acknowledging but decentering colonial relations. It is Land-centred approaches to Indigenous education and forms of inquiry grounded in circularity and understandings of self-in-relationship that provide shared thematics across diverse Indigenous contexts. Land-centred approaches are formed and informed from complex interactions between the natural and spiritual worlds that are conceptual, experiential, relational, and embodied. Land-centred approaches to education and inquiry are grounded in circular, fluid, dynamic, and storied relationships.

Therefore, the core of Land-centred approaches is found in the interconnected relationships between individuals and Iethi'nihsténha Ohwentsia'kékha (Land) that include natural and built environments. It is also my assertion that Land-centred approaches allow for the specificity of what Kovach (2009a) termed as *tribal* ways of knowing among Indigenous nations and linguistic-sharing communities. Tribal can relate to a particular large culture-sharing group, such as Hodenosaunee or Anishinaabe, or it can also refer to specific nations within those larger groups, such as Mohawk, Cayuga, Oneida, Seneca, Onondaga, and Tuscarora (Hodenosaunee) or Ojibwa, Cree, Oji-Cree, Odawa, and Potawatomi (Anishinaabe). Each of these communities of nations is, within the larger culture-sharing group linguistically

and culturally distinct and is informed by both the specificity of land
(lower-case *l*) and connections to Iethi'nihsténha Ohwentsia'kékha –
Land (capital *L*). Pedagogies of Iethi'nihsténha Ohwentsia'kékha incorporate both overarching and shared connections to Land and circularity
while also addressing the specificities of land and understandings of
self-in-relationship.

Iethi'nihsténha Ohwentsia'kékha – (Re)actualizing

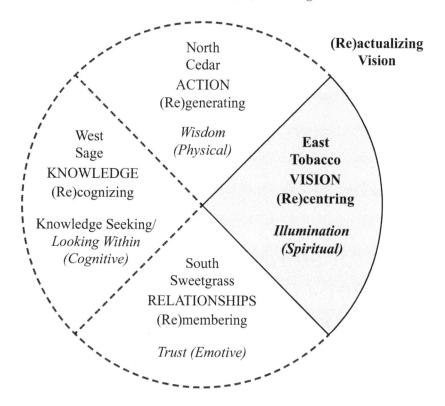

In Section 4 I examined the ways Indigenous knowledges may be (re)cognized in contemporary contexts and the pathways through which they might coexist with Eurocentric knowledges in distinct and intellectually sovereign relationships between knowledge systems. I also explore language use and the ways language informs thought and vice versa in interconnected circular relationships. Last, I consider the ways Land-centred approaches to education might provide an alternative framework for decolonizing processes, as well as the ways the fluidity of community informs understandings of Land and self-in-relationship.

The concepts of Iethi'nihsténha Ohwentsia'kékha (Land) and the process of (re)actualizing in this section is intended to provide a critical examination of Iethi'nihsténha Ohwentsia'kékha in relation to the challenges, tensions, and contradictions of conducting this work within the academy. I offer some practical examples from my experiences in Sioux Lookout and in southern Ontario, as well as some conclusions and implications for transformative practices. I explore the ways Iethi'nihsténha Ohwentsia'kékha is distinct from two of the current and trendy approaches that have developed in an attempt to address the limitations of the dominant and prevailing ways of *doing* education: culturally responsive and place-based education. I also discuss the ways Iethi'nihsténha Ohwentsia'kékha disrupts, challenges, and resists embedded colonial relations of power and privilege in culturally responsive and place-based education. Further, this section is an articulation of the culmination of my understandings of the relationship between current scholarship regarding Land in education and the implications for praxis. In essence, this section allows our iterative journey to continue through the circle to form the foundation for (re)imagining, (re)theorizing, and (re)visioning, Land-centred approaches to education.

10 Tensions, Challenges, and Contradictions

Deconstruction has proven helpful in its insistence that we pay attention to the exclusions and the silences in narratives. It also impels us to recognize how we all participate in what we criticize. This *critical intimacy* – in contrast to the scholarly distance that is so often highly valued – does not allow me to conveniently forget that as I engage in this current critique ... **I nevertheless remain a part of it, privileged and complicit in many ways.**

(Kuokkanen, 2007, p. xiv – emphasis added)

As I sit at my desk in my home office and write this section or am walking my sweet and beautiful chocolate Labrador retriever, Nala, along one of the Grand River trails, contemplating what it means to do this work as a woman of Native and mixed-Euro ancestry, a non-Indigenous language speaker, a First Nations community member, and an academic working in a university, I realize that one of the many challenges in doing this work is in attempting to articulate what cannot be textually articulated – particularly in English. There are many things in this world and the next that individuals, and in this context Indigenous people, are spiritually sensitive and attuned to that cannot, and sometimes should not, be articulated or explained through the voices of dominant Western scientific logic and rationalism. This chapter focuses on the various tensions, challenges, and at times, contradictions of doing this work within the academy. It is an attempt to examine the "so what" question: why should we care now, here – in this time – about Indigenous knowledges and what they have to offer all of us within and outside the academy? Perhaps one may consider this chapter a call to critically examine the conscious and unconscious ways Indigenous knowledges are positioned within academia.

"Word Warriors"

The tensions I have and continue to experience in doing this work are both personal and systemic – and in saying that, these tensions are not to be perceived as dichotomous or necessarily oppositional but are interconnected by the formation of ethical space as defined by Willie Ermine. In a previous chapter I discussed the use of the Guswhenta (Two Row Wampum) analogy for the coexistence of Indigenous and Eurocentric knowledges within education. I believe that this analogy continues to apply to the issues of personal and systemic tensions that arise out of doing this work within the academy. I have, in earlier work, examined the concept of being and/or walking bi-epistemically. The prefix *bi-* refers to "two, twice, double" and is influenced by the Latin *bini*, meaning "twofold or binarial," and relates specifically to scientific terminology. Binarial is more than a construction of difference – it is a construction of opposition. Epistemic or epistemology is a Greek philosophical term relating to the dominant Western concepts of logic and the formalization of knowledge. It addresses questions such as, What can we know? How do we come to know? What are the origins of truths?

As a field of study, epistemology is a consideration of the grounds, nature, and origins of knowledge, as well as of the limits of human understanding. Epistemology is a very large, overwhelming, and abstract concept that does not effectively capture the idea of crossing or walking between concepts or systems of knowledge. Discourses that focus solely on epistemologies can also create constructions of difference that do little to create bridges of understanding between knowledges and systems of coming to know. These epistemological discourses tend to focus on absolutes, such as the determinants of truth, whose truth is privileged, as well as the relativity of truth. I prefer Youngblood Henderson's (2009) notion of trans-systemology as a more effective concept in addressing the complex and tangled tensions, challenges, and contradictions of doing this work across two knowledge systems, particularly as it relates to building bridges of connections while engaging the philosophical principles of the Guswhenta.

The Indigenous intellectual, within the academy, must be able to effectively work with and bridge two distinct knowledge systems.

As previously described the prefix *trans-* refers to "crossing or going beyond," and *systemic* originating from the Late Latin and Greek *systema* pertains to "the arrangement and/or an organized whole" in relation to cosmology and ecology. It came to be used philosophically to refer to a set of correlated principles, facts, and/or ideas. Two forms of systemic tensions existing within academia include dominant Western paradigms and ways of conceptualizing systems and doing the work; the second is the long-established concept of what constitutes legitimized knowledge. The tensions arise when Indigenous intellectuals bring with them into the academy and into their own work Indigenous philosophies that inform ways of knowing, being, and relating in the world, as well as introducing knowledges that have their legitimacy in ancient roots in Turtle Island that are grounded understandings of Land and self-in-relationship. In so doing the Indigenous intellectual often disrupts the status quo – the comfort of long-established taken-for-granted assumptions about ways of being, doing, and relating.

Youngblood Henderson (2009) uses Willie Ermine's concept of ethical space to address the tensions in trans-systemic practices. Youngblood Henderson writes that each knowledge system is represented by two overlapping circles and ethical space is formed where the two knowledge systems encounter each other, interact, and converge. The applications of trans-systemic engagement are that Indigenous professionals (including education as a profession) be given opportunities and appropriate resources within academia to develop to their fullest potential in terms of practice and achievement – the fullest potential as defined by the Indigenous professional community. Youngblood Henderson states that some of these tensions arise from the interactions between Indigenous community and academic professionals who are engaged in defining and perhaps also (re)defining the concepts of professionalism based on the egalitarian coexistence of knowledges, values, and beliefs in both Indigenous and dominant Western perspectives. Current assumptions and institutional systems very often box in Indigenous knowledges, ways of perceiving the world, and the work that we do. The box is the imposed classification, surveillance, and bounded applications of Indigenous knowledge within academia, as well as the defining, articulating, and legitimizing of the intellectual based on dominant Westernized criterion.

One of the many issues Indigenous people working with or within the academy frequently confront is finding their place among the *legitimized* intellectuals within some of the established disciplines. The pressure to conform creates contexts of opposition, resistance, and marginalization in taking a stance for one's own Indigenous professionalism, or acquiescence and struggling with feelings of loss of one's Indigeneity to find acceptance as an intellectual within long-established systems. Further, for all academics, but particularly for Indigenous intellectuals, there are the complex issues concerning what knowledge can or should be shared, as well as educating other academics and students on protocols that must be adhered to.

Indigenous intellectuals constantly navigate the tensions and challenges between professional or academic notions of intellectualism and culture-centred and grounded intellectualism. Gramsci (1971) argues that there are two types of intellectuals: (1) traditional or professional, and (2) organic. According to Gramsci, traditional intellectuals are immersed in relations of power and privilege, are steeped in dominant Western scientific logic and rationalism, and regard themselves as autonomous. Organic intellectuals are context specific. That is, their ideas and aspirations coincide with the culture-sharing group to whom they organically belong and are characterized by political and social activism. Gramsci asserts that all human beings are philosophers by nature (though not necessarily formally recognized as such) and that each culture-sharing group has the ability to develop intellectuals from within. Turner (2006), a member of the Temagami First Nation in Northern Ontario, refers to organic intellectuals as *word warriors*.

Word warriors stand in the gap – they engage both dominant Western intellectual, social, and political practices and Indigenous philosophies – all the while working to meet the needs of community (as defined by those communities) and doing so in ways that balance Indigenous philosophies and traditions within contemporary contexts. Similarly, Kuhn (1962) writes that the highest standard comes from community acknowledgment, which in the current context of word warriors is the Indigenous community locally and at large. Word warriors, engaging the philosophies of the Guswhenta, work trans-systemically with Indigenous and Eurocentric knowledges, all the while protecting and centring Indigenous thought as a distinct knowledge system within the academy. Word warriors, while working trans-systemically within academia, are not, as some may criticize, lacking in cultural and spiritual experiences. Word warriors, by virtue of working within the deep structures of Indigenous thought, are connected to Iethi'nihsténha Ohwentsia'kékha (Land) and understandings of self-in-relationship (through kinship ties, as well as cultural, spiritual, and ceremonial practices and experiences).

Challenges that I have observed and personally encountered within the academy include the resistances to Indigenous intellectualism and the challenge to find the spaces to define for myself what that might look like and the ways it may be relevant for me as a person of First Nations and mixed-Euro ancestry. For me, intellectualism based on Indigeneity is an organic and fluid process of articulation grounded in understandings of Iethi'nihsténha Ohwentsia'kékha (Land), self-in-relationship, circularity, and iterativity that is continually evolving as I develop my sense of being within the context of community and Indigenous intellectualism, particularly as I continue to negotiate and make connections inherent in the complex historical and contemporary relationships between community and academia. Having said that I must state with all earnestness and gratitude that I have been very fortunate to have had key individuals both within and outside academia (locally, nationally, and internationally) who have come along side my canoe, have been and continue to be encouraging and supportive, providing helpful feedback while creating opportunities and opening spaces for me to do this work.

Another of the many tensions in engaging this work is seeking the balance in acknowledging and building on the work of others while finding the place where I am expected to *own* the knowledge I am deemed to have created. For instance Kuhn (1962) writes about two theorists and the absurd controversy about which one of them apparently discovered oxygen – as if (and Kuhn also acknowledges) it is possible to claim for oneself the discovery and knowledge of something that already exists – the very breath of creation is proof that oxygen is a part of all life in some way or form. I do not believe nor am I comfortable with the notion that I, or anyone, can own knowledge – particularly ancient knowledges, since whatever paradigms I may have articulated belong to the community or collective. Even in instances where stories or songs may belong to specific communities or families, knowledge is shared with permission, respect, understanding, and acknowledgment. In working trans-systemically the Indigenous intellectual must constantly struggle with tensions pertaining to balancing the (re)generating and (re)actualizing of ancient knowledges, being ever mindful of acknowledging our teachers (Land and human) and all those who have laid the foundational work for what we do, while understanding the pressures to find the spaces where they are able identify what has been created beyond the work of others. Ownership of knowledge runs counter to Indigenous philosophies and is not a position that a word warrior would take up. Having said that, word warriors can, under certain conditions, be positioned by the community to be carriers or keepers of knowledge(s).

Ethics of Protocol

The principles of the Guswhenta indicate that while there are ways for two knowledge systems to inform or influence one another, there are some tensions in working trans-systemically to ensure Indigenous knowledges remain centrally positioned, distinct, and protected from co-optation or appropriation in a world that seeks to define, to classify, and many times to commodify Indigeneity. Appropriation can include material aspects of culture (style of clothing and adornments, foods, artefacts, and cultural/spiritual representations); however, it can also include spirituality, values, beliefs, philosophies, and interpretations of knowledges, stories, ceremonies, and ways of knowing and being. Haig-Brown (2010) refers to this form of appropriation as "cultural theft." We must take seriously issues of appropriation and co-optation in any discussion relating to the integration or infusion of Indigenous and Eurocentric knowledges within the academy and in particular within Indigenous education.

Conversely, I have also encountered scholars within the academy (non-Indigenous professors/educators, teacher candidates, and graduate students, just to name a few) who, with woefully good intentions, are fearful of making errors in judgment that might lead to cultural appropriation. These individuals neglect to follow important cultural protocols in interactions with Elders, community scholars, and communities as a whole. I use the term *fearful* purposefully as some of these individuals have expressed to me directly that they fear that they may be engaging in cultural appropriation if they follow protocols and yet they fail to see the impacts of not respecting these long-established cultural protocols, such as the respectful way to ask Elders or Knowledge Keepers to share their knowledge. For educators, this might include a request for the sharing of time and knowledge with a class. Tensions arise in finding the balance between understandings of appropriation and important adherences to cultural protocols.

One such protocol is the offering of tobacco to an Elder or Knowledge Keeper/Holder when making a request. The National Aboriginal Health Organization[1] has listed the offering of tobacco as the generally accepted protocol among many First Nations, Métis, and Inuit peoples, although the specificity of protocols vary from nation to nation – land to land. Protocols are critical to the ethics of establishing and maintaining relationships and are foundational to the nations they belong to. In other words protocols are grounded in Iethi'nihsténha Ohwentsia'kékha (Land), understandings of self-in-relationship, and what I have called the *ethics of protocol* based on relationship, respect, relevance, reciprocity, and responsibility. Kirkness and Barnhardt (1991) refer to the four R's (respect, relevance, reciprocity, and responsibility) in relation to higher education. Styres, Zinga, Bennett, and Bomberry (2010) build on these to discuss the five R's (relationship, respect, relevance, reciprocity, and responsibility) in relation to Indigenous research contexts. For my own use, I will discuss these same five R's in connection to the ethics of protocol. Protocol refers to an established code of procedure or conduct in any group, organization, or situation. In understandings of Iethi'nihsténha Ohwentsia'kékha (Land), the ethics of protocol refers to the official ceremonies that establish the ethical procedures for engaging with Indigenous communities as a whole and more particularly, Chiefs, Clan Mothers, Elders, Knowledge Keepers/Holders, and community scholars. While a general concept of ethics gestures to the rightness or wrongness of particular motives, intentions, actions, and/or behaviours, for me it also refers to the process of respectfully adhering to cultural practices. Sometimes, when I have raised the issue of community protocols and the importance of adhering to them with academics, I have been told that following protocols and building relationships is a waste of time and resources – it takes time away from doing the *real* work. While it is true that adhering to protocols and building relationships can and often does take time – it is a necessary and critical part of *doing* the *real* work. It is far better to take the time necessary to build relationships and attempt to respect and follow protocols – and risk possibly making some mistakes along the journey – than to do nothing and risk offence by replicating dehumanizing and de-relationalizing research and education.

Doctrine of Discovery?

This leads into another challenge of doing this work within the academy, which is the resistances that are often brought to bear when introducing into the academy as a whole and within specific disciplines what are considered new knowledges and paradigms as well as the *discovery* of what are perceived as *new* knowledges. Specifically I am referring to the ways Indigenous knowledges and paradigms are perceived as *new*. I believe it is very important for me to be clear on this point – Indigenous knowledges are not new and are grounded in ancient traditions, knowledges, and very old pedagogies that are foundational to and arise from understandings of Iethi'nihsténha Ohwentsia'kékha (Land), self-in-relationship, circularity, and iterativity. Kuhn (1962) would probably agree with Kuokkanen (2007) that "the university is founded on a key ideal of the [dominant] Western intellectual tradition known as rationalism. The premise being: truth exists independently of human perception" (Kuokkanen, 2007, p. 12). Western institutions, such as academia, establish guidelines for the legitimizing of theory and its practical applications – they also provide the foundations for which patterns of *discovery* are considered new knowledge, the ways new patterns of discovery may and may not occur, and who may *own* the knowledge arising from the discovery. These patterns of discovery find their roots in what Swamp (2010) calls the "Doctrine of Discovery" established as a legal right by the Papal Bulls of 1452 and 1493 issued under Pope Alexander VI. This Doctrine was a legally established world view held by the Roman Christian church, which swept across Europe. This world view, according to Swamp, provided the context whereby Christians (in the broadest sense) believed (and perhaps still do) it was their duty to take for their own any lands they came into contact with. If the lands were inhabited by people considered non-Christians,[2] the Christians, under the Doctrine of Discovery, had a legal right to recognize those lands as *terra nullus* (empty lands) and to *appropriate* the lands for their own use.

The perpetuation of the Doctrine of Discovery as a world view continues to have implications for Indigenous people and knowledges within Western institutions, such as the academy. The Doctrine of Discovery in contemporary academic contexts extends well beyond the idea of empty lands (although there is a general failure to care to know or acknowledge whose traditional lands these institutions are built on) to include an erasure of Indigenous people and their knowledges by either failing to acknowledge their legitimacy or by appropriation. Kuhn (1962) argues that there are specific characteristics under which new phenomena may emerge within the academy: "(1) an awareness of anomaly (or counterinstances) in a paradigm; (2) gradual and simultaneous emergence of observational and conceptual recognition; and (3) the consequent change of paradigm categories and procedures are often accompanied by resistance" (pp. 62–5). These resistances resulting from emerging knowledges are quite often preceded by periods of what Kuhn calls "professional insecurities," leading to a critical crisis of destruction and reconstruction. Granted, Kuhn was talking about the (re)structures of scientific revolution, but I believe that the same principles apply across disciplines. So many times I questioned whether the violence premised by Kuhn is really an accurate account of what occurs in introducing work, such as this text, into the academy. Yet the various tensions and resistances that I, and indeed other scholars who would introduce Indigenous thought, have experienced might suggest that violence does exist and in fact permeates the very foundations of networks and relations of power and the ways they operate. By violence I do not necessarily refer to physicality but to the violence perpetuated spiritually, emotionally, and intellectually. Freire (2003) writes that "there is not one state for dialogue and another for revolution. On the contrary, dialogue is the essence of revolutionary action" (p. 135).

This book could possibly be considered such a form of dialogue – a call to action, if you will – an opportunity to look at and do things differently. New paradigms or patterns of thought can open up opportunities for looking at old problems in new and exciting ways, perhaps finding solutions that could not be found under the old paradigms alone. In academia social scientists frequently defend their research and ways of *doing* research in education within narrowly defined and rigid frameworks.

"Critical Intimacy"

One particular interesting contradiction inherent in this work is the fact that at the very moment I deconstruct and problematize the dominant Western systems embedded in academia, I am fully aware that, in many ways, I am also exceedingly complicit and participatory in the very systems I am problematizing. Kuokkanen (2007) refers to this process as "critical intimacy." I am always aware that as an academic and educator, I am intimately connected to the very system I criticize. I am also always conscious that as an Indigenous person of First Nations and mixed-Euro ancestry within academia, I am embracing the messy fluidity of an insider/outsider perspective and am at once privileged and complicit in so many tangled ways yet also simultaneously disconnected, isolated, and marginalized. This necessitates that I participate in and negotiate multiple discourses that at times contradict, erase, or marginalize the *other* within myself, as well as challenging dichotomous lines of thought while opening up spaces of possibility. This fluid, ambiguous, and organic participation is not only inevitable but necessary, requiring continual (re)negotiation. This work is exceedingly messy, personal, and emotional, which is a pariah in dimensions of Western institutions that find security in maintaining walls of emotionless rationality and are very uncomfortable with and disapproving of the messiness and ambiguity of doing this type of work within the academy – but that messiness and ambiguity are also what make this work so exciting!

One example of what I have been talking about centres on an encounter I had with a young non-Indigenous scholar at an education conference. A colleague and I presented a paper together, and afterwards a discussion ensued that brought forward the particular tensions and complexities of traditional lands, historical and contemporary colonial relations, and, relatedly, land claims issues arising out of current realities within rural and urban environments. The individual asked why it was made out to be so complicated to determine whose traditional lands we were on. The young scholar declared that we simply had to look at the nearest First Nations community and that is whose lands we are on. I responded by stating that because of forced relocations, historical migrations, and other sensitive implications of historical colonial relations it is not that simple. I brought forward the example from my own community, Six Nations, which is outlined more fully in the Introduction. I advised the individual that, from this example we could see that the complex colonial histories of the traditional peoples of this land do not lend themselves to simple declarations of whose traditional lands we may be on.

The young scholar then asked me in light of these complexities how I would resolve land claims issues, particularly in relation to people who had built homes and businesses on what was (and I would add, continues to be) Indigenous land. Did I want the land *simply* given back? Did I want them to be asked to leave? In what ways would Indigenous people be compensated? Would individuals or Canada as a whole (which would ultimately affect individual taxpayers) be asked to pay compensation to Indigenous peoples? What form would that compensation take? After firing these questions in rapid succession, the individual demanded a response in that moment, and I advised that I could not say – that I did not know what the answers were. Greater minds than my own with years of experience in this area are still trying to find solutions to the land claims issues in ways that balance out the areas of concern for all stakeholders while still holding Canada accountable to its treaty and constitutional fiduciary obligations. I went on to calmly explain that the points in question are exceedingly complex. From this person's position of privilege and sense of entitlement, she complained I was being *ferocious* because I chose to address her perceptions of traditional lands and answer her questions in a manner that was different from the ways she demanded. It is interesting to note her choice of the term *ferocious*:[3] it gestures to the cloaked and unspoken racism that Indigenous scholars experience and the position of silence they are expected to assume within academic circles.

This example illustrates another important issue that caught my attention. I want to preface the next discussion by stating that I clearly understand that people have questions, that not everyone has taken an Indigenous studies course nor is required to do so, that many times people quite simply do not know, are unaware, or have never encountered or thought about Indigenous issues. I have taught undergraduate and graduate students who, after learning about Indigenous issues in both current and historical contexts, are upset with an education system that in many cases does not include appropriate and respectful Indigenous content in courses. Having said that, the following discussion focuses not on individuals asking genuine questions and seeking to acquire knowledge but to the persisting drive to homogenize and over-simplify Indigeneity.

I have observed and experienced the tendency for Indigenous people to be expected to be a fount of wisdom and knowledge for all other Indigenous culture-sharing groups. We are, many times, expected to be able to speak authoritatively to the issues of other Indigenous nations, particularly across Canada and sometimes also across North America. While there are some shared themes relating to the broader issues, the particulars may be specific to a localized, contextualized land (lower-case *l*) and the colonial relationship each nation has with Canada. Sometimes both the broader and the more specific issues are so complex and tangled that they have no easy or concrete answers; to expect them is a demonstration of a sense of oversimplification that continues to be the hallmark of perceptions embedded in historical and contemporary colonial relations. Esteemed Māori scholar and author Graham Smith said it best when he spoke at a conference, stating that there are conversations that we need to have among ourselves as Indigenous peoples first and that these conversations need to occur without interference from those who would seek to (re)centre colonial relations.

Opening opportunities for these conversations to take place within the academy and in other academic spaces, particularly because they need to be grounded in Indigenous thought, could present challenges and contradictions as world views collide.

Transformative Practices

Opening up spaces for bringing the philosophical principles of Iethi'nihsténha Ohwentsia'kékha (Land) into the academy has at times been (and in some ways still is) a source of tension and contradiction. The Reggio Emilia approach to schooling asserts that the environment is a third teacher – children and teachers are seen to be the first and second teachers, respectively. Wien (2008) writes that the key to the Reggio philosophical approach to education is "the image of children and teachers as capable, resourceful, powerful protagonists of their own experiences" (p. 6). The environment, in relation to the Reggio conceptualization, relates to the way the environment engages and shapes the learner, particularly in the ways spatial arrangement can facilitate learning with minimal mediation by the educator – in essence the ways the "environment shapes responses, acting as a teacher" (p. 9). Iethi'nihsténha Ohwentsia'kékha goes beyond the spatial arrangement of the environment as an influencing factor to the deeper principles, ontologies, and philosophies grounded in Land. In essence Land is not the third teacher but is central, primary – it is the first relationship, the one that comes before all else. As previously discussed Haig-Brown and Dannenmann (2008) describe land as the first teacher. The idea of first in this instance is not a reflection of dominant Western linear or hierarchical categorization but rather gestures to locating, legitimizing, and grounding pedagogies within the notion that land (lower-case *l*) in all its primacy and centrality is our first teacher – whether we choose to acknowledge it or not. However, Iethi'nihsténha Ohwentsia'kékha goes deeper still – it expresses a relationship before all relationships: the womb. Iethi'nihsténha Ohwentsia'kékha takes into account Land (capital *L*) in all its various elements including water, earth (land – lower-case *l*), and air. We are all born of water – the water was our first environment – Land was our first relationship – the place of our formation and development – our gestation – the place where we enter this world from the spirit world. It was in that environment that Land formed the very core essence of who we are as part of creation. When we are born from water to the earth and take that first breath we continue that relationship – differently but no less intimately, no less sacred.

I have experienced various tensions via some student resistances when bringing Iethi'nihsténha Ohwentsia'kékha (Land) into the curriculum and my own teaching practices. One way of incorporating Land into pedagogies without necessarily declaring it as an explicit course of action in the syllabus is to embed Iethi'nihsténha Ohwentsia'kékha (Land) within the course structure. For example I use the concept of the Three Sisters as one of the multilayered frameworks for structuring learning in course development. I will briefly explain the historical significance of the Three Sisters and then demonstrate the ways this may work in structuring a course. The story of the Three Sisters (corn, beans, and squash) emerged out of the Hodenosaunee Creation story.[4] All Creation stories are sacred stories belonging to specific nations and should not be used inappropriately or without permission – they are not to be used unilaterally as part of a "toolbox." As always it is important to point out here that it is crucial to follow community-specific protocols for any use of story work.

Because of the sacredness of the Creation story, I will recount it here in very general concepts only. While the specificity of the Creation story often changes among the various Hodenosaunee nations, the general premise always remains the same. Sky Woman, who was pregnant, fell through an opening in the sky, grasping at plants as she fell, and eventually, after a long descent, landed on a giant turtle's back – thanks to the air animals who, seeing her falling, flew up to her and brought her gently and safely down. Several of the water animals who also observed her falling tried, failed, and died while trying to bring land from beneath the sea to place on the turtle's back so Sky Woman would have a safe place on which to land. Muskrat was the only animal able to bring up earth clenched in his two fists from beneath the depths of the great water. Sky Woman took that small lump of dirt, placed it in the middle of the turtle's back, and began dancing, following the direction of the sun around the turtle's back. While she danced, the earth grew and life began on Turtle Island (what we know as North America). Eventually Sky Woman gave birth to a daughter who herself eventually became pregnant with twin sons. The daughter died giving birth and her mother, Sky Woman, placed the plants and leaves that she had carried with her from the Sky World onto her daughter's grave. It is said that from the head of the daughter's grave grew the three plants, corn, beans, and squash, known as the Three Sisters, which became the primary life sustaining food for the Hodenosaunee people. The Three Sisters concept is based on very old knowledges wherein each of the sisters work together as interconnected and interdependent elements, each one building on and depending on the strengths of the other for survival. By that I mean that the corn grows tall, strong, and straight, acting as a trellis for the beans to grow up and use to stabilize themselves as they reach for the sun. Together, they provide shade to the squash, which grows along the ground. The wide leaves of the squash act as ground cover, protecting the roots of the corn and bean plants from the sun and weeds while keeping the earth moist.

The concept of the Three Sisters as a model of very old pedagogy is grounded in understandings of Iethi'nihsténha Ohwentsia'kékha, the deep, intimate, and sacred source of all relationships and relates to the ways course design may be structured. For example, in my courses I organize small reading groups, larger class discussions, and regular weekly journaling. Each of these builds on the other and culminates in a final paper, which is essentially, an analysis of the small and large class discussions, class activities, assignments, and an in-depth journal analysis. Students prepare a reading reflection based on a threefold response (read, reflect, and respond). The small group discussions are like the corn growing tall and straight, providing the basis and stability for the larger class discussions. The large class discussions build out of the small group discussions, centring on core concepts or questions arising out of and across each of the readings and related in-class activities. The large class discussions are representative of the beans, which wind around the corn for stability while reaching for the sun to grow, develop, and blossom. The weekly journaling is the squash growing along the ground, providing shade and protection for the roots of the other plants. As a whole the Three Sisters approach to pedagogy creates a balanced approach to the course structure, providing each student with varied opportunities to participate in and be responsible for his or her own learning from their own positions of strength. Of course, depending on context and instructor preference, this model may be successfully implemented without explicitly providing the background knowledge – the students are made aware of the course expectations and overall structure but not necessarily the rationale. This pedagogical approach opens opportunities to embed core principles of Iethi'nihsténha Ohwentsia'kékha (Land) directly into the very foundation of any course.

One of the many questions and areas of critical analysis to be addressed in the final paper is, what are you taking away from this course? In analysing their journals, in-class activities, and readings, and answering that question, students are provided opportunities to critically examine their own resistances and any awkwardness they may have felt while charting their learning journey through the course. Several undergraduate students have pointed out that the courses are structured unlike any courses they have previously taken, and some have even said that they were initially confused and frustrated at the push to be so deeply reflexive while articulating the depth of their learning journey through the course. One student advised me one semester later that the course she took with me was the only one where she remembered the readings, content, and what she took away from the course – in her own words her learning was *transformative*. Another student declared the whole process to be completely unacademic and that she felt she had wasted her time on the course. We once again find ourselves at the place where we can say with certainty that we all exist in intimate relationship with Land, whether we choose to acknowledge it or not.

This work, while potentially transformative, is not without its resistances, particularly when opening up discussions concerning the ways various issues relate to Indigeneity. Some students indicated that they perceive these discussions as pushy and unwelcomed – as pushing Indigeneity too much into the classroom in a course that may not be specifically designated as an Indigenous studies course – one student stated, "this is not what we signed up for." This is particularly interesting because these students become aware of my background when I introduce myself the first day of class. I find these resistances to be similar in some ways to those expressed by James (2001), who encountered active student resistances to having a black teacher, simply because they had never had a black teacher before. James wrote that students indicated in course evaluations that they should have been made aware ahead of time they would have a black teacher so they could have been better prepared – *so that they knew what they were signing up for*. The students in his article indicated on the course evaluations they felt this rationale to be an adequate explanation for all the expressions of resistances James encountered within the courses.

James (2001) questioned why it would be important for students to be forewarned that their teacher was black before entering that first class. Similarly, I question why it is perceived as biased when an Indigenous teacher explicitly incorporates Indigeneity and understandings of Land into curriculum and course content outside a specifically designated

Indigenous course. One example of this resistance arose when I taught a racism and constructions of race course where we examined several aspects of racism within Canadian contexts. The students were made very aware through the syllabus and in-class discussions that no examination of race within the Canadian context would be complete without considering Indigenous perspectives. Further, since individuals in the class can and should only speak from their own perspective, as a teacher of First Nations ancestry I would be using that position to segue into other aspects of racism and constructions of race. Despite these active preparations some students remained steadfastly resistant – which, by the way, is an example of the ongoing compartmentalization of Indigeneity in academia. It is, as suggested by Leroy Little Bear (2000), as if there are two world views colliding.

Another tension experienced in relation to this work is connected to the reality and impact of colonial relations embedded deep within the conscious and unconscious psyche of the academic community, which includes faculty, staff, and students, where Indigenous and dominant Western world views collide and compete for space. Little Bear (2000) writes that within these spaces objectivity and control are illusionary. Haig-Brown (2008) writes that "dismissive critique based in cries of essentialism has allowed scholars immersed in [dominant] Western/ Euro-Canadian (and American) discourses to continue to relegate Indigenous thought to some marginal space while colonial relations proceed apace and unexamined" (p. 16). We must always begin these discourses from somewhere and, building from the discussions relating to discourse in earlier chapters, I add Loomba's (2005) assertion that discourse is "a whole field or domain within which language is used in particular ways. This domain is rooted in human practices, institutions and actions" (p. 38). If, as Horton and Freire (1990) have stated and I have articulated elsewhere, we make the road by walking then that journey must begin with a single movement forward. At times that first step begins with a question, a commitment to attempt to articulate the inarticulatable, and a search for more effective answers. Yet having said that, I find it so incredibly ironic that more than five hundred years after contact I/we are still having to articulate and defend the *so what* question – why should we care about Indigenous knowledges or what they have to offer? I gesture to an understanding of whose traditional lands these dominant Western institutions are built on – on whose lands are the knowledges constructed that are resisted in these institutions? Whose stories still carry knowledges arising from Land? Is

Iethi'nihsténha Ohwentsia'kékha still the primary relationship, the first before all else, whether one chooses to acknowledge and respect it or not? The answer is and should be a resounding yes!

One way of acknowledging the legitimacy of Indigenous knowledges within current Western informed institutions, such as academia, is to (re)actualize the ways Indigenous knowledges are conceptualized and used through the principles of the Guswhenta (Two Row Wampum Treaty) as expressions of trans-systemic practices. I return to the (re)generating principles of the Guswhenta, as articulated in Chapter 8, to look at the ways Indigenous and Eurocentric knowledges, philosophies, and principles might coexist and inform transformative practices. Many Indigenous Elders, Knowledge Keepers, and community scholars have indicated that within the guiding principles of the Guswhenta, individuals and or governing bodies must each remain in their own vessel or, in attempting to straddle the vessels, risk falling between and face disaster. I do agree with this position but I also believe that the spaces between the two vessels or world views is not neutral or vacant but can be considered ethical space where individuals may create cognitive bridges of understanding that connect two world views. However, more often than not the realities of historical and contemporary colonial relationships produce a wake between the two vessels in which the waters are turbulent, treacherous, and unpredictable, and the attempted pathways of connections are similarly treacherous and unpredictable. As suggested by Ermine (2007, 2005) these spaces are the uncharted waters of ambiguity, abstractness, messiness, and uncertainty where two knowledge systems are poised to engage one another. It is, as Youngblood Henderson (2009) argues, "a zone of confrontation … a space where no single knowledge or way controls; it is the extraordinary realm of change, paradigm shifts and divergent ways of knowing and acting" (p. 64). It can be a place of radical transformation. Because Indigenous and Eurocentric world views encompass sharp distinctions, it is sometimes in the mutual acknowledgment and negotiation (rather than in deflection and avoidance) of the turbulent and messy spaces between these two vessels that opportunities open for transformative approaches to pedagogies within education that respect and acknowledge Iethi'nihsténha Ohwentsia'kékha.

To accomplish this we all, Indigenous and non-Indigenous peoples alike, need to venture into the messiness beyond the vessel of dominant Western academia; step outside our offices, classrooms, virtual spaces, and libraries and go out onto the land, into architecturally or naturally formed green spaces, onto the waterways (natural or built), and into the streets. Break down the barriers of previously held assumptions, paradigms, and ideologies – be willing to walk with ambiguity and emotion, and ask the tough and risky questions, to step outside ourselves to listen to Iethi'nihsténha Ohwentsia'kékha (Land) and what *she* has to say to each of us.[5] Iethi'nihsténha Ohwentsia'kékha is a storied place – a place of journeying, struggle, and transformation. Building on the concepts of storying and journeying as outlined in Chapter 1 it is my continued assertion that "teaching is a storied act. To teach is to develop a living text" (Styres, 2011, p. 719).

11 Coyote as Trickster

> We locate all we do in relation to the lands and the Aboriginal peoples who
> have lived with those lands.
>
> (Haig-Brown & Hodson, 2009, p. 167)

This chapter begins with my journey with Coyote and the Two Eyes
story as told by Terry Tafoya in Jo-Ann Archibald's (2008) book *Indigenous Storywork: Educating the Heart, Mind, Body, and Spirit*. I became
familiar with Coyote and the Two Eyes story in relation to my initial
thinking around a two worlds approach to Indigenous education, as
well as my own position and identity in relation to my work. As my
thoughts have shifted and transformed into Land-centred approaches
to education, Coyote, in all of his forms, remains a familiar friend.
Coyote, as one of the trickster characters in Native American storytelling, is a metamorph. Metamorph originates from the Latin and Greek
metamorphosis, meaning "to transform or change shape." The prefix
meta- is "a change of state, place, or condition of being"; the term *morph*
originates from the Greek *Morpheus*, a character in Greek mythology
known as a dream shaper. According to Ovid (AD. 8/2004), Morpheus could transform his shape and appear to others in dreams as
a messenger of the Gods. Dreaming and morphing are shared themes
woven throughout both Greek and Indigenous stories. These shared
themes provide the pedagogical context for considering the ways trickster characters and the life lessons they teach us might inform Indigenous understandings within English; in this way understandings of
Iethi'nihsténha Ohwentsia'kékha (Land) may transcend cultural and
linguistic boundaries.

The concept of morphing reflects the process of change, transformation, or transition from one form or image to another. Coyote's metamorphosis occurs through various storied contexts – humour, farce, sarcasm, self-ridicule, and the nonsensical. There are several trickster characters that are threaded throughout First Nations, Métis, and Inuit storytelling, such as the Raven, Coyote, Nanabush, Nanabozho, and Hä-qweh-da-ět-gǎh or Sawiskera (sometimes known as Left-Handed Twin). Coyote as a trickster carries the lessons that teach us about life and the ways of being in relationship with one another, creation, and Iethi'nihsténha Ohwentsia'kékha (Land). Trickster characters are constantly journeying, making mistakes, struggling, transforming, and journeying again. As I have discussed many times throughout this book, stories are circular, with many entry points into the story and with many other stories layered within and between the stories.

Inception

I enter this particular story with a practicum that I proposed as part of my dissertation course requirements. The practicum was designed with guidance from my then supervisor, Dr Celia Haig-Brown, to explore the ways I might draw on land (lower-case *l*) in developing pedagogy. One of the outcomes of the practicum was to design and co-teach courses as part of the Bachelor of Education Primary/Junior (Aboriginal) program offered by Brock University in the Northern Nishnawbe Aski Territory. The courses in the program are designed around a three-week intensive model, and students drive or fly in from their respective communities, depending on their location within the Nishnawbe Aski Territory, to one of two lodges (subject to availability) in the Sioux Lookout district. With a few exceptions the students were at that time teaching in their communities with a Native Teaching Certificate. This program is one way that the Nishnawbe Aski communities have identified as a viable option for overcoming the various challenges their teachers face in earning a full undergraduate university degree with Ontario College of Teachers Certification. It is a consistent challenge for the students in this program to arrange adequate child care, manage community and family crises, and certainly not least, ensure their classrooms are covered for the three weeks they will be at the courses. While I had prior knowledge and experience with this program through my involvement with the Program Development Committee, this was my first experience teaching in it. I worked with a close friend and colleague to redevelop and implement the two existing courses.

The redeveloping of the courses posed certain challenges around integrating and privileging Indigenous ways of knowing into what were mainstream course content. Further, I was also attempting to draw on the ways my initial understandings of land might inform the course content. My colleague and I quite literally sat side by side at the computer working on reconceptualizing the courses. We had been working for a while when I realized that, in my view, things were not going well – we were not incorporating land or Indigeneity into the course content in ways I felt would be relevant and meaningful. I became silent as I struggled with my own vision for drawing on land in the course development and its current direction. The very air was pregnant with awkwardness – how was I to tell a then-senior colleague that I was unhappy with the direction she was going with the course development? When she asked what was bothering me, I remained silent for a moment and then indicated that the current conceptualization was not working for me. She then became silent – and then we both were silent. My silence was a waiting silence. I was waiting to see how she would respond – it was a pivotal moment. She broke the silence by asking me what was not working and how I conceptualized the course. I then explained that I saw the course structured in a circle format around the elements: vision, relationship, knowledge, and action – very much like the logic framing this book. We then went onto develop integrative assignments for each course. That is, the function of the assignments for each course was designed to be seamlessly integrated across both courses. Iterative circularity as a key element of land, a concept threaded throughout this book, formed the basis for all assignments and coursework, evaluative strategies, and course evaluations. Thus began our journey with land (I had not yet capitalized my understandings of Land – see chapters 1 and 2) and we left for what would, for me, be the first of two journeys to Sioux Lookout to teach.

Lessons from Land

As I said earlier, I had been journeying with a familiar friend, Coyote the Trickster. Immediately on crossing the bridge into the Sioux Lookout district, Coyote (in actual physical animal form) was there to greet me on the side of the road, just inside the border of the town. I noticed Coyote immediately and without thinking wondered aloud what lessons he might have for me on this journey with land. While this story is focused on my own connections to the land I was to work in, I also want to focus the following discussion on some of the student stories and the ways we were all able to draw on Land (as I have come to know Land both as a fundamental sentient being and as a philosophical construct) in the classroom.

In the first year teaching in Sioux Lookout, we focused our efforts on welcoming Land into the classroom and introducing the concept to students. Every day began with one student taking responsibility for doing an opening of his or her choice. The students signed up ahead of time and planned whatever opening they felt appropriate to begin the day. The opening can take place in several contexts, such as in the classroom, out on the land, or in the sharing lodge around the fire. An opening brings us together and helps begin the day with good thoughts and a sense of togetherness, and it is an acknowledgment of what I have come to know as Iethi'nihsténha Ohwentsia'kékha (Land) – in this initial understanding Land did indeed become our first teacher.

Another key Land-centred activity was the concept of vision questing. As discussed in the introduction to Section 1, visioning comes from the eastern door of illumination and is a word connected to the act of seeing, envisioning, dreaming, or imagining something in a deeply intimate and spiritual sense. To quest is the act of seeking something. Vision questing, is the act of seeking a vision that connects the natural and theoretical with the spiritual. In the case of Land-centred activities students were instructed to take the core concepts arising out of daily course content and apply them to their understandings of land as first teacher. Students were asked to go out on the land to reflect on and find symbolic representations of the ways Land was informing their understandings of the course content. These representations could take on various forms, such as journaling, drawings, photos, or physical elements of Land, such as branches, pieces of bark, rocks, feathers, pine cones, or snow balls, while being respectful by not taking or removing anything that would damage or destroy Land in any way – Iethi'nihsténha Ohwentsia'kékha (Land) in her role as our first teacher cautions and encourages us to engage Land in deeply respectful, meaningful, and relevant ways. These representations were to be shared with the larger group, usually at the end of the day or at the conclusion of a difficult lesson, either in the sharing lodge, at the water's edge, along pathways, tree lines, or in the classroom.

Following are some examples of these vision quests. The first day of classes the students were sent on a vision quest and were asked to find ways Land was informing their initial understanding of pedagogies. The students were advised that this was to be a personal reflection and not a social activity. It is important to note here that as instructors we always participated in all of the Land-centred activities, which helped us draw on Land in our own classroom practices. On returning to the sharing lodge it became immediately clear that there was a common theme among the symbolic representations. The shared theme was of a tree with deeply embedded roots grounding the tree into the land. However, each student had a specific and unique representation of that understanding based on his or her own lived experiences. Generally and across all the presentations, the tree trunk represented pedagogies and classroom practices, the roots grounded learning in Land that provided all the sustenance and stability the tree needed not just to survive but to thrive in that environment. Finally, the branches represented the learning outcomes and the leaves the diverse learning experiences of the students. I remain in awe at the consistent depth of understanding and sharing that occurred because of these Land-centred activities.

On another occasion after working on difficult and challenging concepts, we all decided to go down to the docks by the lake to debrief in a sharing circle. It is important to note that when doing circle work in any context there are certain generally shared protocols to adhere to. These include but are not limited to the following:

- State the specific focus or theme clearly at the beginning of the circle. This helps everyone collect their thoughts and keep the dialogue on track.
- Sometimes a talking rock, feather, or stick is passed around the circle from one person to the next as each takes a turn to speak.
- Only the person holding the special object speaks, letting the individual speak uninterrupted. Individuals speak only for themselves and what is on their mind;
- Everyone who wants to speak should be given the chance. However, an individual has the right to pass if she or he so chooses.
- The beginning of a sharing circle is not the time to respond directly to another individual in the circle but rather to reflect deeply on one's own thoughts and feelings. Everyone does not have to agree with each other, but everyone is treated equally and with respect.

- The special object may be passed around the circle again if the mediator feels or notices that someone wants to respond to something or if the dialogue is not yet complete. With each journey around the circle, the sharing becomes deeper and more open.

Following these protocols, I decided to use the symbol that I had chosen during the first vision quest to represent my own understandings of the ways land is our primary teacher for our debriefing. My symbolic representation was a rock that was solid, was dense, and had circular layers of colour in it. In my vision the various layers represented the dimensions of meaning inherent in the stories of my and the students' ancestors that are etched and layered deep into the foundational bedrock of Iethi'nihsténha Ohwentsia'kékha (Land). The circle pattern represents the ways stories continuously teach us with, each iterative repetition adding depth and dimension to each retelling. The denseness and layering of the rock was the perfect symbol to be passed around as each individual debriefed after a dense session. The sharing and debriefing was emotive and poignant. One student who had been particularly quiet throughout the course began opening up during this sharing circle.

Following another session where the students were struggling in preparing for an assignment that focused on the spiritual, emotional, intellectual, and physical growth and development of children, I sent them on another visioning on Land to find a symbol that reflected their work and understanding about their ideas. We met at the water and my colleague used a pinecone, the symbolic representation from her first vision quest, to initiate this sharing circle. She indicated that, for her, the pinecone represented the ways infants are born all the same, tightly compacted, and then they open up, spread out, and discover many different possibilities. Two students, picking up on the pinecone idea, indicated that, for them, the pinecone symbolized the ways children needed to be nurtured and cared for to grow up strong and straight, if not they will wither and fail to thrive – that children are gifts to be honoured and nurtured. There was significant snow still on the ground after a late spring snowstorm and another student picked up a handful of snow while silently and slowly forming a snowball. She then articulated that the snowball symbolized how children may be moulded and shaped and that we leave impressions on them the same way we do when forming a snowball. Someone else chose one of the muffins he had brought with him from the lodge as his symbol. He said that if you put all the correct ingredients into the recipe and follow the directions, you will achieve success. However, if you leave out ingredients or cut corners, it will not taste very good. It is the baker who has ruined the muffin – the muffin is not responsible for the baker having failed to follow the recipe.

Throughout that first year I journeyed with Coyote – struggling, transforming, and journeying again – learning from Iethi'nihsténha Ohwentsia'kékha (Land) and incorporating those reflections and understandings into pedagogy and course content. My colleague and I would often walk together after class through the trails along the lakes experiencing Iethi'nihsténha Ohwentsia'kékha – many times in silence listening, each in our own way, to those deep teachings she had for us. We would then go late into the evening sharing and reflecting on our blossoming understandings while using the outcomes of our personal reflections, the sharing circles, and Land-centred activities to inform and refine the course content for the following day. We focused a great deal that first year on welcoming Land into the learning environment and our own teaching practices. In our final sharing circle each student expressed an intense emotionality relating to his or her experiences of Land, particularly because for some, this was a completely new experience. Further, all students indicated they were seriously thinking about ways of taking up and incorporating what they have learned about Land as their first teacher into their own practices.

On the final morning before our final sharing circle we played a slide show we had put together for the students based on all the experiences over our three weeks together. The students were asked not to talk to one another but in deep and intimate self-reflection were instructed to go out onto the Land and reflect on their individual and collective experiences and what they had seen in the slide show, and to (re)member the ways Iethi'nihsténha Ohwentsia'kékha (Land) forms that deeply intimate and spiritual primary relationship – the one that comes before all else – and to come back with a symbolic representation of why each of them chose the difficult and challenging path of being away from their communities and families to engage in this work here, at this time. With very little communication so as not to disrupt the reflexivity and sacred profoundness of the experience, we met in the sharing lodge once again for a final time and sat across from one another around that sacred fire. To acknowledge and respect the sacredness of that moment I chose to pass the sacred eagle feather and this, in very general terms, is what they shared.[1]

The first student who shared chose a dead leaf and a twig with buds. The dead leaf symbolized the loss of traditional values and ways of being in the world. The buds represented the work and sacrifices that all the students were doing in that moment to make things better for their communities. The twig itself was a representation of the process of life-long learning. The tree that the twig came from grows and is nurtured by Mother Earth, which provides sunlight, water, and nutrients – very much the ways a teacher nourishes students. Every fall the leaves return to the earth – they go back to the ground and represent Land. The seeds also go back to Land, learning and giving back, being faithful, and being given the gift of life. Another student chose the formation of the land to represent his journey through the two courses. He stated that at one time his people used to have to remember the various nuances and formations of the land to be able to find their way home – in this way Land has always been and continues to be our first teacher – it is how we find our way home. The next student who shared chose the sharing lodge as her symbolic representation because it was the place where we shared our thoughts, ideas, and dreams – it was a place of joy, smiles, and tears. It connected us as parents, teachers, and students. It was a representation of all of us. The fourth student in the sharing circle chose a seed as her symbolic representation. She indicated that a seed represents the birth of a child. To flourish plants need sun, water, nutrients, and love. Similarly, children need love, guidance, teachings, loving physical contact, and smiles to flourish. The next student stated that the water was the symbol of her journey because in life we all go through some rough patches, like the turbulence in rough waters, such as rapids. At times our lives can be similar to the lake, which may be calm in the morning and yet unexpected things can happen. However, when we journey through the treacherous and uncertain rapids, there is always an end and a return to calm and safe waters. Finally, we journeyed through the circle with the last student returning us to the notion of trees. This student brought forward the concept of the roots of trees, which, for her, represented who they were and where they came from as Onkwehonwe people and that the purpose in their experiences is one way of coming back to traditions and understanding some of the ways to incorporate those teachings in their own practices. She then went on to say that they are each responsible for guiding their own journeying and being grounded in their own understandings of Land. Daily joint journaling sessions opened up spaces and opportunities for us, as instructors, to debrief, to (re)member, to reflect on student responses to Land-centred activities, and to share our experiences with each other through simultaneous recording on our laptops.

My experiences the second year differed from the first year in unexpected and critical ways. The first year was guided by Coyote the Trickster and characterized by journeying, struggle, transformation, and journeying again. In this way it was intense, immersive, and purposeful. The greatest challenge was remaining open to all the various life lessons and experiences of Iethi'nihsténha Ohwentsia'kékha through Coyote the Trickster. The second year I was deeper along in my understandings and experiences of Iethi'nihsténha Ohwentsia'kékha and felt I was more centred and grounded. When I began to notice that the concept of bringing Land into the learning environment was not being experienced by the students or in the learning environment as I had expected I felt concerned. I worried that perhaps we had somehow lost some of our initial vision; that perhaps I was not as far along in my understandings of Iethi'nihsténha Ohwentsia'kékha as I had thought. It was only during an early evening walk along the lake that it became clear that we were both feeling the same way. Our discussion revealed that what we were experiencing was the move from explicitly bringing Land into the learning environment to one where it was implicitly embedded in everything we, as instructors, together with the students did. We had both worked so diligently and purposefully in that first year to ensure that Iethi'nihsténha Ohwentsia'kékha was welcome and incorporated in the classroom that Land, in the second year, had become an inseparable part of our everyday learning experiences. The students had told us in a sharing circle that during the year between our courses, while they were working in their respective communities, they had been diligently incorporating Iethi'nihsténha Ohwentsia'kékha into their own personal and professional practices. The work that the students had done over the year was reflected in the ways each of them approached and completed their assignments and presentations, which were immersed in their (re)membered, (re)cognized, and (re)generated understandings of the connections between the course content and Land.

Another crucial experience was that the learning environment seamlessly moved from inside the classroom out onto the land with increasing frequency. Lectures, preparation for assignments, presentations, and small and large group discussions all began to take place out on the land in various places throughout the fishing lodge – sitting in grassy areas, under trees, on porches/decks, at the dock, on picnic tables, and, of course, in the sharing lodge. We made a shift from reliance on technology, such as Power Point slides, for lectures to relying more fully on Iethi'nihsténha Ohwentsia'kékha as our first teacher and primary source for making deeper connections between course content and students' personal experiences.

Rural to Urban Contexts

Moving from rural to urban contexts, Iethi'nihsténha Ohwentsia'kékha (Land) continues to have relevance to all of the ways we work to understand the deeper connections each of us has with the land we inhabit. In schools and universities located within urban settings we can continue to engage in various activities that take students and instructors/faculty outside the boundedness of the panopticon onto the land. While many of the activities, course content, and structures transitioned well from rural to urban contexts, I continually explore ways to incorporate Iethi'nihsténha Ohwentsia'kékha into urban landscapes. Soundscapes and photovoice provide two very interesting examples of activities that can be adapted and modified for pedagogies of Land.

Soundscape activities are one way of experiencing Land within built environments. Soundscapes are a concept developed by Murray Schafer, Canadian music composer and environmentalist, in 1969 as a way for students to experience natural acoustic landscapes.[2] There are many examples of soundscape activities designed to assist in getting started that are listed on several artistic, environmental, and place-based education websites.[3] Soundscape activities focus on the ways sounds are experienced to express feelings and create impressions or stories. By quieting our inner self, sitting or standing still, and listening to the sounds all around us, we can experience these activities independently and reflexively. Students can sketch or journal where and what various sounds occurred, write short stories or poems, or create more complex audio/visual presentations. Students can also create performance tableaux or dramatic representations of their experiences. This type of exercise can be done as an in-class activity or as a short-duration assignment.

Another way to experience Land across diverse contexts is through the use of photovoice. Photovoice is a concept originally developed by Caroline Wang in 1955 as a participatory method of recording and communicating auto-ethnographical experiences.[4] In the context of this work photovoice uses a series of successive images as a way for students to reflect on and express their own experiences with Land, particularly in the ways we experience Iethi'nihsténha Ohwentsia'kékha. This activity is time intensive and requires access to visual equipment, such as digital cameras or other video-capturing devices (video-cameras, laptops, I-pads, tablets, cell phones, etc.), together with applicable software. This type of assignment would need to be given out at the beginning of a course culminating in an end of term presentation.

Regardless of whether we teach in rural or urban contexts, as educators and practitioners, I believe Iethi'nihsténha Ohwentsia'kékha must be the very bedrock on which we conceptualize and create course structures; classroom practices; and course content including activities, assignments, and evaluative strategies. Without question Iethi'nihsténha Ohwentsia'kékha (Land) is a philosophy of teaching that I believe has implications for transformative teaching and learning practices.

12 Conclusions and Implications: Iethi'nihsténha Ohwentsia'kékha – Beyond Responsiveness and Place-Based Education

Generally transformative teaching practices involve moving beyond what Freire (2003) refers to as banking education. Banking education is a pedagogy that involves the teacher as the sole expert and repository of knowledge depositing information into the mind of a student who is perceived as coming into the learning environment knowing nothing. In this context children are perceived as tabula rasa – that is, as lacking mental content and sociocultural positioning – blank slates. Freire asserts, as do I, that this form of education is oppressive and dehumanizing. Transformative practices, in the context of Iethi'nihsténha Ohwentsia'kékha (Land), transcend Western informed banking practices and ways of *doing* education to understandings of pedagogies that privilege Land in both concrete materialism *and* philosophical principles. So why is Iethi'nihsténha Ohwentsia'kékha so relevant now?

Iethi'nihsténha Ohwentsia'kékha goes beyond the environment or place as a source of learning – it goes beyond environmental education for sustainability – it goes beyond acknowledging the cultural diversity of students in content and practices. Iethi'nihsténha Ohwentsia'kékha encompasses the spiritual, philosophical, and ontological principles inherent in the fundamental being of Land. Many academics have tried to fit the notions of Land into what is generally understood to be culturally responsive and/or place-based education; however, the result of such attempts is the stepsister and glass slipper effect. In other words they do not fit each other. I want to be very clear that when I talk about Iethi'nihsténha Ohwentsia'kékha I am *not* referring either to culturally responsive or place-based education (as it has come to be understood in the North American context). Iethi'nihsténha Ohwentsia'kékha is distinct from culturally responsive and place-based education in some very critical aspects.

Beyond Responsive Pedagogies

In addressing the challenges and tensions of standardization related to teaching, learning, and assessment practices Gay (2010) proposes a culturally responsive pedagogy (CRP). Gay defines culturally responsive teaching (CRT) as "using the cultural knowledge, prior experiences, frames of reference, and performance styles of ethnically diverse students" (p. 31) to create a context of relevance. Gay, a well-known international expert in multicultural education, argues that educators must interrupt their own positionalities and taken-for-granted assumptions to critically consider the ways these lead to various constructions of race. Some of the main goals of CRT are (1) student success based on high expectations and academic achievement; (2) effective and active citizenship; (3) acknowledgment and acceptance of cultural diversity evidenced through curriculum content and classroom practices; (4) community engagement; and (5) an ethics of caring.

While CRT is a crucial first step it does not go far enough in addressing the ways CRP continues to remain embedded in relations of power and privilege within an education system grounded in dominant Western ideologies. Gay writes that *empowerment* of ethnically diverse students is a fundamental goal of CRP. The concept of empowerment is a Western construct that lies in relations of privilege and power, where those having positions of privilege can confer power on those who are not privileged and are seen as power*less* – it remains a deficit theorizing practice. Further, as long as CRT remains in the control and at the discretion of individual teachers or specific schools it will not be applied universally. Implementing CRT and CRP does not erase the fact that these practices continue to remain embedded in the relations of power and privilege found in Eurocentrically informed education policies and practices.

Beyond Place-Based Pedagogies

The term place-based education originated with the foundational work of Laurie Lane-Zucker of the Orion Society and Dr John Elder of Middlebury College and was first used in the early 1990s. Place-based education generally provides students with an immersive experience in the history, culture, and ecology of their environment. Place-based education across North America generally focuses on issues of conservationism and environmental sustainability. Greenwood is an associate professor and Canada Research Chair at Lakehead University and is a well-known place-based educator. His work seeks to bridge inquiry into environment, culture, and education with a focus on environmentalism and sustainability. In searching for deeper and more meaningful connections for what he has come to define as place-conscious education (rather than place-based), Greenwood (2009) writes that place-based education continues to be grounded in relations of power and privilege that also serve to perpetuate and maintain the urban and rural dichotomy. Greenwood, following a performance by Indigenous visual/performance artist and lecturer LisaNa Redbear, writes that it is crucial to be aware of and refrain from tendencies towards *mis*appropriation or denial through the romanticizing, simplification, and idealization of Indigenous knowledges and ways of being. Referring back to my earlier discussion on the ethics of protocol, it is my view that any form of appropriation is not simply misguided or misplaced but instead is completely unethical.

Another issue needing to be addressed in the notion that dominant Western-based schooling (including place-based or culturally responsive education) is perceived as progressive and trendy while Iethi'nihsténha Ohwentsia'kékha (Land) grounded in Indigenous thought is often regarded as quaint, romantic, and archaic. Understandings of Land, particularly the philosophy of Iethi'nihsténha Ohwentsia'kékha, are indeed progressive, dynamic, and relevant both locally and globally – "Land is the only thing that lasts life to life" (Erdrich, 1988, p. 33).

Both culturally responsive and place-based education discourses focus on aspects of citizenship, community engagement, and localized constructions of place while failing to recognize the deeper historical connections that Indigenous people, indeed all people, have to the natural or built places they currently occupy.

Building from all previous discussions relating to space, place, and Land, land (lower-case *l*) becomes more than material geography when it is intimately, relationally, spiritually, and relevantly inhabited through storying and ceremony. Storying takes seriously both the historical and the contemporary tracks of Indigeneity as well as the complex, tangled, and at times, contradictory historical and contemporary colonial relations. Greenwood's (2009) argument that we are all "embodied and

emplaced people connected to other embodied and emplaced people …
and that most conversations about schooling are silent about the deeper,
emplaced and embodied past" (n.p.) resonates with understandings of
Land and self-in-relationship. Greenwood also insists that these conversations tend to focus on school itself rather than the ways we *do* education. Greenwood, after being deeply and critically influenced by the
provocative work of Redbear, emphatically writes that it is not about
"making school more meaningful or contributing to community life. It
is about remembering a deeper and wider narrative of living and learning in connection with others and with the land" (n.p.).

Iethi'nihsténha Ohwentsia'kékha disrupts, challenges, and resists
dominant Western pedagogies, including culturally responsive and
place-based education, by positioning and taking seriously education within the context of Indigeneity and Indigenous knowledges, as
well as by opening opportunities for critically examining the various
complex layers and tensions inherent in historical and contemporary
colonial relations. Iethi'nihsténha Ohwentsia'kékha takes seriously and
centrally positions Indigenous thought as a theoretical framework for
understanding self-in-relationship, the deeper and broader historical
and contemporary connections to Land, and the ways we think about
and *do* education.

Philosophy as Wampum

As stated in the introductory chapter, Iethi'nihsténha Ohwentsia'kékha
is not a *statement* of Indigenous philosophy, which would be far too prescriptive; nor is this a toolbox or a list of best practices – Iethi'nihsténha
Ohwentsia'kékha is a wampum philosophy of education created from
the tangled strings and chipped beads of (re)membering, (re)cogniz-
ing, and (re)generating ancient knowledges and very old pedagogies
within contemporary contexts. While resisting a prescriptive statement
about Iethi'nihsténha Ohwentsia'kékha as an Indigenous philosophy of education, I can gesture to an overarching articulation based
on shared themes across diverse contexts while also addressing the
specificity of land and sociocultural, sociopolitical, and sociolinguistic
uniqueness characterizing Indigenous people locally, nationally, and
internationally.

Iethi'nihsténha Ohwentsia'kékha wampum is an articulation of
the breadth, depth, and scope of self-in-relationship with Land.
Iethi'nihsténha Ohwentsia'kékha as an Indigenous wampum philosophy

of education is an expression of reality in flux grounded in Land through embodied understandings of self-in-relationship, ceremony, spirituality, circularity, and iterativity, as well as connections to specific home lands (urban and rural), culture, and kinship ties. I would like to leave you with the words of Eber Hampton (1995):

> *Standing on the earth with the smell of spring in the air, may we accept each other's right to live, to define, to think, and to speak.*

Notes

Introduction

1 The Hodenosaunee Confederacy comprises 52 hereditary chiefs representing each of the Six Nations. It was established by the Peacemaker, who is considered by the Hodenosaunee to be one of the "great philosophers and organizers in human history" (Akwesasne Notes, 1978, p. 31).

2 The traditional self-identifying term *Hodenosaunee* is thought by some community leaders who support the elected system within the Six Nations Territory to be a politically charged and contested designation. They prefer the use of the term *Onkwehonwe*, meaning "original people."

3 See http://historymatters.gmu.edu/d/4929: "Kill the Indian, and Save the Man": Capt. Richard H. Pratt on the Education of Native Americans.

4 According to the *Oxford English Dictionary* (2011), *remembering* as a verb refers to being able to bring to one's mind an awareness of someone or something from the past; the prefix *re-* is an expression of intensive force denoting "once more; afresh; anew"; the root *member* is Latin for "mindful" or "call to mind." The addition of *-ing* denotes progressive action, an active doing. In this context setting the *re* in brackets emphasizes the intense expression of being mindful or bringing something back to mind again in new contemporary ways.

5 See also Jennings (1984), Johnston (1964), and Shimony (1994) for additional information.

6 The Peacemaker, we are told, was born among the Huron people and arrived first in the land of the Kanien'kehá:ka, the People of the Flint, known to the English as the Mohawks. The story is that "he crossed Lake Ontario in a stone Canoe" in order to establish "a union of peace under the principles the Hodenosaunee understand to be the natural laws of the

universe" (Lyons, 1992, p. 34). I have been told that his actual name is considered so sacred that it is not to be either spoken or written and so I have
not included it here.

7 Pronounced Yeti-knee-STUNH-ha (nh is nazal) Oh-when-ja-GAY-kuh.

1 Iethi'nihsténha Ohwentsia'kékha: Land, Circularity, and Storying

1 *Good* in this context is not intended to reinforce dualistic constructs, such as
good and evil or good and bad, but to put forward the understanding that
to do something is a good way is to act respectfully, responsibly, and with
great integrity.

2 Cognitive imperialism sets the criteria for determining what is and is not
legitimate knowledge and cultural capital – it denies the cultural currency
of one group by legitimizing one world view, one language, one set of
values and beliefs against which all others are judged.

3 See also Archibald (2008), Bishop & Glynn (1999), Eshkibok-Trudeau (2000),
Fixico (2003), Graveline (1998), Hampton (1995), Hodson (2004), Kovach
(2009a, 2009b), Smith (2004), Stewart-Harawira (2005), Styres (2008), and
Tafoya (1995).

4 *Abstract* in this context refers to Land as an Indigenous philosophy or ideology that exists beyond concrete connections to home lands/landscapes.

5 For further information see Serim (1998).

6 For further information see Anishnawbe Health Toronto (2000).

7 Kanien'kehá:ka (meaning "People of the Flint") are one of the original five
nations of the Hodenosaunee confederacy.

8 *Storying* refers to how we describe in story our experiences through personal, community, national, and global narratives (Styres, 2008, p. 75).

2 Iethi'nihsténha Ohwentsia'kékha: Space, Place, and Land

1 This duality is not to be construed as dichotomous, oppositional, or binarial
but rather expresses the ways Land embodies two simultaneously interconnected and interdependent conceptualizations.

2 See also Haig-Brown (2005), Haig-Brown & Dannenmann (2002, 2008),
Haig-Brown & Hodson (2009), Styres (2011), Styres, Haig-Brown, & Blimkie
(2013), and Zinga & Styres (2011).

3 *Built* in this context refers to human-made rather than anything made out of
or from the natural world.

4 While the men perform the haka with aggressive posturing, the women
demonstrate grace and elegance.

3 Self-in-Relationship

1 *Ecology* refers to seeking an understanding of the ways living organisms relate to each other and to their environment.
2 *Cosmology* refers to the study of the physical universe in relation to time and space.
3 These *-isms* refer to a set of values and beliefs that form and underpin philosophies, ideologies, doctrines, and practices.
4 A Mohawk word referring to the original people of Turtle Island (North America).

4 "You're Not the Indian I Had in Mind"

1 King (2003).
2 Citizenship, in this context, includes but is not limited to the allegiance and participation, whether by birth or by choice of an individual, to a particular Indigenous nation's traditional or elected political systems, community, and nationhood, together with all of the rights and responsibilities associated with that citizenship. It is not intended to represent citizenship in relation to the nation of Canada to which some First Nations people do not claim citizenship. However, it also does not exclude such designation because some Native people claim allegiance to both their own First Nation and to the nation of Canada or the United States of America.
3 *Indigeneity* is defined as "the quality and state of being Indigenous."
4 As indicated in Chapter 1, the Confederacy is the traditional political system of the Hodenosaunee people.
5 See also Mohawk (1989) and Porter (1993, 2008).

Section Three: Knowledge – (Re)cognizing

1 See http://www.theturtlelodge.org for additional information.

5 Sacred Fires: Contemporary (Re)memberings of Ancient Knowledges and Very Old Pedagogies

1 See Akwesasne Notes (1978), Mohawk (1989), Porter (1993, 2008), and Wall (2001).
2 See also Archibald (2008) – Sto:lo; Erdrich (1999, 2004) – Chippewa; Horne (Horne & McBeth, 1998) – Shoshone; Joe (1996) – Mi'Kmaq; Silko (1977) – Pueblo; and Woodworth (2010) – Mohawk.

6 Relations of Privilege – Relations of Power

1 The term *network* refers to a system of interconnections. *Relations* are the ways individuals, the natural world, built environments, and institutions are connected within the system. Both terms denote fluidity, action, and movement. Networks and relations of power are interconnected and interdependent.

2 *Transfer* refers to the movement of something from one place to another; in this context it is the movement of power from one group of individuals to another. *Confer* refers to the granting of a right on someone; in this case it is the granting of power to a group without any loss or movement from the original holder.

7 Land and Circularity: An Indigenous Philosophical Approach to Thought

1 *Paradigms* generally refer to a set pattern of beliefs, thought processes, or world view underlying theoretical concepts, particularly as they relate to science. In this context it relates to dominant Western scientific and philosophical thought.

2 See Chapter 2 for a detailed description.

8 Indigenous and Dominant Western Philosophies: A Bridge Too Far?

1 This author's conceptualization of Kawagley into the model of circularity is used throughout this work.

2 In the late 1970s and into the 80s Kāterina Mataira, a Māori language scholar and educator, as well as philosopher and artisan, was instrumental in developing and implementing the first kura kaupa, te reo Māori revitalization using the Cuisenaire rod learning method (CRLM) – (aka the Silent Way). CRLM is a method of teaching language that uses coloured rods to teach rudimentary and increasingly more complex language structures. Kāterina, having learned the method developed by Caleb Gattegno, re-conceptualized it using te reo Māori and philosophies – thus the Te Ataarangi language movement was born and it became instrumental in revitalizing the Māori language. From this language movement Kāterina, along with Pita Sharples, in 1985 established the first Kohanga Reo at the Hoani Waititi Marae in Auckland. The Kohanga Reo or language nests were developed for preschool children and their primary caregivers to be "nested" in the language.

3 For Te Aho Matua to be enacted into legislation, it had to be translated from Māori into English. The first English version was philosophically far

removed from its original Māori roots. The principles, philosophies, and spiritual essence did not easily translate into English. While reluctant and with good reason, Kāterina Mataira was asked to take responsibility for translating Te Aho Matua into English to ensure that, as much as is possible, the original spirit of the philosophy was effectively communicated through the translated version. Te Aho Matua exists as a living document that keeps evolving, but it is crucial to note that the original writers wanted to ensure that it would not become enshrined as a tapu (sacred) document. The document itself is not tapu – rather it contains the philosophies we live by – it is a guideline.

4 See the TDSB website for additional information: http://www.tdsb.on.ca/findyour/schools.aspx?schno=5360.

5 See Ahkwesáhsne Freedom School for further information at http://freedom-school.org/index.php/about-us.

6 See http://www.collectionscanada.gc.ca/obj/s4/f2/dsk2/ftp01/MQ39172.pdf for additional information.

7 See Thomas (1978) for more detailed information.

9 Indigenous Languages and Thought: A Verb-Oriented Reality

1 I am aware of the various criticisms and controversies that surround the Sapir-Whorf hypothesis by linguistic purists. However, I believe his work has relevance to the points I am making.

2 A gerund is a verb functioning as a noun in a sentence. In English these verb forms usually end in -ing.

3 Dan Moohawk Alford (1946–2002), Gah-wonh-nos-doh Alma Greene (1896–1983), Vine Deloria Jr. (1933–2005), Black Elk (1863–1950), Esther B. Horne (1909–99), Rita Joe (1932–2007), Chief Oren Lyons (1930–), John Mohawk (1945–2006), Luther Standing Bear (1868–1939), Chief Leon Shenandoah (1914–96), Leslie M. Silko (1948–), to name only a few.

4 Foucault, M. (1982). In J. Harkness (Trans.), *This is not a pipe: Ceci n'est pas une pipe*. Berkeley, CA: University of California Press.

10 Tensions, Challenges, and Contradictions

1 See http://www.naho.ca/media-centre/interviewing-elders-guidelines for additional information.

2 The term *non-Christian* is used in reference to and as defined in the Papal Bulls issued by Pope Alexander VI on behalf of the Roman Christian church.

3 The *Oxford English Dictionary* and *Online Etymology Dictionary* tell us that
   the word *ferocious* originates from the Latin *ferocitatem*, which translates
   to "wild-looking," and is intimately connected to the Late Latin *salvaticus*
   or Old French *sauvage* (English, "savage"). Both *ferocious* and *savage* refer
   to a wildness, primitiveness, and animalism, which, undoubtedly is a
   dehumanizing description.

4 I want to acknowledge and thank the teachers from my community as well
   as textually who have taught me the Creation story. For my purposes I am
   drawing on a general (re)telling both of what I have been told and of the
   story published in a text called *Traditional Teachings*, published by the North
   American Indian Travelling College (1984, August), which is a collection of
   traditional teachings compiled by my Mohawk brothers and sisters from
   Ahkwesáhsne in collaboration with Chiefs, Faithkeepers, and Elders from
   Six Nations. The stated intent of the text is to share the teachings for future
   generations of Hodenosaunee people who are looking to find their way
   back to their spiritual ways of life. These traditional and sacred stories are
   not intended to be used by "other races and nationalities" (p. vi).

5 Land is seen by many Indigenous nations as a female entity because of her
   ability to give, sustain, and nourish life. See also Hampton (1995), North
   American Indian Travelling College (1984), Porter (2008), and Youngblood
   Henderson (2000a, 2000b) for additional information.

11 Coyote as Trickster

1 Ethics approval was granted by Brock University for the work that was
   done during these courses. Individual student consent was also obtained to
   use their words; however, in respect for the sacredness of this sharing circle
   and to protect student anonymity, I write only in general terms, omitting
   specific references to individuals or contexts.

2 For additional information, see Schafer (1969).

3 For some examples see http://nationalgeographic.org/archive/xpeditions/
   activities/10/gasounds.html?ar_a=1; http://www.exploratorium.edu/
   listen/activities/soundscapes/deploy/activity_soundscapes.php; http://
   artsonline2.tki.org.nz/resources/lessons/music/soundscape/extension_
   e.php, and http://science.lotsoflessons.com/sound.html.

4 For additional information, see Wang & Burris (1997).

References

Abram, D. (2007, March). Storytelling and wonder. *Gatherings*. Retrieved December 5, 2011, from http://www.ecopsychology.org/journal/ezine/archive4/storytelling.html

Absolon, K., & Willett, C. (2005). Putting ourselves forward: Location in Aboriginal research. In L. Brown & S. Strega (Eds.), *Research as resistance: Critical, Indigenous & anti-oppressive approaches* (pp. 97–126). Toronto, ON: Canadian Scholars' Press/Women's Press.

Akwesasne Notes (Ed.). (1978). *A basic call to consciousness*. Summertown, TN: Native Voices.

Alfred, T. (1999). *Peace, power & righteousness: An Indigenous manifesto*. Don Mills, ON: Oxford University Press.

Alfred, T. (2005). *Wasáse: Indigenous pathways of action and freedom*. Peterborough, ON: Broadview Press.

Alfred, T. (2008). Opening words. In L. Simpson (Ed.), *Lighting the eighth fire: The liberation, resurgence, and protection of Indigenous nations* (pp. 9–11). Winnipeg, MB: Arbeiter Ring Publishing.

Anishnawbe Health Toronto. (2000). *The four sacred medicines*. Toronto, ON: Author.

Anzaldúa, G. (1999). *Borderlands/la frontera: The new mestiza* (3rd ed.). San Francisco, CA: Aunt Lute Books.

Archibald, J. (2008). *Indigenous storywork: Educating the heart, mind, body and spirit*. Vancouver, BC: UBC Press.

Armstrong, J. (1998). Land speaking. In S. J. Ortiz (Ed.), *Speaking for generations: Native writers on writing* (pp. 174–94). Tucson, AZ: University of Arizona Press.

Assembly of First Nations. (2011). *First Nation elementary and secondary education: A discussion guide*. Ottawa, ON: Author.

Bachelard, G. (1994). *The poetics of space: The classic look at how we experience intimate places* (M. Jolas, Trans.). Boston, MA: Beacon Press. (Original work published 1958)

Bailey, S. (2008, February 6). NDP launches campaign to help "Third World" Native schools. *Tekawennake*, p. 16.

Basso, K. H. (1996). *Wisdom sits in places: Landscape and language among the Western Apache*. Albuquerque, NM: University of New Mexico Press.

Battiste, M., & Youngblood Henderson, J. S. (2000). *Protecting Indigenous knowledge and heritage: A global challenge*. Saskatoon, SK: Purich Publishing Ltd.

Benton-Banai, E. (1988). *The Mishomis book: The voice of the Ojibway*. Hayward, WI: Indian Country Communications Inc.

Bhabha, H. K. (1994). *The location of culture*. New York, NY: Routledge Publishing.

Bishop, R., & Berryman, M. (2006). *Culture speaks: Cultural relationships and classroom learning*. Wellington, ANZ: Huia Publishers.

Bishop, R., & Glynn, T. (1999). *Culture counts: Changing power relations in education*. New York, NY: Zed Books Ltd.

Bohm, D. (1980). *Wholeness and the implicate order*. New York, NY: Routledge Publishing.

Bohm, D., & Peat, D. (1987). *Science, order, and creativity*. New York, NY: Routledge Publishing.

Burkhart, B. Y. (2004). What Coyote and Thales can teach us: An outline of American Indian epistemology. In A. Waters (Ed.), *American Indian thought* (pp. 15–26). Malden, MA: Blackwell Publishing.

Cajete, G. (1994). *Look to the mountain: An ecology of Indigenous education*. Skyland, NC: Kivaki Press.

Cajete, G. (1999). "Look to the mountain": Reflections on Indigenous ecology. In G. Cajete (Ed.), *A people's ecology: Explorations in sustainable living* (pp. 1–20). Santa Fe, NM: Clear Light Publishers.

Cajete, G. (2000). *Native science: Natural laws of interdependence*. Santa Fe, NM: Clear Light Publishers.

Casey, E. S. (1996). How to get from space to place in a fairly short stretch of time: Phenomenological prolegomena. In S. Feld & K. Basso (Eds.), *Senses of place* (pp. 13–52). Santa Fe, MN: School of American Research Press.

Daffron, B. (2013, July 12). Gravel mining puts Kiowa sacred place in peril. Retrieved from http://indiancountrytodaymedianetwork. com/2013/07/12/gravel-mining-puts-kiowa-sacred-place-peril-150378

Davis, W. (2009). *The wayfinders: Why ancient wisdom matters in the modern world*. Toronto, ON: House of Anansi Press.

Dellaflora, A. (Producer & Director). (2005). *The language of spirituality: Exploring the connections between modern science, ancient wisdom and language* [Documentary]. http://www.thelanguageofspirituality.com

Deloria, V. (1973). *God is red.* New York, NY: Dell Publishing Co.

Deloria, V., & Wildcat, D. R. (2001). *Power and place: Indian education in America.* Golden, CO: Fulcrum Resources.

Descartes, R. (2006). *A discourse on the method* (I. MacLean, Trans.). New York, NY: Oxford University Press. (Original work published 1637)

Duranti, A. (1997). *Linguistic anthropology.* New York, NY: Cambridge University Press. http://dx.doi.org/10.1017/CBO9780511810190.

Erdrich, L. (1988). *Tracks.* New York, NY: Henry Holt and Company, Inc.

Erdrich, L. (1999). *The antelope wife.* New York, NY: Harper Perennial.

Erdrich, L. (2004). *Four souls: A novel.* New York, NY: Harper Perennial.

Ermine, W. (2005, May). *Ethical space: Transforming relations.* Paper presented at the National Gatherings on Indigenous Knowledge, Rankin Inlet, NU.

Ermine, W. (2007). The ethical space of engagement. *Indigenous Law Journal at the University of Toronto Faculty of Law, 6*(1), 193–203.

Eshkibok-Trudeau, M. (2000). Circular vision – Through Native eyes. In N. Roger (Ed.), *Voice of the Drum: Indigenous Education and Culture* (pp. 25–34). Brandon, MB: Kingfisher Publications.

Feld, S. (1996). Waterfalls of song: An acoustemology of place resounding in Bosavi, Paupa New Guinea. In S. Feld & K. Basso (Eds.), *Senses of place* (pp. 91–135). Santa Fe, NM: School of American Research Advanced Seminar Series.

Feld, S., & Basso, K. (1996). Introduction. In S. Feld & K. Basso (Eds.), *Senses of place* (pp 3–11). Santa Fe, NM: School of American Research Advanced Seminar Series.

Fixico, D. (2003). *The American Indian mind in a linear world: American Indian studies & traditional knowledge.* New York, NY: Routledge.

Foucault, M. (1977). *Power/knowledge: Selected interviews & other writings, 1972–1977.* New York, NY: Pantheon Books.

Foucault, M. (1982). *This is not a pipe:* Ceci n'est pas une pipe (J. Harkness, Trans.). Berkeley and Los Angeles, CA: University of California Press.

Foucault, M. (1988). *Politics, philosophy, culture: Interviews and other writings, 1977–1984.* New York, NY: Routledge Publishing.

Foucault, M. (1995). *Discipline & punish: The birth of the prison* (2nd ed.). Originally published in France as Surveiller et Punir: Naissance de la prison in 1975. New York, NY: Random House.

Four Arrows, Cajete, C., & Lee, J. (2010). *Critical neurophilosophy & Indigenous wisdom.* Rotterdam, The Netherlands: Sense Publishers.

Freire, P. (2003). *Pedagogy of the oppressed* (30th anniversary ed.). New York, NY: The Continuum Publishing Group.

Freire, P., & Macedo, D. (1987). *Literacy: Reading the word and the world.* Westport, CT: Bergin & Garvey.

Gay, G. (2010). *Culturally responsive teaching: Theory, research, and practice* (2nd ed.). New York, NY: Teachers College Press.

Gee, J. P. (2008). *Social linguistics and literacies: Ideology in discourses* (3rd ed.). New York, NY: Routledge.

George-Kanentiio, D. (2000). *Iroquois culture & commentary.* Santa Fe, NM: Clear Light Publishers.

Gleason, P. (1983). Identifying identity: A semantic history. *Journal of American History, 69*(4), 910–31. http://dx.doi.org/10.2307/1901196

Gopnik, A. (2014, May 26). Word magic: How much really gets lost in translation? *The New Yorker,* p. 36–9.

Gramsci, A. (1971). The intellectuals. In G. N. Smith & Q. Hoare (Eds. & Trans.), *Selections from the prison notebooks* (pp. 3–14). New York, NY: International Publishers.

Grande, S. (2004). *Red pedagogy: Native American social and political thought.* Lanham, MA: Rowman & Littlefield Publishers.

Grant, A. (2004). *Finding my talk: How fourteen Native women reclaimed their lives after residential school.* Calgary, Alberta: Fifth House.

Graveline, F. J. (1998). *Circle works: Transforming Eurocentric consciousness.* Halifax, NS: Fernwood Publishing.

Greenwood, D. A. (2009). Place, survivance and white remembrance: A decolonizing challenge to rural education in mobile modernity. *Journal of Research in Rural Education, 24*(10), 1–6. Retrieved June 4, 2012, from http://jrre.vmhost.psu.edu/wp-content/uploads/2014/02/24-10.pdf

Gribbin, J. (2002). *Science: A history, 1543–2001.* London, England: Penguin Books.

Gumperz, J., & Levinson, S. (1996a). Introduction: Linguistic relativity re-examined. In J. Gumperz & S. Levinson (Eds.), *Rethinking linguistic relativity* (pp. 1–18). New York, NY: Cambridge University Press.

Haig-Brown, C. (1988). *Resistance and renewal: Surviving the Indian residential school.* Vancouver, BC: Arsenal Pulp Press.

Haig-Brown, C. (2005). Toward a pedagogy of the land: The Indigenous knowledge Instructors' program. In L. Pease-Alvarez & S. Schecter (Eds.), *Learning, teaching, and community: Contributions of situated and participatory approaches to educational innovation* (pp. 89–108). Mahwah, NJ: Lawrence Erlbaum Associates.

Haig-Brown, C. (2008). Taking Indigenous thought seriously: A rant on globalization with some cautionary notes. *Journal of the Canadian Association for Curriculum Studies, 6*(2), 8–24. (Document ID: 16859)

Haig-Brown, C. (2010). Indigenous thought, appropriation, and non-Aboriginal people. *Canadian Journal of Education, 33*(4), 925–50.

Haig-Brown, C., & Dannenmann, K. (2002). A pedagogy of the land: Dreams of respectful relations. *McGill Journal of Education, 37*(3), 451–68.

Haig-Brown, C., & Dannenmann, K. (2008). The land is the first teacher: The Indigenous knowledge instructors' program. In Z. Bekerman & E. Kopelowitz (Eds.), *Cultural education-cultural sustainability: Minority, diaspora, Indigenous, and ethno-religious groups in multicultural societies* (pp. 245–66). New York, NY: Routledge.

Haig-Brown, C., & Hodson, J. (2009). Starting with the land: Toward Indigenous thought in Canadian education. In P. Woods & G. Woods (Eds.), *Alternative education for the 21st century: Philosophies, approaches, visions* (pp. 167–87). New York, NY: Palgrave MacMillan. http://dx.doi.org/10.1057/9780230618367_10.

Hallett, R. R. (2009). Logic and reason. Retrieved from https://web.archive.org/web/20100915173553/http://www.helium.com/items/1420944-logic-and-reason

Hampton, E. (1995). Towards a redefinition of Indian-education. In M. Battiste & J. Barman (Eds.), *First Nations education in Canada: The circle unfolds* (pp. 5–42). Vancouver, BC: UBC Press.

Health Canada. (2010). *Acting on what we know: Preventing youth suicide in First Nations*. Retrieved from http://www.hc-sc.gc.ca/fniah-spnia/pubs/promotion/_suicide/prev_youth-jeunes/index-eng.php#tphp

Hodson, J. (2004). *Learning and healing: A wellness pedagogy for Aboriginal teacher education*. Unpublished master's thesis, Brock University, St. Catharines, Ontario, Canada.

Honderich, T. (1995). *The Oxford companion to philosophy*. Oxford, NY: Oxford University Press.

Horne, E., & McBeth, S. (1998). *Essie's story: The life and legacy of a Shoshone teacher*. Lincoln, NE: University of Nebraska Press.

Horton, M., & Freire, P. (1990). *We make the road by walking: Conversations on education and social change*. Philadelphia, PA: Temple University Press.

Indian Act, Revised Statues of Canada. (1985, c. I-5). Retrieved from the Justice Laws website: http://laws-lois.justice.gc.ca/eng/acts/i-5/

Indigenous and Northern Affairs Canada. (2005). *Elementary/secondary education enrolment statistics 96–97 to 04–05*. Microsoft Excel worksheet estimates, prepared by Matthew Chan, INAC.

James, C. E. (2001). I've never had a black teacher before. In C. E. James & A. Shad (Eds.), *Talking about identity: Encounters in race, ethnicity, and language* (pp. 150–67). Toronto, ON: Between the Lines.

Jennings, F. (1984). *The ambiguous Iroquois empire.* New York, NY: W. W. Norton & Company.

Joe, R. (1996). *Song of Rita Joe: Autobiography of a Mi'kmaq poet.* Charlottetown, PEI: Ragweed Press.

Johnston, C. (1964). *The Valley of the Six Nations: A collection of documents on the Indian lands of the Grand River.* Toronto, ON: University of Toronto Press.

Jojola, T. (2004). Notes on identity, time, space, and place. In A. Waters (Ed.), *American Indian thought* (pp. 87–96). Malden, MA: Blackwell Publishing.

Kawagley, A. O. (2006). *A Yupiaq worldview: A pathway to ecology and spirit* (2nd ed.). Longrove, ILL: Waveland Press, Inc.

Kawagley, A. O., Norris-Tull, D., & Norris-Tull, R. (1998). The Indigenous worldview of Yupiaq Culture: Its scientific nature and relevance to the practice and teaching of science. *Journal of Research in Science Teaching, 35*(2), 133–44. http://dx.doi.org/10.1002/(SICI)1098-2736(199802)35:2<133::AID-TEA4>3.0.CO;2-T

Killion, U. (2006). *A modern Chinese journey to the west: Economic globalization and dualism.* New York, NY: Nova Science Publishers.

King, T. (2003). *The truth about stories: A Native narrative.* Toronto, ON: House of Anansi Press.

Kirkness, V. J., & Barnhardt, R. (1991). First Nations and higher education: The 4R's – respect, relevance, reciprocity, responsibility. *Journal of Native American Indian, 30*(3), 1–10. Retrieved January 15, 2010, from http://www.ankn.uaf.edu/IEW/winhec/FourRs2ndEd.html

Kovach, M. E. (2009a). *Indigenous methodologies: Characteristics, conversations, and contexts.* Toronto, ON: University of Toronto Press.

Kovach, M. E. (2009b). Being Indigenous in the academy: Creating space for Indigenous scholars. In A. M. Timpson (Ed.), *First nations, first thoughts: the impact of Indigenous thought in Canada* (pp. 51–73). Vancouver, BC: UBC Press.

Kuhn, T. S. (1962). *The structure of scientific revolutions* (3rd ed.). Chicago, IL: The University of Chicago Press.

Kulchyski, P. (2005). *Like the sound of a drum: Aboriginal cultural politics in Denendeh and Nunavut.* Winnipeg, MB: University of Manitoba Press.

Kuokkanen, R. (2007). *Reshaping the university: Responsibility, Indigenous epistemes, and the logic of the gift.* Vancouver, BC: UBC Press.

Laduke, W. (1999). *All our relations: Native struggle for land and life.* Cambridge, MA: South End Press.

Lee, P. (1996). *The Whorf theory complex: A critical reconstruction.* Philadelphia, PA: Johns Benjamin Publishing Company. http://dx.doi.org/10.1075/sihols.81

Lefebvre, H. (1991). *The production of space* (D. Nicholson-Smith, Trans.). Malden, MA: Blackwell Publishing. (Original work published 1974).

Levine, J. (Producer), & Attenborough, R. (Director). (1977). A bridge too far [DVD]. United States of America: Joseph Levine Productions.

Little Bear, L. (2000). Jagged worldviews colliding. In M. Battiste (Ed.), *Reclaiming Indigenous voice and vision* (pp. 77–85). Vancouver, BC: UBC Press.

Locke, J. (2010). *Some thoughts concerning education* (classic reprint series). Charleston, SC: Forgotten Books.

Loomba, A. (2005). *Colonialism/postcolonialism* (2nd ed.). New York: Routledge.

Lorde, A. (1981). The master's tools will never dismantle the master's house. In G. Anzaldúa & C. Moraga (Eds.), *This bridge called my back* (pp. 98–101). Watertown, MA: Persephone Press.

Lyons, O. (1992). The American Indian in the past. In O. Lyons & J. Mohawk (Eds.), *Exiled in the land of the free: Democracy, Indian nations and the U.S. Constitution* (pp. 13–42). Santa Fe, NM: Clear Light Publishers.

Maracle, K. (n.d.). Wampum. Retrieved March 24, 2011 from http://www.wampumshop.com.

Matlack, G. (1997). Four centuries of forest clearance and regeneration in the hinterland of a large city. *Journal of Biogeography, 24*(3), 281–95. http://dx.doi.org/10.1046/j.1365-2699.1997.00108.x

McCarthy, T. (2010). Dęˀni:s nisaˀsgaoˀdę?: Haudenosaunee clans and the reconstruction of traditional Haudenosaunee identity, citizenship, and nationhood. *American Indian Culture and Research Journal, 34*(2), 81–101. http://dx.doi.org/10.17953/aicr.34.2.yv6n3n601523m65k

McIntosh, P. (1988). *White privilege and male privilege: A personal account of coming to see correspondences through work in women's studies* (Working Paper No. 189). Wellesley, MA: Wellesley College Centre for Research on Women.

McLean, S. (2010, November 24). PhD student defends thesis in Mi'gmaw language, a York first. *YFile.* Retrieved from http://yfile.news.yorku.ca/2010/11/24/phd-student-defends-thesis-in-migmaw-language-a-york-first/

McTighe, F. (2011, July 12). Chief Speaker joins Kainai chieftanship. *Macleod Gazette.* Retrieved from http://www.fortmacleodgazette.com/2011/chief-speaker-joins-kainai-chieftanship

Mendelson, M. (2008). Improving education on reserves: A First Nations education authority act. Ottawa, ON: Caledon Institute of Social Policy. Retrieved September 3, 2008, from http://www.caledoninst.org/Publications/PDF/684ENG.pdf

Metallic, F. (2008). Strengthening our relations in Gespe'gewa'gi, the seventh district of Mi'gma'gi. In L. Simpson (Ed.), *Lighting the eighth fire: The liberation, resurgence, and protection of Indigenous nations* (pp. 59–71). Winnipeg, MB: Arbeiter Ring Publishing.

Meyer, J. W. (1977). The effects of education as an institution. *American Journal of Sociology, 83*(1), 55–77. http://dx.doi.org/10.1086/226506

Mohawk, J. (1989). John Mohawk (Seneca): Origins of Iroquois political thought. In J. Bruchac (Ed.), *New voices from the longhouse: An anthology of contemporary Iroquois writing* (pp. 218–28). Ann Arbor, MI: Greenfield Review Press.

Momaday, N. S. (1997). *The man made of words: Essays, stories, passages.* New York, NY: St. Martin's Griffin.

Morgan, D. (2003). Appropriation, appreciation, accommodation: Indigenous wisdoms and knowledges in higher education. *International Review of Education, 49*(1), 35–49. http://dx.doi.org/10.1023/A:1022937003545

National Indian Brotherhood. (1972). *Indian control of Indian education. Policy paper presented to the Minister of Indian Affairs and Northern Development by the National Indian Brotherhood in response to the federal government's 1969 "White Paper" of Aboriginal policy reform.* Ottawa, ON: Author.

Neihardt, J. G. (2008). *Black Elk speaks: Being the life story of a holy man of the Oglala Sioux* (2nd ed.). New York, NY: State University of New York Press.

Nishnawbe Aski Nation. (2016). About us. Retrieved November 1, 2016, from http://www.nan.on.ca/article/about-us-3.asp

Nock, D., & Haig-Brown, C. (2006). Introduction. In C. Haig-Brown & D. Nock (Eds.), *With good intentions: Euro-Canadian & Aboriginal relations in colonial Canada* (pp. 1–31). Vancouver, BC: UBC Press.

North American Indian Travelling College. (1984). *Traditional teachings.* Cornwall Island, ON: Author.

Oxford English Dictionary. (2011). *Oxford English Dictionary.* Retrieved October 24, 2011, from http://www.oxforddictionaries.com/

Palmater, P. D. (2011). *Beyond blood: Rethinking Indigenous identity.* Saskatoon, SK: Purich Publishing.

Peat, F. D. (2005). *Blackfoot physics: Journey into the Native American universe.* York Beach, ME: Weiser Books.

Peat, F. D. (2007). *Pathways of chance.* Grosset, Italy: Paripublishing.

Porter, T. (1993). *Clanology: Clan system of the Iroquois.* New York, NY: Native North American Travelling College.

Porter, T. (2008). *And grandma said ... Iroquois teachings as passed down through the oral tradition.* Bloomington, IN: Xlibris Corporation.

Pritchard, R. (2004). Humboldtian values in a changing world: Staff and students in German universities. *Oxford Review of Education, 30*(4), 509–28. http://dx.doi.org/10.1080/0305498042000303982

Ridge, B. (2011, January 31). What is a Cherokee? *Tahlequah Daily Press.* Retrieved February 2, 2011, from http://tahlequahdailypress.com/local/x1581529707/What-is-a-Cherokee

Royal Commission on Aboriginal Peoples. (1996). *Royal Commission on Aboriginal Peoples.* Retrieved February 10, 2010, from http://www.collectionscanada.gc.ca/webarchives/20071115053257/http://www.ainc-inac.gc.ca/ch/rcap/sg/sgmm_e.html

Samples, B. (1976). *The metaphoric mind: A celebration of creative consciousness.* Boston, MA: Addison Wesley Publishing Company.

Sarris, G. (1993). *Keeping Slug Woman alive: A holistic approach to American Indian texts.* Berkeley, CA: University of California Press.

Schafer, M. (1969). *The new soundscape: A handbook for the modern music teacher.* Rochester, VT: Destiny Books.

Scollon, R., & Scollon, S. (1981). *Narrative, literacy and face in interethnic Communication volume VII advances in discourse processes.* Norwood, NJ: ABLEX Publishing Corporation.

Serim, F. (1998). Four directions for lifelong learning. Retrieved from http://www.itari.in/categories/lifelonglearning/TheFourDirectionsoflifelonglearning.pdf

Shimony, A. (1994). *Conservatism among the Iroquois at the Six Nations Reserve.* Syracuse, NY: Syracuse University Press.

Shorto, R. (2008). *Descartes' bones: A skeletal history of the conflict between faith and reason.* New York, NY: Random House.

Silko, L. M. (1977). *Ceremony.* New York, NY: Penguin Books.

Simpson, L. (2008). Our elder brothers: The lifeblood of resurgence. In L. Simpson (Ed.), *Lighting the eighth fire: The liberation, resurgence, and protection of Indigenous nations* (pp. 73–87). Winnipeg, MB: Arbeiter Ring Publishing.

Simpson, L. (2011). *Dancing on our turtle's back: Stories of Nishnaabeg re-creation, resurgence and a new emergence.* Winnipeg, MA: Arbeiter Ring Publishing.

Skinner, B. F. (1971). *Beyond freedom and dignity* (1st ed.). New York, NY: Knopf Publishing.

Smith, L. T. (2012). *Decolonizing methodologies: Research and Indigenous peoples* (2nd ed.). New York, NY: Zed Books.

Smith, M. (2004). Crippling the spirit, wounding the soul: Native American spiritual and religious suppression. In A. Waters (Ed.), *American Indian thought* (pp. 97–115). Malden, MA: Blackwell Publishing.

Spivak, G. (1993). *Outside in the teaching machine.* New York, NY: Routledge.

Statistics Canada. (2003). *Aboriginal peoples survey 2001 – Initial findings: Well-being of the non-reserve Aboriginal population.* Ottawa, ON: Author.

Statistics Canada. (2011). *Population projections by Aboriginal identity in Canada: 2006 to 2031.* Ottawa, ON: Author.

Statistics Canada. (2013). *Aboriginal peoples in Canada: First Nations people, Métis and Inuit. National household survey, 2011.* Retrieved from http://www12. statcan.gc.ca/nhs-enm/2011/as-sa/99-011-x/99-011-x2011001-eng.pdf

Stewart-Harawira, M. (2005). *The new imperial order: Indigenous responses to globalization.* New York, NY: Zed Books.

Strong, P. T., & Van Winkle, B. (1996). "Indian blood": Reflections on the reckoning and refiguring of Native North American identity. *Cultural Anthropology, 11*(4), 547–76. http://dx.doi.org/10.1525/ can.1996.11.4.02a00050

Styres, S. (2008). *Language shifting among the Hodenosaunee of Southern Ontario.* Unpublished master's thesis, Brock University, St. Catharines, Ontario, Canada.

Styres, S. (2011). Land as first teacher: A philosophical journeying. *Reflective Practice, 12*(6), 717–31. http://dx.doi.org/10.1080/14623943.2011.601083

Styres, S., Haig-Brown, C., & Blimkie, M. (2013). Toward a pedagogy of land: The urban context. *Canadian Journal of Education, 36*(2), 34–67.

Styres, S., Zinga, D., Bennett, S., & Bomberry, M. (2010). Walking in two worlds: Engaging the space between Indigenous community and academia. *Canadian Journal of Education, 33*(3), 617–48. http://dx.doi.org/10.2307/ canajeducrevucan.33.3.617

Swamp, J. (2010). *Kanikonriio: "Power of a good mind."* In L. Davis (Ed.), *Alliances: Re/envisioning Indigenous-non-Indigenous relationships* (pp. 15–24). Toronto, ON: University of Toronto Press.

Tafoya, T. (1995). Finding harmony: Balancing traditional values with Western science in therapy. *Canadian Journal of Native Education, 21*(Suppl.), 7–27.

Task Force on Aboriginal Languages and Cultures. (2005). *Towards a new beginning: A foundation report for a strategy to revitalize First Nation, Inuit and Métis languages and cultures.* Ottawa, ON: Author.

Taylor, D. M., & Wright, S. C. (1989). Language attitudes in a multilingual northern community. *Canadian Journal of Native Studies, 9*(1), 85–118.

Thomas, J. (1978). *Simcoe Deed; Haldimand Deed; Proclamation, Dec. 22, 1766; Covenant Chain; Two Row Wampum Treaty; Jay Treaty, 1784; Washington Treaty, 1812, 1842; Treaty of Ghent, 1814.* Wilsonville, ON: Sandpiper Press.

Titley, E. B. (1986). *A narrow vision: Duncan Campbell Scott and the administration of Indian affairs in Canada.* Vancouver, BC: University of British Columbia Press.

Tran, V. D. (2001). *Reason, rationality, and reasonableness: Vietnamese philosophical studies, 1.* Washington, DC: Council for Research in Values and Philosophy.

Tuck, E., & Yang, E. W. (2012). Decolonization is not a metaphor. *Decolonization, 1*(1), 1–40.

Turner, D. (2006). *This is not a peace pipe: Towards a critical Indigenous philosophy.* Toronto, ON: University of Toronto Press.

UNESCO. (2003). *Education in a multilingual world* (UNESCO Education Position Paper). Retrieved February 8, 2008, from http://unesdoc.unesco. org/images/0012/001297/129728e.pdf

Vermeulen, J. (1998). Edward Sapir. In J. Verschueren, J.-O. Östman, J. Blommaert, & C. Bulcaen (Eds.), Handbook of pragmatics (1998 Installment) (pp. 1-16–1-34). Amsterdam, The Netherlands: John Benjamins Publishing.

Wall, S. (2001). *To become a human being: The message of Tadodaho Chief Leon Shenandoah.* Charlottesville, VA: Hampton Roads Publishing, Inc.

Wang, C., & Burris, M. A. (1997). Photovoice: Concept, methodology and use for participatory needs assessment. *Health Education & Behavior, 24*(3), 369–87.

Waters, A. (2004a). Language matters: Nondiscrete nonbinary dualism. In A. Waters (Ed.), *American Indian thought* (pp. 97–115). Malden, MA: Blackwell Publishing.

Waters, A. (2004b). Ontology of identity and interstitial being. In A. Waters (Ed.), *American Indian thought* (pp. 153–70). Malden, MA: Blackwell Publishing.

Wien, C. (2008). Emergent curriculum. In C. A. Wien (Ed.), *Emergent curriculum in the primary classroom: Interpreting the Reggio Emilia approach in schools* (pp. 5–16). New York, NY: Teachers College Press.

Wilshire, B. (2006). On the very idea of "a worldview" and of "alternative worldviews." In Four Arrows (Don Trent Jacobs) (Ed.), *Unlearning the language of conquest: Scholars expose the anti-Indianism in America* (pp. 260–72). Austin, TX: University of Texas Press.

Wilson, S. (2008). *Research is ceremony: Indigenous research methods.* Winnipeg, MB: Fernwood Publishing.

Woodworth, W. (2010). Iroquoian Condolence practised on a civic scale. In L. Davis (Ed.), *Alliances: Re/envisioning Indigenous-non-Indigenous relationships* (pp. 25–41). Toronto, ON: University of Toronto Press.

Wurm, S. A. (Ed.). (2001). *Atlas of the world's languages in danger of disappearing.* Paris, France: United Nations Educational, Scientific and Cultural Organization.

Youngblood Henderson, J. S. (2000a). Ayukpachi: Empowering Aboriginal thought. In M. Battiste (Ed.), *Reclaiming Indigenous voice and vision* (pp. 248–78). Vancouver, BC: UBC Press.

Youngblood Henderson, J. S. (2000b). The context of the state of nature. In M. Battiste (Ed.), *Reclaiming Indigenous voice and vision* (pp. 11–38). Vancouver, BC: UBC Press.

Youngblood Henderson, J. S. (2008). *Indigenous diplomacy and the rights of peoples: Achieving UN recognition.* Saskatoon, SK: Purich Publishing Limited.

Youngblood Henderson, J. S. (2009). *When learning draws us in like magnets, our heart and brain connect to animate our worldviews in practice.* Saskatoon, SK: University of Saskatchewan, Aboriginal Education Research Centre. Retrieved from http://www.aerc.usask.ca

Zinga, D., & Styres, S. (2011). Land as pedagogy: Tensions, challenges, and contradictions. *First Nations Perspectives, 3,* 59–83.

Index

Page numbers with (f) refer to figures.